PENN STATION

View of main entrance to Penn Station, New York, at Seventh Avenue and 32nd. Street, shortly after opening in 1910.

PENN STATION

IT'S TUNNELS AND SIDE RODDERS

By

Fred Westing

SUPERIOR PUBLISHING COMPANY - SEATTLE

Library of Congress Cataloging in Publication Data

Westing, Frederick, 1903-
   Penn Station.

   Reprint of the 1912 ed. of History of the Engineering, construction, and equipment of the Pennsylvania
Railroad Company's New York terminal and approaches,
edited by W. Couper: p.
   Includes index.
   1. Pennsylvania Railroad. 2. New York. Pennsyl-
vania Station. 3. Railroads — United States —
Electrification. 4. Electric locomotives — United
States. I. Couper, William, 1884-   ed. History of
the engineering, construction, and equipment of the
Pennsylvania Railroad Company's New York terminal and
approaches. 1978. II. Title.
TF25.P4W47   1978   625.1'8'097471   78-2557
ISBN 0-87564-529-1

FIRST EDITION

PRINTED IN THE UNITED STATES OF AMERICA

DEDICATION

Dedicated to the engineering organization of WESTINGHOUSE CHURCH KERR & COMPANY, one of the greatest in their day and, also to WALTER CRAIG KERR, their President, who contributed so much to their excellent reputation. Regarding this Company's association with the Penn Station project (less tunnels) it was said "The magnitude and variety of the engineering work which was awarded to WESTINGHOUSE CHURCH KERR & COMPANY, was unprecedented in the annals of the profession."

PREFACE

This book contains two parts. The first is a reprint of a rare and valuable book describing original Penn Station's architectural and engineering details including the river tunnels. These tubes were an integral and vitally essential part of the Pennsylvania Railroad Company's, direct rail entrance into New York City's Manhattan Island. Its descriptive material was authoritatively written by men who worked on the complexities associated with such a gigantic task.

Penn Station, appropriately called "A Temple of Transportation," and "an architectural gem," combined in the highest degree the primary function of such an edifice, capable of meeting the exacting demands of railroad transportation, with a building of monumental dignity. Unlike some contemporary railroad stations, there was to be no compromise by using "air rights" for non-railroad office space, and to this the Company adhered. Only in the splendid and impressive arcade were located some few floor-level shops representing a small concession to commercialism.

The second part of the book represents my contribution. In it are described and illustrated through text and captions, types and classes of jack-shaft, side-rod drive electric locomotives. These "motors" initially, and later, contributed immeasurably to the project's success, without which, it may well at that time have foundered.

In bringing Pennsylvania Railroad passengers into New York City, and that classic station by direct rail connection, a lasting tribute to the memory of its great President, Alexander Johnston Cassatt, should ever belong. His sudden, and unexpected death on December 28, 1906, tragically prevented him from seeing the culmination of this vast enterprise which he had so resolutely advanced.

Frederick Westing

ACKNOWLEDGMENTS

To my ever patient wife Marge, who has been of inestimable help to me in the production of my articles and books. And to Miss Elva Ferguson former Librarian of the Pennsylvania Library, whose unfailing kindness and courtesy was of great assistance in obtaining off-the-record material and some exceptional illustrations of the DD1 electric locomotives in the early days of their operation.

Transactions of the American Society of Civil Engineers, were consulted, and some items quoted verbatim from comments made by George Gibbs and Norman W. Storer. Track layouts on the Pennsylvania Tunnel & Terminal Railroad Company were also from the Transactions of the ASCE.

The British publication "ENGINEERING" was responsible for the splendid elevation drawing of the original L5 class electric locomotive No. 3930.

Various Locomotive Dictionary's and Cyclopedia's as well as Railway Age provided some data, but, with few exceptions the illustrations are from the author's own collection. Two very good photos, however, showing "N" tower at the west end of Manhattan Transfer, and another showing the approach tracks to Sunnyside Yard, together with some Long Island Trackage, were furnished through the kindness of James J. Lynch, Jr.

Frederick Westing

Drexel Hill, May 1977

TABLE OF CONTENTS
COVERING SIDE-RODDERS

POSTSCRIPT

In using a book reprint for the first part of this publication I wanted to provide the atmosphere of a specific period in Pennsylvania Railroad history showing the Pennsy as it was in the days of its pristine splendor indicated by the book's publication date of 1912. I also acted in an editorial capacity regarding the reprinted book and found several omissions. These, however, were run down and completely included.

I have refrained from including illustrations of the present day and far less imposing Penn Station which is covered by a pseudo Madison Square Garden, and a bland-looking office building. Also eliminated are views of the original station after its interior was mutilated by garish "catch penny" devices and other eyesores. This paraphernalia desecrated what was once a railroad station capable of being equated architecturally with the finest classical examples of ancient Greece and Rome.

Another objective of mine was to make this valuable reprinted book available to a greater number of people interested in Pennsy and Manhattan Island nostalgia. Difficulty in obtaining photographs of the original Penn Station's interior and exterior and the improbability of running down pictures of the personalities involved in this project prompted my action in using the reprinted book for the first section of the completed book.

With one exception no alternating-current (AC) locomotives or Multiple-Unit (MU) trains are shown. The exception which is illustrated in my section of the book, is the photo taken by the author from the cab of GG-1, No. 4831 on a tangent section of the "highline" while hauling an express westbound at 70 mph. Its purpose was to show how the highline looked from the "front end" while it still retained the third-rails used by direct-current (DC) locomotives.

Another reason for omitting AC equipment was to be consistent with the time-frame involved. A sidelight not generally known to many is the fact that in 1920, some MU trains made up of DC Long Island Railroad rolling stock were used to carry passengers between Penn Station and Manhattan Transfer. This took place during the early evening rush hour. These trains were scheduled to run between the locomotive hauled trains. I rode them occasionally when I worked at Penn Station. This arrangement enabled residents of Newark, Harrison, and Jersey City, or surrounding locations, to make swifter connections with Hudson & Manhattan trains, thereby, making earlier arrivals at their homes.

Frederick Westing

HISTORY OF THE ENGINEERING
CONSTRUCTION AND EQUIPMENT OF THE

PENNSYLVANIA
RAILROAD COMPANY'S

NEW YORK TERMINAL
AND APPROACHES

PUBLISHED BY ISAAC H. BLANCHARD
COMPANY NEW YORK

NINETEEN HUNDRED AND TWELVE

EDITED BY WM. COUPER, FORMER ACT-
ING SECRETARY BOARD OF ENGINEERS

PENNSYLVANIA STATION, NEW YORK CITY, THE LARGEST RAILROAD TERMINAL IN THE WORLD

TABLE OF CONTENTS

LIST OF ILLUSTRATIONS

LIST OF ILLUSTRATIONS
(*CONTINUED*)

WILLIAM COUPER, ACT'G SEC'Y   ALFRED NOBLE   CHAS. M. JACOBS   GEORGE GIBBS
SAMUEL REA   GEN'L CHAS. W. RAYMOND, CHAIRMAN

MR. SAM'L REA AND BOARD OF ENGINEERS, PENNSYLVANIA TUNNEL AND TERMINAL RAILROAD

FOREWORD

WM. COUPER

NEW YORK CITY, the metropolis of the Western Hemisphere, includes within its corporate limits 327 square miles. Much of the land is still under cultivation and is unknown to thousands of people who daily visit the city, for to the vast majority of the visitors New York City is the Borough of Manhattan, which in reality is a small island comprising about 7 per cent of the area of the entire city. However, when we consider that more people live on the little island of Manhattan than in the states of Vermont, Montana, Delaware, Idaho, Wyoming, Utah, Arizona and New Mexico combined, we see the necessity which has, within the past few years, led to the construction of no less than fifteen separate and distinct subaqueous tunnels connecting this island with the surrounding territory.

The advantages, and in fact the commercial necessity, of establishing a terminus in the mercantile and monetary center of the country are obvious and only the great cost of the undertaking and the physical difficulties to be overcome have prevented the railroads terminating on the west shore of the Hudson River from fully meeting the transportation requirements of the community.

The ferry-boat, which is admittedly a makeshift, was for years the sole means of reaching the city from the West and South for all railroads, save those using the one terminal formerly existing in the city proper. The ferries are doomed, for not only is their operation hampered by the congested harbor traffic but passengers are subjected to delays on account of fog; further, the time consumed in reaching business or hotel districts from the water-front adds half an hour to the journey and entails the use of another means of transportation after the railroad company has fulfilled its contract.

There are a number of subaqueous tunnels in operation in this country and travel through them is no longer a novelty. However, as tunnel work is of necessity carried on under land or water, few people have a chance of seeing the operations necessary to create these sub-surface highways, and it is one of the purposes of this book to familiarize all who may be interested with the methods employed and the results obtained in the execution of the most colossal and comprehensive project for the improvement of railroad terminal facilities which has ever been undertaken.

The project may be resolved into several well defined divisions:

1. The Meadows Division, from Manhattan Transfer, near Harrison, N.J., to the New Jersey tunnel portals.

2. The North River Division, from the New Jersey portals to Ninth Avenue, New York City.

3. The East River Division, from Ninth Avenue, New York City, eastward excluding the station.

4. The station building, auxiliary buildings and operating facilities.

These will be described in detail separately, in order that the continuity of the progress of construction in each case may be preserved.

The history of the establishment of a terminal in the heart of New York begins properly with the lease of the United Railroads of New Jersey by the Pennsylvania Railroad in 1871, when the eastern terminus of the system was extended from Philadelphia to New York. The project is not, as has been the popular impression, the outcome of a sudden inspiration in recent years but is the logical result of long and detailed study of various schemes, all having as their ultimate purpose the establishing of a terminal in New York City.

The extension of the Pennsylvania Railroad System to the Hudson River and thence by ferry to New York established it as one of the leading trunk lines of the country. If any plans were at that time considered providing for an extension into New York they were dropped on account of the panic of 1873, the effect of which extended over a number of years and made prohibitory the enormous outlay of money necessary to overcome the seemingly insurmountable difficulties.

Meanwhile, the progress of work on the Hudson tunnel was closely followed. This tunnel was started in 1874, but four years later construction was held up by injunction only to be abandoned in 1880, when twenty lives were lost as the result of one accident—caused by a "blow-out." The use of this tunnel was considered to be purely a rapid transit proposition, for electric traction was undeveloped and the operation of standard trains drawn by self-contained locomotives, whether impelled by coal, coke or oil, was prohibitive on account of smoke in case of the usage of the first and noxious fumes in case of either of the other fuels.

One of the first methods of entering the city to be given serious consideration involved the construction of a high-level bridge over the Hudson River, this was in 1884. The bridge was to rise 135 feet in the clear and its approach reached a terminal near Desbrosses and Canal Streets. One of the difficulties encountered was that the Government would not countenance the erection of piers between the pierhead lines of the river on account of the congested harbor conditions and in consequence the span of the bridge would have had to be about twice that of the Brooklyn Bridge, a record yet unattained. The project was, however, thought by bridge engineers to be perfectly feasible. Consideration of the bridge project was brought to a close by the panic of 1884, one of the most disastrous ever experienced in this country. The advocates of the bridge scheme continued to evolve their plans and petitioned for, and in 1890 received from Congress a charter providing for interstate traffic via a bridge over the Hudson River. Plans for a bridge and its approaches were approved by the Secretary of War, providing for a single span between pierhead lines. The bridge was to cross the river near Twenty-third Street and the terminal was to have been located near Sixth Avenue and Twenty-sixth Street. This scheme was given serious consideration but it was feared that financial difficulties would arise owing to investors questioning the validity of the Federal charter. However, as the result of a test suit in condemnation the Supreme Court of the United States finally handed down a decision fully establishing the charter powers of the bridge company.

The general scheme evolved for operating the bridge was for the various railroads terminating on the west bank of the Hudson to extend their transportation facilities across the river into New York City; it being estimated that there would be 900,000 loaded passenger equipment cars per annum, of which the Pennsylvania Railroad was requested to furnish 200,000. The estimated cost of the bridge project was about $95,000,000.

In 1900, the Pennsylvania Railroad agreed to the arrangement and to bear its proportion of the cost involved, but as it was impossible to induce the other railroads to participate and as it was impossible to obtain a charter for a bridge to be used exclusively by a single company, the project was abandoned.

In 1892, Mr. Austin Corbin, president of the Long Island Railroad, approached the Pennsylvania Railroad in an endeavor to interest it in the construction of a tunnel which would connect Jersey City, New York and Brooklyn. It was Mr. Corbin's idea to use these tunnels for standard equipment but other officials considered this not feasible and the work done was consequently based on a rapid transit service. Electric locomotives were to be used for power, multiple-unit traction being undeveloped at the time. It is of interest to know that a tunnel was constructed under Atlantic Avenue, Brooklyn, in 1845 and was operated for a time. The tunnel was, however, eventually filled up. Mr. Corbin made investigations of a number of projects for establishing a terminal for the Long Island Railroad in New York City; one of these following very closely the line as finally constructed.

At the request of Mr. G. B. Roberts, president of the Pennsylvania Railroad, a comprehensive report on the question of "Establishing and Reaching a Railroad Terminal in New York City" was prepared in October, 1892, by Mr. Samuel Rea, who eventually, as vice-president of the companies incorporated to construct the tunnel extension, had charge of the prosecution of the work. This report presented five schemes for entering the city which in brief were as follows:

1. An underground system, distinct from the steam railroad, connecting Jersey City and New York, or Jersey City and Brooklyn via New York.

2. The Hudson River tunnel, which, already partly constructed, was to be completed. Others were to be constructed and trains operated by cable power into New York after detaching the steam locomotives.

3. The establishment of a terminal near Forty-second Street which would have a connection with the Forty-second Street tunnel running to Long Island. This terminal was to have been reached by standard trains conveyed on floats.

4. The establishment of a terminal at Madison Avenue and Thirty-eighth Street, which was to have been reached by a line leaving the main line near Rahway, thence via Staten Island and a three and a half mile subaqueous tunnel under "The Narrows" and a connection with the Long Island Railroad to a high-level bridge crossing over the East River and the intervening streets and elevated railroads. The question of utilizing this terminal for New England trains, which were to be run over a high-level bridge crossing Hell Gate was also discussed and the scheme advocated.

5. A high-level bridge over the Hudson River for freight and passenger traffic. The passenger terminal was to have been located near Madison Square on Sixth Avenue. This scheme also provided for the New England traffic by means of a spur to the New York Central & Hudson River Railroad's tracks and the Forty-second Street tunnel.

All of the projects were discussed in a full and comprehensive manner and this report, prepared ten years before the adoption of the scheme as finally carried out, covers all of the broader features of the New York Extension project.

In the summer of 1901, the extension of the Orleans Railway into Paris and its successful operation by electric power, suggested to the management of the Pennsylvania Railroad that it might offer a solution of its problem. The New York extension is somewhat similar to the layout of the French railroad, on which electric locomotives are substituted for steam locomotives at Austerlitz, from which point the road runs, in tunnel, along the river, although at no time under it, to the Quai d'Orsay Station. It is a matter of national pride that the adoption of electric locomotives was the direct result of an investigation made by a committee sent to the United States to study their performance in the Baltimore tunnel. The evolution of electric traction has revolutionized the operation of terminals reached by tunnels just as the perfection of the internal combustion engine has made possible the conquest of the air—for but a cursory study of aeronautics will show that the theory of planes reached an advanced stage years ago.

The inspection of the extension of the Orleans Railway was made by Mr. A. J. Cassatt, president of the Pennsylvania Railroad, himself, at the cabled request of Mr. Rea. Later in the same year preliminary investigations for the location of the New York tunnel line were made, the general arrangement having been made more flexible by the Pennsylvania acquiring a controlling interest in the Long Island Railroad, thus making it possible to use one terminal for both railroads, effect a physical connection between them, afford an outlet to the New England States and provide for terminal yard facilities on Long Island.

In the latter part of 1901, Mr. Cassatt appointed a commission of engineers, all eminent in their profession, to pass upon the practicability of the undertaking; to determine the best means for carrying it out; to make a careful estimate of its cost; and, if the work was undertaken, to exercise general supervision over its construction. Mr. Cassatt's letter appointing the commission contains the following further instructions:

"You are requested to procure all additional information that may be needed, sparing neither time nor any necessary expense in doing so, for I am sure it is not necessary for me to say that, in view of the magnitude and great cost of the proposed construction, and of the novel engineering questions involved, your studies should be thorough and exhaustive, and should be based upon absolute knowledge of the conditions."

The first meeting of this commission, known as the Board of Engineers, was held January 11, 1902, at which time it was formally organized. The personnel of the Board was as follows:

General Charles W. Raymond, U.S.A., chairman; Messrs. Charles M. Jacobs, Alfred Noble, Gustav Lindenthal and William H. Brown. Mr. George Gibbs was appointed a member of the Board April 9, 1902.

Mr. Jacobs was made chief engineer of the North River Division, which extends from near the New Jersey portals to Ninth Avenue, New York; Mr. Noble, chief engineer of the East River Division, from Ninth Avenue, New York, to Woodside, L.I.; Mr. Brown, chief engineer of the New Jersey Meadows Division, from Harrison, N.J., to the New Jersey portals (on his retirement the work was placed under Mr. A. C. Shand, his successor). Mr. Gibbs was appointed chief engineer of Electric Traction and of the New York Station Construction.

Before any construction whatever was commenced the Board of Engineers gave two consecutive years' consideration to the method of carrying out the project, Messrs. Cassatt and Rea being always at its call. For a period of about one year the Board received proposals from engineers and contractors submitting methods for constructing the subaqueous tunnels. Most of the schemes called for the construction of temporary structures in the rivers between the bulkheads. On account of the heavy river traffic it was thought inadvisable to obstruct the channels and although some of the methods of construction proposed had considerable merit, the shield method with compressed air was finally adopted, this being the only method recommended by the chief engineers.

It was thought that the shield method of tunneling might not be applicable without serious difficulties in material such as that composing the bed of the East River and, in order to have a method in reserve, an extended test was made of the so-called freezing process. This process in brief calls for the construction of a pilot tunnel of small diameter in which pipes, through which brine is circulated, are placed, thus freezing the surrounding material until its arch strength is great enough to allow the removal of the pilot tunnel. The frozen material is then excavated and the lining of the full-sized tunnel erected in the excavation thus formed. The method contained too many elements of uncertainty to justify its adoption and when the shield method proved to be satisfactory the freezing test was discontinued.

In establishing the grades the limiting features were: the elevation of the tracks in the station area, which are from nine to twenty-three feet below mean high water; the depth of the river bulkheads, for it was necessary to pass under or through their foundations; the contour of the river beds, for it was necessary to establish the tunnel sufficiently below the dredging plane to insure them against possible injury from anchors or sunken vessels and to insure ample cover to retain the compressed air during construction without incurring danger from "blow-outs"; and the rise and fall of tide on the Hackensack Meadows—it being necessary for the water to drain away from the tunnel portals. The problem was solved so successfully that the grades to be surmounted are in all cases less than 2 per cent or about 100 feet rise per mile. The enormous electric locomotives have no difficulty starting and accelerating a 550-ton train on the maximum grades. The power may be shut off trains approaching the station from the west some distance out on the Meadows and the train will run to the station, operated by the momentum grade.

In detail will be described later the provisions for the disposal of the vast quantities of material taken from the many excavations; the changes in the city water and sewer system made necessary; the monster girders near Seventh Avenue which, although at present they support a comparatively small load, will uphold skyscrapers yet unplanned; and many of the other features of the work.

For the construction of the line two companies were incorporated, one in New York and the other in New Jersey, in the early part of 1902; these companies were merged in 1907 under the name of the Pennsylvania Tunnel and Terminal Railroad Company, a corporation of both states. The franchise granting the right of extending the line under the Hudson River to a passenger station located in New York City and thence under the East River to a connection with the Long Island Railroad was passed by the Board of Aldermen on December sixteenth and approved by the Mayor on December 23, 1902.

By referring to the map on page 32 it will be seen that the extension leaves the main line about half a mile east of Newark at Manhattan Transfer. Here electric locomotives replace the steam locomotives and vice versa. Thence the line extends across Hackensack Meadows on an embankment, dives under the Palisades of the Hudson, at this point called Bergen Hill, under the North River, the City of New York, the East River and Long Island City—emerging in a large terminal yard.

One of the greatest improvements in local transportation facilities is the completion of the electric rapid transit service between New York and Newark, via the Hudson and Manhattan Railroad. Steam service from the West and South on the Pennsylvania Railroad will be discontinued at Manhattan Transfer, where passengers will take either the rapid transit line to the down-town or business district of New York, or else will continue on to the Pennsylvania Station, which is located in the heart of the shopping, hotel and theater district.

The Tunnel Extension forms the most important part of a general plan for improving the traffic facilities of the Pennsylvania Railroad at New York. The other elements were outlined by Mr. Cassatt in a letter to the Board of Rapid

Transit Railroad Commissioners of the City of New York, dated January 18, 1906, and were, in brief, as follows:

1. The electrification of the Long Island Railroad within city limits.

2. The construction of a freight terminal yard and piers at Greenville, N.J. This is the principal point for the distribution of freight in the district and cars are transported to the various yards on floats.

3. The Bay Ridge Improvement of the Long Island Railroad from Bay Ridge to East New York, involving the establishment of a number of freight stations and the improvement of others in the Borough of Brooklyn.

4. The Atlantic Avenue Improvement in Brooklyn, which eliminated a number of grade crossings by means of tunnels and elevated structures and in addition involved extensive improvements in terminal facilities, both passenger and freight, at Flatbush Avenue, where a connection is made with the city rapid transit system, operating into New York via the Battery tunnel. It is of interest, in the light of recent developments, to note that one of the two controling reasons for adopting the combination elevated and tunnel plan was that at that time no underground railroad carrying on a heavy local traffic had ever been operated by electricity in this country and public opinion prohibited the operation of the entire line, if in tunnel, by steam locomotives.

5. The New York Connecting Railroad, which extends from a connection with the Bay Ridge Improvement through the Borough of Queens to a connection with the New York, New Haven and Hartford Railroad, at Port Morris. This line will cross Hell Gate on a bridge having an arch span of 1,000 feet—the longest in the world. The lower chord of this bridge will be 135 feet above the water and 90,000 tons of steel will have to be fabricated for its erection. Passenger service to and from New England will be operated over this line, via the Pennsylvania Station, to the west and south and the freight will be carried via Bay Ridge, Brooklyn, to the Greenville Freight Yard.

6. The Glendale Cut-off of the Long Island Railroad, which materially reduces the distance between New York and Rockaway Beach.

7. New piers and docks in Newtown Creek near its confluence with the East River.

8. Electrification of the road between Newark and Jersey City.

As a general rule the efficiency of a railroad is directly proportional to its terminal facilities. The cost of these facilities is, however, very great, as will be seen from the following statement giving the estimated cost of the most thorough and comprehensive project of terminal improvements ever undertaken:

*New York Extension and Station including interchange yards at Harrison, N.J., and Sunnyside, L.I., P. T. & T. R.R. Co.	$100,000,000
Long Island Railroad electrification, Bay Ridge and Atlantic Avenue Improvements, Glendale Cut-off, freight yards and new equipment	35,000,000
New York Connecting Railroad, to be built jointly by the Pennsylvania R.R. Co. and the New York, New Haven and Hartford R.R. Co., about,	14,000,000
Pennsylvania Railroad improvements in the State of New Jersey, electrification of line from Jersey City to Park Place, Newark, Greenville freight line and terminal on New York Bay	10,000,000
Total	$159,000,000

*"The New York Tunnel Extension of the Pennsylvania Railroad," by Brigadier-General Chas. W. Raymond, Transactions American Society of Civil Engineers, vol. lxviii., p. 9, September 1910.

It is interesting to note in passing that the entire island of Manhattan once sold for less than one six-millionth part of this sum of money.

The station building, a mammoth structure than which but three larger buildings exist, is located in the heart of the city one block from Herald Square. There is no question when approaching the station that it is aught else than a railroad terminal although the entrance has the aspect of a monumental gateway. As we enter, the daring color treatment is at once apparent. The pleasing effect of the travertine, of which the interior is constructed and which has since the days of Roman ascendancy been a favorite building material abroad, pervades the atmosphere and adds a thrill which is tempered only by the silence—an awesome silence when we realize that there is no audible evidence of the hastening throngs seen all around us.

Immediately inside the entrance there are a number of high-class shops in which may be purchased articles of all descriptions needed by travelers. For the convenience of travelers spacious waiting rooms have been provided in addition to which there is a retiring room where ladies may sit or lounge in comfort and privacy; an engagement room for the use of out-of-town people who have but a few minutes in the city and wish to hold a meeting; a thoroughly equipped emergency hospital with attendant physician; and private rooms in which funeral parties may await the departure of trains apart from the general public.

The most salient feature of the station is the main waiting-room; so large is it that many of the best known hostelries in the country could be placed in this one room. Spaced about the lofty travertine walls are enormous Corinthian columns, standing on pedestals, which support the coffered vaulted ceiling. At the north and south ends of the room there are colonnades of Ionic columns and immediately below the six large lunette windows which surround the room are panels on which have been painted conventionalized maps in colors blending with the beautiful, warm, sunny color of the travertine. Travertine has not been used in this country for building purposes before but its use is no experiment. The exterior of the Colosseum, the Castle of St. Angelo, the Quirinal Palace, the Cathedral of St. Peter's and, in fact, nearly all of the Roman palaces are constructed with this stone. About this room are grouped the facilities usually found in railroad waiting-rooms.

Passing out of the waiting-room toward the west we enter an enclosure, known as the Concourse, surrounded by granite walls and covered with a glass roof supported by tall, graceful latticed steel columns. From the Concourse the traveler passes to his train, this being clearly defined by indicators showing the destination and time of departure.

Immediately below the Concourse, is the so-called Exit Concourse, used by travelers arriving in New York. The entire layout has been so schemed that it is impossible for the inbound and outbound traffic to oppose each other and thereby cause congestion.

A boon to the commuter are the luxurious pay toilets. Luxurious, you say. Yes, and why? Mr. Commuter has a dinner or theater engagement. In the good old days he had to engage a room at his club or a hotel, change his clothes there, return to the hotel at the end of the evening, secure his suitcase and then hustle to the station. Now he goes to the station, where in the morning he checked his suitcase, engages a so-called pay toilet, which in reality is a small room built of Carrara glass provided in addition to the usual toilet facilities with a wash-basin, towel, soap, whisk, mirror and chair. Here he changes his clothes, shaves if he wishes, and after rechecking his suitcase proceeds to keep his engagement. For a small coin he has fulfilled all requirements and saved a trip at a later hour in the evening.

A waiting-room designed for the exclusive use of the patrons of the Long Island Railroad, is located in the northeast corner of the station about twenty-five feet below the street level. Outside of the New York district this would be a large waiting-room but it would be possible to wander about the Pennsylvania Station a long time before you became aware of its existence, were it not for the dignified bronze signs which form a blazed trail not only to this waiting-room but to all facilities. So cunningly have these signs been placed that a stranger has simply to glance about him to find the way to any facility, part of the station, or city street emblazoned and the direction clearly indicated.

It is summer and the cool, airy, spacious halls, ventilated by the most modern methods, form a haven from the intense heat radiated by the street pavements and the skyscrapers. On the other hand, it is winter and we marvel that a building occupying two entire city blocks can be heated so skilfully that we know it is heated only when we seek shelter from the outside blast or go out to face it. The same ducts through which cool air is forced in the summer are our benefactors in winter, the only difference being that the air has first been forced over radiators heated by exhaust steam from the boilers.

Where are the boilers located, in the engine-room? Yes, but the engine-room of the station is a separate building, eight stories high, nearby. Here are located the heating and lighting facilities; the pumps for forcing the water through the miles of piping in the station; the machinery developing power for operating the elevators, switches, signals and sump pumps, which eject drainage to the city sewers not only from the station area but from the tunnels.

The power for operating the trains and for almost all other facilities save those taken care of by the Service Plant is generated at Long Island City, in a huge power plant near the Long Island Railroad ferry slips. The economic advantages of concentrating the generation of power at one point are many and great and cannot be attained with a number of self-contained steam locomotives.

One of the departments which is not ordinarily associated by the traveler with a railroad is the restaurant department. In walking through the great halls one can hardly realize that far above there are culinary facilities for feeding ten thousand people daily. Aside from the elaborate arrangements for preparing the food a multiplicity of refrigerators, storage rooms and many service rooms have been provided which, with the elevator system necessary to convey the food to the traveler in the restaurant below, form a little world unthought of by the patron who sees only the waiters moving silently about on the cork floor.

One has but to glance about to realize that emphasis has been placed entirely upon results—strength, safety, permanency—rather than upon the money it cost to attain them. And yet so rapidly was the entire project prosecuted that but eighty-seven months elapsed between the time actual construction was started and the departure of the first revenue train. The station, which was completed in seventy-nine months, is the largest building in the world constructed at one time. Three structures—the Vatican, the Tuileries and the St. Petersburg Winter Palace—surpass it in area, but centuries elapsed in their construction.

How many of your letters have gone astray in the mail? Few people have missed so many that they cannot answer promptly. The efficiency of the mail service is directly attributable to the tireless energy of the Government officials extending over many years, but the modern idea of mail service entails besides surety of transit, rapid transit; and here the railroad is concerned. At present about forty per cent of the New York out-of-town mail is received and despatched by the Pennsylvania Railroad and to expedite its movement the Government is erecting on a site, purchased from the railroad, adjoining the station a new post-office which, when completed, will be a monumental structure covering about four acres. As the building, part of which is now completed and in operation, is located directly over the station tracks it is obvious that the tracks on which mail cars may stand while being loaded are limited in number and extent. Consequently, to handle the enormous amount of mail, which on heavy days amounts to about 260 tons, with the greatest despatch elaborate mail handling machinery has been designed and installed. As a general rule the outgoing mail is taken care of by spiral chutes and horizontal conveyors, while inbound mail is carried from the cars to the post-office by horizontal conveyors and bucket lifts. These mechanical devices in conjunction with elevators on which truck loads of mail are handled provide a mail-handling system far in advance of anything of its kind ever before attempted. It is, however, necessary to keep pace with the times and we must not forget that no longer ago than 1864 there was but one post-office car in the United States, whereas in 1909 there were 1,350 post-office cars and 3,800 compartment cars, usually consisting of baggage cars with a compartment reserved for mail.

It is prohibitive in an introductory paper to treat of details which would, among other things, include the countless labor-saving contrivances installed throughout the line. So efficient are these devices that the number of employees necessary to operate the entire terminal division, extending from Manhattan Transfer, N.J., to Woodside, L.I., is less than half the number required to operate a large department store.

Extraordinary efforts were made during the construction period to safeguard the health of employees. Of necessity the clothing worn by them would become wet, or at least damp, but on the morrow they would be dry again, for each man's locker was heated by steam; hot coffee was always on tap and it was served to the tunnel workers under the rivers once during each shift; a medical corps was maintained on the work and, in fact, many features of a nature not usually found on construction work were provided. This policy has been continued and the railroad has fitted up for the men who now operate the line a luxurious club, conducted under the auspices of the Pennsylvania Railroad Young Men's Christian Association. Here the employees may exercise in the gymnasium, read, divert themselves with games of many kinds or lounge in the commodious reception room.

Many are the devices which have been installed to enhance the safety of the traveler and the signal system is the most thorough and elaborate ever undertaken. Unusual conditions had to be met because of the limited clearances, necessity for frequent train movement, difficulty of locating permanent signals and restricted field of vision in the underground yard. One thousand, five hundred and thirty miles of signal wire were used on the terminal division, which itself is less than fourteen miles long. The vast outlay of money required to install these vigilant sentinels of safety is repaid by the feeling of security instilled in passengers by their presence and efficiency, and in the consequent increase of travel—for the keynote of the signal system is found in the old maxim: "An ounce of prevention is worth a pound of cure." An open switch, a broken rail or another train in the section ahead throws the signal to danger. If, for some reason, any part of the signal system gets out of order or fails to work properly the signal immediately goes to danger and assures the safety of the passenger even when the apparatus is not working properly. As in all modern railroad practice the men in the towers, knowing the exact conditions at the terminal, divert the trains to the proper track and the engineer, knowing that the towerman has set the route, confidently proceeds, guided by the interlocked signals, with the assurance that a collision is impossible—for once the operator has set a combination of switches he cannot add another to it without first breaking the whole.

The signal layout in a way determines the capacity of a terminal and this phase of the project was given long and careful study, but the capacity of the

Pennsylvania Station would in any case be greater than that of most terminals because there are so few stub-end tracks. The main line tracks from the North River tunnels diverge so as to reach any one of the twenty-one standing tracks in the station. More than 80 per cent of these tracks converge to the tunnels under the East River at the east end of the station, through which the Long Island Railroad trains operate and the Pennsylvania trains run to the large terminal yard, called Sunnyside Yard, located on Long Island.

On our way to this yard five viaducts carrying the city streets are passed under and the train enters the yard proper by a loop track, thereby making it unnecessary to turn observation cars, diners, and similar equipment and materially reduces the shifting of baggage and mail cars. All appliances used in modern yard operation have been provided. Cleaners swarm over the cars both inside and outside; hard by there is a shed fitted for the exclusive purpose of carpet cleaning. Commissary attendants hustle here and there stocking cars with edibles, ice and water. Pullmans comprise about 40 per cent of the cars handled and the yard service on this equipment is especially heavy. Just as the finished produce of the kitchen is delivered to the restaurant, just so the fully made-up and appointed train is delivered from the yard for use of passengers at the station. Few travelers give a thought to the labor which has been expended by the air-brake, steam heat, electrical and car inspectors, icemen, watermen, switchmen, cleaners and many other classes of employees in preparing the train for service, but all trains must be complete in every detail for the very purpose of keeping the traveler's mind from dwelling on this phase of the operation and to achieve this perfection a small army of men is required.

The entire project is monumental and the Pennsylvania Railroad has, through the Board of Directors, erected at the main entrance of the station tablets briefly outlining the historic features of the construction and immortalizing the names of those who have been foremost in the prosecution of the work. These tablets are the only memorials in the building with one exception. In a niche, overlooking the vast waiting-room, is the heroic bronze statue of Alexander Johnston Cassatt, to whose foresight, courage and ability the achievement of the extension of the Pennsylvania Railroad System into New York City is mainly due.

The foregoing sketch of the general features of the tunnel extension project would be sadly incomplete without quoting the words of Brigadier-General Charles W. Raymond, chairman of the Board of Engineers, in paying "a tribute of admiration and respect to the memory of the late A. J. Cassatt, president of the Pennsylvania Railroad Company, to whom the conception, design and execution of the project are mainly due. His education and experience as a civil engineer, his thorough knowledge of all the details of railroad construction, operation and management, gained by long and varied service, the directness, clearness and strength of his mind, and his great executive ability, placed him at the head of the railroad men of the country. In the consideration of great problems, whether of transportation, finance, commerce or political economy, he was almost unequaled, owing to the breadth, originality and decisiveness of his character; yet his manner to his subordinates was so direct and simple that he seemed unconscious of his own superiority. Great as it is, the New York plan of improvement is only one item in a far-reaching scheme of development which became the policy of the Pennsylvania Railroad Company through Mr. Cassatt's advice and influence, yet his strongest interest was doubtless centered in the New York works. It is the sincere regret of all connected with the design and execution of the project that he did not live to see its completion."*

* "The New York Tunnel Extension of the Pennsylvania Railroad," Transactions American Society of Civil Engineers, vol. lxviii., p. 31, September 1910.

A.J. CASSATT

ALEXANDER·JOHNSTON·CASSATT
PRESIDENT·PENNSYLVANIA·RAILROAD·COMPANY
1899–1906

WHOSE·FORESIGHT·COURAGE·AND·ABILITY·ACHIEVED
THE·EXTENSION·OF·THE·PENNSYLVANIA·RAILROAD·SYSTEM
INTO·NEW·YORK·CITY

THE PROCEEDINGS AT THE DEDICATION OF THE CASSATT MEMORIAL

TO honor his memory and his achievements, the Board of Directors of the Pennsylvania Railroad Company erected a statue of Mr. Cassatt in the new station at Seventh Avenue and Thirty-second Street, New York City, which, at the unostentatious but dignified opening on August 1, 1910, was unveiled in the presence of the directors and officers of the Pennsylvania System.

On that occasion, Mr. Samuel Rea, second vice-president of the Company, in charge of the construction of the New York Tunnel Extension and Station, stated: "We are here to-day to honor the memory of the late president of the Pennsylvania Railroad Company, Mr. A. J. Cassatt, and to unveil the statue as a tribute to his genius. Mr. Cuyler, chairman of the Memorial Committee, will now present the statue to the Company, and Mr. McCrea, president, will, on its behalf, accept the same."

Mr. T. DeWitt Cuyler, in presenting the statue to the Company, said: "We are gathered here to-day to take part in an event which marks one of the most important epochs in the history of the Pennsylvania Railroad. With the unveiling of the statue, before which we stand, it is proposed, sir, that you should officially declare the station open for purposes for which it was built. The occasion calls for no ostentatious ceremonies or elaborate words. These massive walls and columns speak in their severe simplicity and majestic silence far more eloquently than human tongue could give utterance to, and so too this splendid statue which we are now to look upon in the greatness of the genius and the simplicity of the character of the man, finds a fitting resting place amid these surroundings. It has been the privilege and duty of the directors to have here placed this portrait of Mr. Cassatt, and how well the artist has done his work, all will attest. We ask you, as the head of this great corporation, to take this statue into your keeping and to unveil it to the public eye so that all men may know, as the inscription so aptly tells, 'whose foresight, courage and ability achieved the extension of the Pennsylvania Railroad System into New York City.'"

In accepting the statue Mr. James McCrea, on behalf of the Company, said: "On behalf of the Board of Directors of the Pennsylvania Railroad Company, I accept this noble statue of Mr. Cassatt. It is fitting and proper that this unveiling should be coincident with the official opening of the great terminal which the Pennsylvania Railroad Company has, prompted by his foresight and courage, builded for itself in this, America's greatest city. As the years roll around, the greater will be the tribute to the genius of Mr. Cassatt—and it is a source of greatest pleasure to those who had the privilege of knowing him, to feel that there has been erected to his memory, in so fitting a place, a statue that will so truly express to those who follow, the manner of man he was. As a fitting conclusion to these ceremonies, I now declare this station officially opened."

THE FORMAL OPENING OF THE PENNSYLVANIA STATION, AUGUST 1, 1910
AT WHICH THE STATUE OF A. J. CASSATT WAS UNVEILED
(See key on next page)

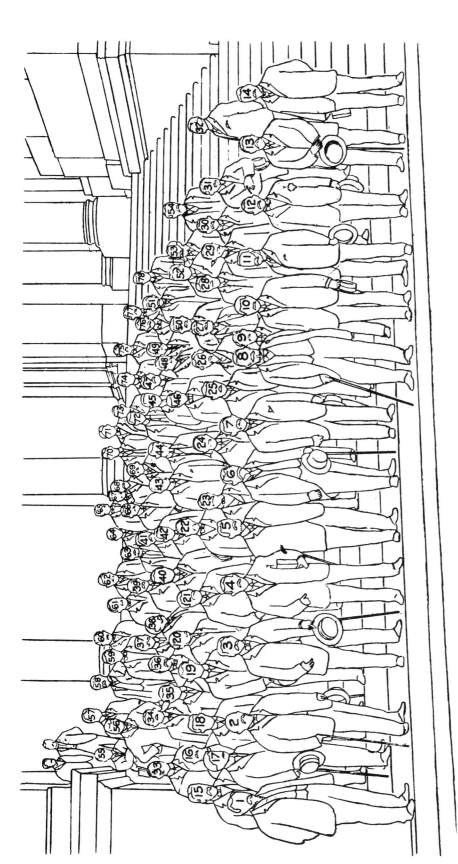

KEY TO GROUP PORTRAIT ON PREVIOUS PAGE

1. H. Walters, *Director, N.C. Ry. Co.*
2. Gen. Chas. W. Raymond, *Chairman, Board of Engineers.*
3. Rudulph Ellis, *Director, P.R.R. Co.*
4. J. B. Thayer, *3rd V.P., P.R.R. Co.*
5. C. Stuart Patterson, *Director, P.R.R. Co.*
6. C. A. Griscom, *Director, P.R.R. Co.*
7. Chas. E. Pugh, *1st V.P., P.R.R. Co.*
8. James McCrea, *President, P.R.R. Co.*
9. Lewis Neilson, *Secretary, P.R.R. Co.*
10. Samuel Rea, *2nd V.P., P.R.R. Co.*
11. Jno. P. Green, *President, W.N.Y. & P. Ry. Co.*
12. J. J. Turner, *2nd and V.P., Penna. Co.*
13. Ralph Peters, *President, L.I.R.R. Co.*
14. E. B. Taylor, *3rd V.P., Penna. Co.*
15. G. Lindenthal, *Consulting Engineer.*
16. P. Huggins, *Trainer for Mr. Cassatt.*
17. E. B. Cassatt, *Son of A. J. Cassatt.*
18. R. K. Cassatt, *Son of A. J. Cassatt.*
19. Wm. Couper, *Sec., Board of Engineers.*
20. I. Richardson, *Asst. to 3rd V.P., P.R.R. Co.*
21. Geo. W. Boyd, *Gen. Pass. Agent, P.R.R. Co.*
22. W. W. Atterbury, *5th V.P., P.R.R. Co.*
23. Geo. Wood, *Director, P.R.R. Co.*
24. H. Tatnall, *4th V.P., P.R.R. Co.*
25. T. DeWitt Cuyler, *Director, P.R.R. Co.*
26. Wm. H. Barnes, *Director, P.R.R. Co.*
27. John D. Crimmins, *Director, P.T. & T. R.R. Co.*
28. Wm. A. Patton, *Asst. to President, P.R.R. Co.*
29. A. J. County, *Asst. to 2nd V.P., P.R.R. Co.*
30. Wm. S. Richardson, *of McKim, Mead & White.*
31. A. A. Weinman, *Sculptor of Statue of A. J. Cassatt.*
32. D. T. Webster, *of McKim, Mead & White.*
33. G. D. Ogden, *Asst. Gen. Freight Agent.*
34. S. C. Long, *Gen. Supt., Western Penna. Div.*
35. W. Plunkett Stewart, *Son-in-law of A. J. Cassatt.*
36. James Forgie, *Engr., North River Div.*
37. Frank E. Haff, *Sec., L.I.R.R. Co.*
38. J. B. Hutchinson, *Asst. to 1st V.P., P.R.R. Co.*
39. M. Trump, *Gen. Supt. Trans., P.R.R. Co.*
40. J. F. Fahnestock, *Treas., P.R.R. Co.*
41. E. F. Brooks, *Gen. Supt., P., B. & W. R.R. Co.*
42. R. C. Wright, *Gen. Frt. Agt., P.R.R. Co.*
43. H. Large, *Coal Frt. Agt., P.R.R. Co.*
44. I. C. Johnson, *Supt. of Telegraph, P.R.R. Co.*
45. L. R. Zollinger, *Engr., M. of Way, P.R.R. Co.*
46. J. G. Rodgers, *Asst. to Gen. Mgr., P.R.R. Co.*
47. Montgomery Smith, *Asst. Prchsng. Agt., P.R.R. Co.*
48. A. C. Shand, *Chf. Engr., P.R.R. Co.*
49. E. B. Temple, *Asst. Chf. Engr., P.R.R. Co.*
50. E. P. Bates, *Gen. Frt. Agt., P.R.R. Co.*
51. Geo. M. Ball, *Mgr., Empire Line.*
52. R. L. O'Donnel, *Gen. Supt., B. & A.V. Div.*
53. A. W. Gibbs, *Gen. Supt. Motive Power, P.R.R. Co.*
54. J. U. Crawford, *Engr. of Branch Lines, P.R.R. Co.*
55. E. T. Mander, *Pass. Train Master, N.Y. Div.*
56. R. H. Newbern, *Supt. Insurance Dept.*
57. A. B. Bierck, *Auditor, L.I.R.R. Co.*
58. T. Postlethwaite, *Asst. to President, P.R.R. Co.*
59. J. B. Fisher, *Supt., N.Y. Div.*
60. G. H. De Long, *Div. Ticket Agt.*
61. G. H. Cobb, *Div. Frt. Agt.*
62. F. L. Sheppard, *Gen. Supt., N.J. Div.*
63. A. L. Langdon, *Traffic Mgr., L.I.R.R. Co.*
64. H. M. Smith, *Gen. Pass. Agt., L.I.R.R. Co.*
65. L. H. Barker, *Resident Engr., Sunnyside Yard.*
66. C. M. Sheaffer, *Supt., Pass. Transportation, P.R.R. Co.*
67. R. M. Pile, *Asst. Gen. Pass. Agt., P.R.R. Co.*
68. Geo. H. Grone, *Asst. Prchsng. Agt., P.R.R. Co.*
69. Colin Studds, *Eastern Pass. Agt., P.R.R. Co.*
70. D. N. Bell, *Asst. Gen. Pass. Agt., P.R.R. Co.*
71. C. S. Krick, *Supt. P.T. & T. R.R. Co.*
72. C. L. Addison, *Asst. to Pres., L.I.R.R. Co.*
73. J. F. Keany, *Attorney, L.I.R.R. Co.*
74. F. Murray, *Asst. to Chf. Engr., P.R.R. Co.*
75. G. C. Clarke, *Resident Engr., East River Div.*
76. E. R. Hill, *Asst. to Chf. Engr., E.T. & S.C., P.T. & T. R.R. Co.*
77. Geo. Gibbs, *Chf. Engr., E.T. & S.C., P.T. & T. R.R. Co.*
78. C. M. Bunting, *Comptroller, P.R.R. Co.*

21

JAMES McCREA,
President Pennsylvania Railroad Company

JAMES McCREA, the son of Dr. James Alexander and Ann B. Foster McCrea, and a descendant of one of the oldest families of Pennsylvania, was born in Philadelphia May 1, 1848. He bears the name of his first American ancestor, who came to Pennsylvania in 1776 from Londonderry, Ireland, as a representative of large banking interests. From him the line of descent is traced through his son John, who married Mary Pleasants, and their son James A. McCrea.

Mr. McCrea was educated at the school of Rev. John W. Fairies and the Pennsylvania Polytechnic College, where he acquired his education in civil engineering. His railway service began in June, 1865, as rodman and assistant engineer of the Connellsville & Southern Pennsylvania Railroad, in which position he served until December, 1867, when he became rodman on the construction of the Wilmington & Reading Railroad. In September, 1868, he was engaged as assistant engineer on the Allegheny Valley Railroad, where he remained until March, 1871.

On March 1, 1871, Mr. McCrea entered the service of the Pennsylvania Railroad as principal assistant engineer in the Construction Department. From this time on his career is marked by dates which indicate his rapid advancement through nearly all the intermediate positions from the lowest to the highest in the company's service.

On August 1, 1874, Mr. McCrea was transferred to the position of assistant engineer of maintenance of way of the Philadelphia Division, becoming superintendent of the Middle Division on January 1, 1875, and assuming the important post of superintendent of the New York Division on October 15, 1878.

On May 1, 1882, Mr. McCrea began his long connection with the Western lines of the Pennsylvania System as manager of the Southwest System, with headquarters at Columbus, Ohio. October 10, 1885, he was advanced to the post of general manager of all the Pennsylvania lines west of Pittsburgh, and then to fourth vice-president on October 19, 1887; second vice-president March 1, 1890, and first vice-president on April 23, 1891.

Mr. McCrea held this position for sixteen years, maintaining a close supervision of all the problems of transportation, engineering, finance and traffic, the solution of which was represented in the marked development of the system west of Pittsburgh under his direction. Through his connection with the Pennsylvania lines west of Pittsburgh, Mr. McCrea became president of the Vandalia Railroad Company, Grand Rapids & Indiana Railway Company, Cleveland, Akron & Columbus Railway Company, the Cincinnati & Muskingum Valley Railway Company, and a large number of lesser companies.

While residing in Pittsburgh Mr. McCrea was, in February, 1898, elected a trustee of the University of Pennsylvania, succeeding Honorable John Scott, former United States Senator. This was the first time in the history of the University that a trustee had been chosen who resided outside of the city of Philadelphia, and his election indicated the policy of the University to make its influence co-extensive with the boundaries of the Commonwealth. After holding the office of trustee for about five years, Mr. McCrea resigned on May 29, 1903, because the location of his residence made it impossible for him to attend the meetings of the Board with as much regularity as he deemed necessary.

Mr. McCrea was elected director of the Pennsylvania Railroad Company on June 9, 1899, at the time of the election of Mr. Cassatt as president, and on January 2, 1907, was elected president of the Pennsylvania Railroad Company, following the death of Mr. Cassatt in December, 1906. Shortly after assuming the presidency of the Pennsylvania Railroad Company, Mr. McCrea was elected president of the Philadelphia, Baltimore & Washington Railroad Company, the Northern Central Railway Company, the West Jersey & Seashore Railroad Company, the Pennsylvania Company, and the Pittsburgh, Cincinnati, Chicago & St. Louis Railway Company.

JAMES McCREA
PRESIDENT
OF THE PENNSYLVANIA RAILROAD

SAMUEL REA
FIRST VICE PRESIDENT
OF THE PENNSYLVANIA RAILROAD

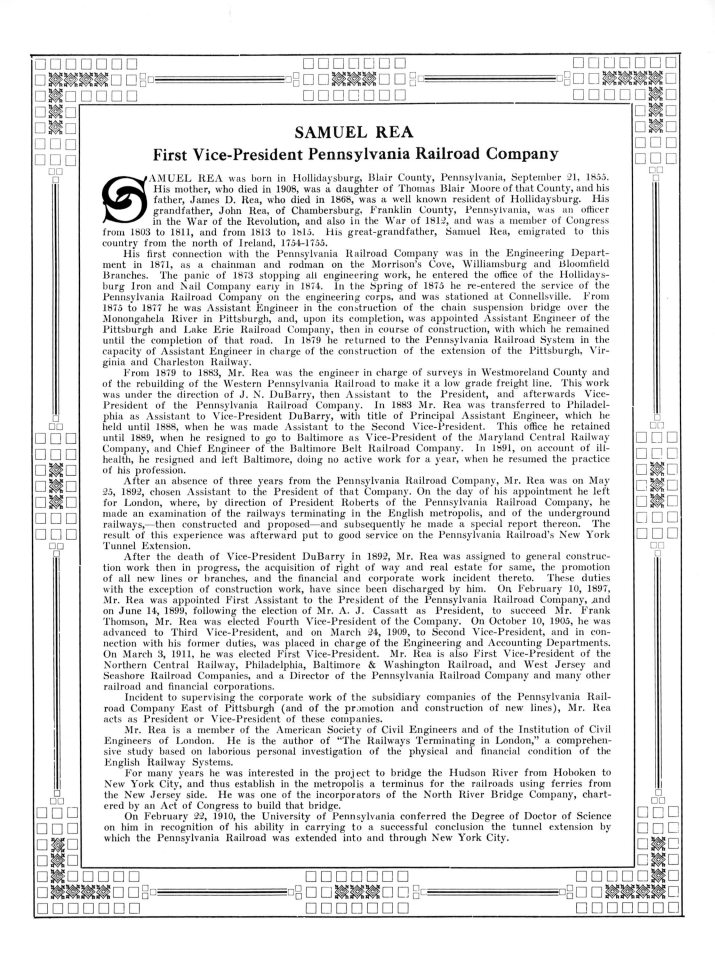

SAMUEL REA
First Vice-President Pennsylvania Railroad Company

SAMUEL REA was born in Hollidaysburg, Blair County, Pennsylvania, September 21, 1855. His mother, who died in 1908, was a daughter of Thomas Blair Moore of that County, and his father, James D. Rea, who died in 1868, was a well known resident of Hollidaysburg. His grandfather, John Rea, of Chambersburg, Franklin County, Pennsylvania, was an officer in the War of the Revolution, and also in the War of 1812, and was a member of Congress from 1803 to 1811, and from 1813 to 1815. His great-grandfather, Samuel Rea, emigrated to this country from the north of Ireland, 1754-1755.

His first connection with the Pennsylvania Railroad Company was in the Engineering Department in 1871, as a chainman and rodman on the Morrison's Cove, Williamsburg and Bloomfield Branches. The panic of 1873 stopping all engineering work, he entered the office of the Hollidaysburg Iron and Nail Company early in 1874. In the Spring of 1875 he re-entered the service of the Pennsylvania Railroad Company on the engineering corps, and was stationed at Connellsville. From 1875 to 1877 he was Assistant Engineer in the construction of the chain suspension bridge over the Monongahela River in Pittsburgh, and, upon its completion, was appointed Assistant Engineer of the Pittsburgh and Lake Erie Railroad Company, then in course of construction, with which he remained until the completion of that road. In 1879 he returned to the Pennsylvania Railroad System in the capacity of Assistant Engineer in charge of the construction of the extension of the Pittsburgh, Virginia and Charleston Railway.

From 1879 to 1883, Mr. Rea was the engineer in charge of surveys in Westmoreland County and of the rebuilding of the Western Pennsylvania Railroad to make it a low grade freight line. This work was under the direction of J. N. DuBarry, then Assistant to the President, and afterwards Vice-President of the Pennsylvania Railroad Company. In 1883 Mr. Rea was transferred to Philadelphia as Assistant to Vice-President DuBarry, with title of Principal Assistant Engineer, which he held until 1888, when he was made Assistant to the Second Vice-President. This office he retained until 1889, when he resigned to go to Baltimore as Vice-President of the Maryland Central Railway Company, and Chief Engineer of the Baltimore Belt Railroad Company. In 1891, on account of ill-health, he resigned and left Baltimore, doing no active work for a year, when he resumed the practice of his profession.

After an absence of three years from the Pennsylvania Railroad Company, Mr. Rea was on May 25, 1892, chosen Assistant to the President of that Company. On the day of his appointment he left for London, where, by direction of President Roberts of the Pennsylvania Railroad Company, he made an examination of the railways terminating in the English metropolis, and of the underground railways,—then constructed and proposed—and subsequently he made a special report thereon. The result of this experience was afterward put to good service on the Pennsylvania Railroad's New York Tunnel Extension.

After the death of Vice-President DuBarry in 1892, Mr. Rea was assigned to general construction work then in progress, the acquisition of right of way and real estate for same, the promotion of all new lines or branches, and the financial and corporate work incident thereto. These duties with the exception of construction work, have since been discharged by him. On February 10, 1897, Mr. Rea was appointed First Assistant to the President of the Pennsylvania Railroad Company, and on June 14, 1899, following the election of Mr. A. J. Cassatt as President, to succeed Mr. Frank Thomson, Mr. Rea was elected Fourth Vice-President of the Company. On October 10, 1905, he was advanced to Third Vice-President, and on March 24, 1909, to Second Vice-President, and in connection with his former duties, was placed in charge of the Engineering and Accounting Departments. On March 3, 1911, he was elected First Vice-President. Mr. Rea is also First Vice-President of the Northern Central Railway, Philadelphia, Baltimore & Washington Railroad, and West Jersey and Seashore Railroad Companies, and a Director of the Pennsylvania Railroad Company and many other railroad and financial corporations.

Incident to supervising the corporate work of the subsidiary companies of the Pennsylvania Railroad Company East of Pittsburgh (and of the promotion and construction of new lines), Mr. Rea acts as President or Vice-President of these companies.

Mr. Rea is a member of the American Society of Civil Engineers and of the Institution of Civil Engineers of London. He is the author of "The Railways Terminating in London," a comprehensive study based on laborious personal investigation of the physical and financial condition of the English Railway Systems.

For many years he was interested in the project to bridge the Hudson River from Hoboken to New York City, and thus establish in the metropolis a terminus for the railroads using ferries from the New Jersey side. He was one of the incorporators of the North River Bridge Company, chartered by an Act of Congress to build that bridge.

On February 22, 1910, the University of Pennsylvania conferred the Degree of Doctor of Science on him in recognition of his ability in carrying to a successful conclusion the tunnel extension by which the Pennsylvania Railroad was extended into and through New York City.

GEN.
CHAS. W. RAYMOND
U.S.A.

CHAIRMAN
BOARD
OF
ENGINEERS

ALBERT J. COUNTY
ASST. TO FIRST VICE PRESIDENT
PENNSYLVANIA RAILROAD

HORACE G. BOOZ
ASST. CHIEF ENGINEER
PENNSYLVANIA RAILROAD

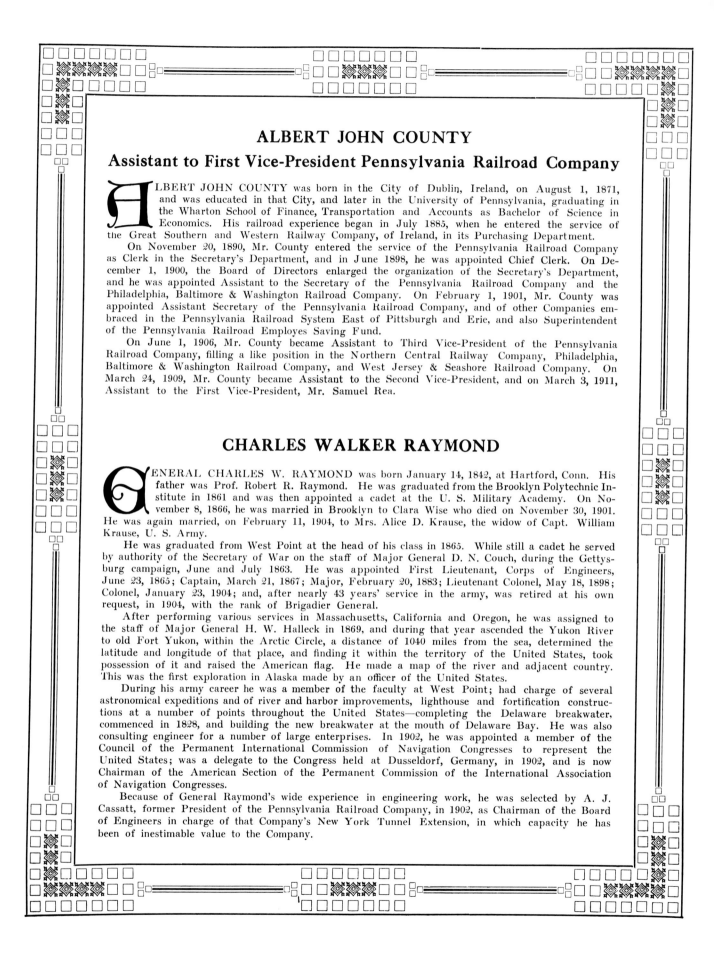

ALBERT JOHN COUNTY
Assistant to First Vice-President Pennsylvania Railroad Company

ALBERT JOHN COUNTY was born in the City of Dublin, Ireland, on August 1, 1871, and was educated in that City, and later in the University of Pennsylvania, graduating in the Wharton School of Finance, Transportation and Accounts as Bachelor of Science in Economics. His railroad experience began in July 1885, when he entered the service of the Great Southern and Western Railway Company, of Ireland, in its Purchasing Department.

On November 20, 1890, Mr. County entered the service of the Pennsylvania Railroad Company as Clerk in the Secretary's Department, and in June 1898, he was appointed Chief Clerk. On December 1, 1900, the Board of Directors enlarged the organization of the Secretary's Department, and he was appointed Assistant to the Secretary of the Pennsylvania Railroad Company and the Philadelphia, Baltimore & Washington Railroad Company. On February 1, 1901, Mr. County was appointed Assistant Secretary of the Pennsylvania Railroad Company, and of other Companies embraced in the Pennsylvania Railroad System East of Pittsburgh and Erie, and also Superintendent of the Pennsylvania Railroad Employes Saving Fund.

On June 1, 1906, Mr. County became Assistant to Third Vice-President of the Pennsylvania Railroad Company, filling a like position in the Northern Central Railway Company, Philadelphia, Baltimore & Washington Railroad Company, and West Jersey & Seashore Railroad Company. On March 24, 1909, Mr. County became Assistant to the Second Vice-President, and on March 3, 1911, Assistant to the First Vice-President, Mr. Samuel Rea.

CHARLES WALKER RAYMOND

GENERAL CHARLES W. RAYMOND was born January 14, 1842, at Hartford, Conn. His father was Prof. Robert R. Raymond. He was graduated from the Brooklyn Polytechnic Institute in 1861 and was then appointed a cadet at the U. S. Military Academy. On November 8, 1866, he was married in Brooklyn to Clara Wise who died on November 30, 1901. He was again married, on February 11, 1904, to Mrs. Alice D. Krause, the widow of Capt. William Krause, U. S. Army.

He was graduated from West Point at the head of his class in 1865. While still a cadet he served by authority of the Secretary of War on the staff of Major General D. N. Couch, during the Gettysburg campaign, June and July 1863. He was appointed First Lieutenant, Corps of Engineers, June 23, 1865; Captain, March 21, 1867; Major, February 20, 1883; Lieutenant Colonel, May 18, 1898; Colonel, January 23, 1904; and, after nearly 43 years' service in the army, was retired at his own request, in 1904, with the rank of Brigadier General.

After performing various services in Massachusetts, California and Oregon, he was assigned to the staff of Major General H. W. Halleck in 1869, and during that year ascended the Yukon River to old Fort Yukon, within the Arctic Circle, a distance of 1040 miles from the sea, determined the latitude and longitude of that place, and finding it within the territory of the United States, took possession of it and raised the American flag. He made a map of the river and adjacent country. This was the first exploration in Alaska made by an officer of the United States.

During his army career he was a member of the faculty at West Point; had charge of several astronomical expeditions and of river and harbor improvements, lighthouse and fortification constructions at a number of points throughout the United States—completing the Delaware breakwater, commenced in 1828, and building the new breakwater at the mouth of Delaware Bay. He was also consulting engineer for a number of large enterprises. In 1902, he was appointed a member of the Council of the Permanent International Commission of Navigation Congresses to represent the United States; was a delegate to the Congress held at Dusseldorf, Germany, in 1902, and is now Chairman of the American Section of the Permanent Commission of the International Association of Navigation Congresses.

Because of General Raymond's wide experience in engineering work, he was selected by A. J. Cassatt, former President of the Pennsylvania Railroad Company, in 1902, as Chairman of the Board of Engineers in charge of that Company's New York Tunnel Extension, in which capacity he has been of inestimable value to the Company.

Meadows Division and Manhattan Transfer

WM. H. BROWN   .   .   *Chief Engineer*
Retired March 1, 1906, and Succeeded by

ALEXANDER C. SHAND   *Chief Engineer*

EDWARD B. TEMPLE, *Ass't Chief Engineer*

WM. C. BOWLES   *Engineer of Construction*

MONOGRAPH
by
EDWARD B. TEMPLE
Assistant Chief Engineer Pennsylvania Railroad

WM. H. BROWN

EDW. B. TEMPLE   ALEX. C. SHAND   WM. C. BOWLES

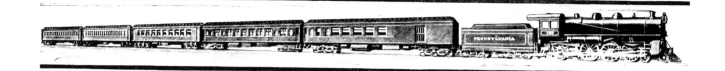

THE NEW YORK TUNNEL EXTENSION OF THE PENNSYLVANIA RAILROAD

MEADOWS DIVISION AND MANHATTAN TRANSFER*

THAT part of the New York Extension of the Pennsylvania Railroad lying west of the portals of the Bergen Hill Tunnels has been divided into two sections: First, known as the Manhattan Transfer Station and Yard; second, the Meadows Division of the Pennsylvania Tunnel and Terminal Railroad, which is a double-track railroad, 5.08 miles long, west of the western portals of the Bergen Hill Tunnels.

Manhattan Transfer Station and Yard.—The necessities for the improvements at this point are two-fold: First, as a place to change motive power from steam to electric, and *vice versa;* second, as a transfer for passengers from trains destined to the new station at Seventh Avenue and Thirty-third Street, New York City, to steam or rapid transit trains destined to the present Jersey City Station, or to the lower part of New York City *via* the Hudson and Manhattan Tunnels, and *vice versa.*

The time required to make this change of motive power, or to transfer passengers, does not exceed 3½ minutes.

The plan at Manhattan Transfer provides two platforms, each 1,100 feet long and 28 feet wide, having ample shelters and waiting rooms, connected by a twelve-foot tunnel under the tracks, provision being made for two additional platforms when necessity requires their construction. The platforms are supported on walls of reinforced concrete, with an overhang to provide a refuge for employees from passing trains. The concrete walls are supported on wooden piles, prevented from spreading by ⅞-inch tie-rods at ten-foot intervals, and embedded in concrete under the paving of the platform. The surface of the platforms, with the exception of the edges, is brick, on a concrete base; and, if settlement occurs, the bricks can be taken up and re-surfaced. The tops of the platforms are on a level with the floors of the cars, so that passengers may enter or leave trains without using steps.

There are four main running tracks, one adjacent to each side of the two platforms, providing standing room for four of the longest trains, two in each direction, or double the number of trains of ordinary length, so that passengers having to transfer from a train destined to the Pennsylvania Station at Thirty-third Street to a train destined for the Jersey City Station or the Hudson

and Manhattan Tunnels merely cross the platform. Between the two interior main tracks are two shifting tracks, so that between the platforms there will be two passenger tracks on which trains will stop to change motive power and transfer passengers, and two shifting tracks for rapid despatching of the empty engines and motors, each of the four tracks being fifteen feet from center to center to allow for uncoupling and inspection of cars.

An efficient system of connections and cross-overs is provided for all tracks, and there is ample storage capacity for ten steam engines at the western end of the platforms and twenty electric engines at the eastern end, both of which are conveniently located for quick movement, with provision for additional storage tracks, if required. Steam engines, upon being disconnected, are quickly sent to the main engine storage yard, and by the use of a loop track no turntable is required. The main engine storage yard is located south of the running tracks adjoining the bulkhead along the Passaic River, where provision is made for the storage of twenty engines. There are two 50,000-gallon water tanks, an ash-pit, inspection-pit, work-pit, sand-hopper, and the necessary buildings.

It was at first planned to locate a power-house and car and engine repair shops in the yard, but as the ultimate extent of the electrification of the New York Division cannot now be determined, the facilities in the large power-house in Long Island City, and in the shop and round-house in the Meadows Yard of the New York Division, were increased to provide for the power and repairs necessary for the next few years.

There is ample room at Harrison, and plans have been prepared providing for storage and light repair of cars, steam and electric locomotives and rapid transit trains, if the future demands require such construction at this place.

The rapid transit line extends from Park Place, Newark, to Manhattan Transfer, and thence over the present line of the Pennsylvania Railroad, which is electrified, to a junction with the Hudson and Manhattan Railroad Company's tunnel tracks at Prior Street, Jersey City. It was constructed and is owned by the Pennsylvania Railroad Company. A joint and frequent through

---

* Condensed from Transactions Am. Soc. C. E. Paper No. 1153. Page 75. Permission Am. Soc. C. E. Permission Mr. E. B. Temple, Asst. Chief Engineer P.R.R.

Concrete Telegraph and Telephone Pole Line

Hackensack Drawbridge

Manhattan Transfer Station

Power Transmission Line

service is now conducted by both companies between Park Place, Newark, and the terminal of the Hudson and Manhattan Railroad, in New York City, by the use of multiple-unit trains similar to those now being operated in the Hudson and Manhatan tunnels. These trains pick up and discharge Pennsylvania Railroad passengers at Manhattan Transfer, so that all passengers bound for lower New York City, who desire to use the tunnel service, now make the change at Manhattan Transfer instead of at Jersey City as heretofore. Provision is made for two additional platforms, each 1,100 feet long, to accommodate the rapid transit trains when the present platforms prove inadequate. The existing passenger tracks between the Manhattan Transfer and Summit Avenue, Jersey City, where a new local passenger station has been constructed, are being used jointly by steam and electric trains.

The embankment at Manhattan Transfer was made, under contract dated July 21, 1906, with Henry Steers, Incorporated, of New York City, of cellar earth from New York City, and with rock and earth excavated from the Pennsylvania Station and cross-town tunnels. It was necessary to construct 1,000 feet of stone and crib bulkhead along the bank of the Passaic River. The plan of the yard was prepared by a committee of operating, electrical, and engineering officers, consisting of Mr. F. L. Sheppard, General Superintendent, New Jersey Division, Pennsylvania Railroad Company; George Gibbs, Chief Engineer, Electric Traction and Station Construction, Pennsylvania Tunnel and Terminal Railroad Company; Mr. J. A. McCrea, General Superintendent, Long Island Railroad Company; Mr. C. S. Krick, Superintendent, Pennsylvania Tunnel and Terminal Railroad Company; Mr. A. M. Parker, then Principal Assistant Engineer, New Jersey Division, Pennsylvania Railroad Company, now Superintendent, Allegheny Division; and approved by Mr. A. C. Shand, Chief Engineer, Pennsylvania Railroad Company, and Chief Engineer, Meadows Division, Pennsylvania Tunnel and Terminal Railroad Company.

Meadows Division, Pennsylvania Tunnel and Terminal Railroad.—The two main tracks ascending through Manhattan Transfer continue on an embankment to a point five hundred feet west of the west abutment of the bridge over the New York Division tracks, which is the point of beginning of the Pennsylvania Tunnel and Terminal Railroad. From this point the line extends in a general northeasterly direction, crossing the Hackensack River, skirting the base of Snake Hill, and thence to the approach cut to Bergen Hill Tunnels. The embankment varies in height from twenty-five to thirty feet above the surface of the meadows.

On this Division the following bridges were necessary:

Pennsylvania Railroad, New York Division Passenger and Newark Freight Tracks;

Delaware, Lackawanna and Western Railroad, Morris and Essex Division;

Newark and Jersey City Turnpike;

Public Service Corporation Right of Way;

Erie Railroad, Newark and Paterson Branch;

Belleville Road, and Jersey City Water Company's Pipe Line;

Greenwood Lake Railroad (Erie Railroad), Arlington Branch;

Hackensack River;

Greenwood Lake Railroad (Erie Railroad), Reconstructed Line;

Delaware, Lackawanna and Western Railroad, Boonton Branch;

Erie Railroad, Passenger Tracks;

Bridge of eleven spans over proposed yard tracks, Erie Railroad;

County Road;

Secaucus Road;

New York, Susquehanna and Western Railroad;

Northern Railroad of New Jersey.

The alignment for this distance consists of 3.57 miles of tangent and three curves, two of which are 0° 30′ each, one of the latter being at the western end of the Division, and the other adjoining Snake Hill; the third is a regular curve of 1° 54′ on the east-bound track, and a compound curve with a maximum of 2° on the west-bound track, the variation being due to the track spacing of thirty-seven feet from center to center in the Bergen Hill Tunnels, while on the Meadows Division it is thirteen feet from center to center.

The profile was adopted to give eighteen feet of clearance from the under side of the bridges to the top of the rail of the Erie Railroad branches, twenty-one feet to the top of the rail of its main line, nineteen feet to the top of the rail of the Delaware, Lackawanna and Western Railroad, and a clearance of twenty-four feet above high water in the Hackensack River. With the exception of that portion of the line adjoining the Bergen Hill Tunnels, where it was necessary to continue the 1.3% grade up to the bridge over the Northern Railroad of New Jersey, and the east-bound ascending grade of 0.5% from the Manhattan Transfer platforms to the bridge over the New York Division tracks, the grades do not exceed 0.3 per cent.

When the construction of the embankment was commenced, it was expected that there would be considerable trouble by settlement due to the displacement of the soft material underlying the surface of the meadows to a depth of from ten to fifteen feet; but, the embankment as completed has settled very little. The section east of the Hackensack River was made, in great part, of rock. The embankment was built under two contracts, one for the work east of the crossing of the Boonton Branch of the Delaware, Lackawanna and Western Railroad, under contract dated January 15, 1907, with H. S. Kerbaugh, Incorporated, the material being taken from the borrow-pit in narrow-gauge cars and dumped from a strong pile trestle along the total length of the section, the same being completed in nineteen months; the other for the embankment west of the Boonton Branch, Delaware, Lackawanna and Western Railroad, under contract dated April 10, 1906, with Henry Steers, Incorporated, of New York City, the material, consisting partly of cellar earth, and partly of rock and earth excavated from other sections of the Pennsylvania Tunnel and Terminal Railroad, being brought on scows up the Hackensack and Passaic Rivers from New York City. The material was handled expeditiously from the scows by orange-peel buckets operated from the shore, deposited in standard-gauge dump-cars, and transported by locomotives at one time used on the elevated railroads in New York City. No

Open *Closed*

HACKENSACK DRAWBRIDGE

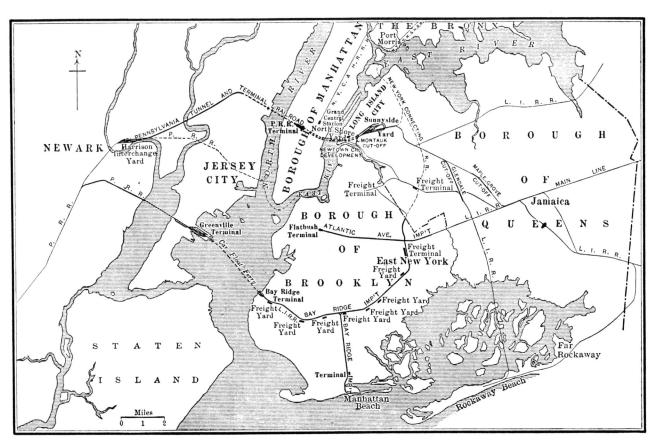

MAP OF THE PENNSYLVANIA R. R. CO.'S NEW YORK TUNNEL EXTENSION AND CONNECTIONS

excavation whatever was required on the Meadows Divison or in the Harrison Yard.

The substructures for all the bridges, except the Hackensack River Draw-bridge, are of concrete, without reinforcement, heavy enough to withstand the ordinary earth pressure for the exposed height. With the exception of three bridges, foundations were built on clay and sand; these three, on account of excessive depth of soft material, were built on piles. In some cases loose stone was deposited back of the foundations for a width of 10 or 12 ft. after the mud had been removed. This precaution has prevented trouble due to the thrust of the high embankments on the saturated material. Masonry for all these bridges was constructed under contract dated August 21st, 1905, with McMullen and McDermott, of New York City. The superstructure consisted principally of half-through girders, floor of I-beams, filled solid with concrete, on top of which were placed five layers of Hydrex felt, and water-proofing compound, protected by a layer of sand and grouted brick from the stone ballast.

The bridges over the New York Division passenger and Newark freight tracks of the Pennsylvania Railroad, and the main-line tracks of the Delaware, Lackawanna and Western Railroad, at the west end of the Meadows Division, are separated by 300 ft. of embankment. The skew angle is 9°, the total length of each bridge being about 450 ft. The floors consist of I-beams embedded in concrete.

The Hackensack River Draw-bridge consists of six spans of deck plate girders, each 110 feet long, and a draw-span 300 feet long, operated by two 70 horse-power electric motors. The masonry was constructed under contract dated August 25, 1905, with the Drake and Stratton Company, of Philadelphia; and the steel-work was furnished and erected by the Pennsylvania Steel Company, of Steelton, Pa. An important and interesting feature of the draw-bridge is the lift rail, and new rail-locking device. Mitered rails are used, with sufficient opening between the ends to prevent binding at times of expansion. It was deemed advisable that the mitered joint should occur on the abutment, or fixed span, instead of at the opening at the end of the draw. The lift rail, therefore, was a necessity; and the design was perfected. It consists of lift-rails, 8 feet 4 inches long, moving vertically 8 inches at the free end, reinforced on both sides by sliding steel castings, which are lifted with the rail; when the latter is dropped in place, the wedges on the castings engage at the abutment and heel joints and at one intermediate point in dove-tailed wedge seats, insuring tight contact with the rail, and absolute fast-

ening to the deck of the bridge. The objection to the ordinary lift-rail, which in lowering must make its own joint by seating in tight boxes, has been that any slight deviation from a true line would prevent the rail from seating itself properly. This objection has been entirely overcome in this design, by allowing liberal clearance on all seats, and securing rigidity by the sliding bars and wedges which are connected with the interlocking system, so that it is impossible for a clear signal to be given unless the lift-rails and wedges are in their proper positions. This device has been operated successfully on the New York and Long Branch Railroad bridge over Raritan Bay for the last eighteen months.

Each of the two main tracks on the Meadows Division, and all the main tracks at Manhattan Transfer are of standard construction, with Pennsylvania Section, 1909, 100-pound, open-hearth steel rails, and stone ballast. Every fifth tie is made 9 feet 5 inches long, to carry the third rail for the electric current, and all joints of the running rails are bonded for the same purpose. Track-laying on the Meadows, and in Harrison Transfer Yard, was done under contract with Henry Steers, Incorporated, of New York City.

Mr. Samuel Rea, First Vice-president, Pennsylvania Railroad Company, is the executive officer under whose direction the work was carried on. Mr. William H. Brown, Chief Engineer, Pennsylvania Railroad Company, and Chief Engineer of the Meadows Division, also a member of the Board of Engineers of the tunnel extension, until his retirement by age limit on February 28, 1906, located and started the construction of the line from Harrison to the western portals of the Bergen Hill Tunnels, which latter point was the westernmost limit of authority of the Board of Engineers. Mr. A. C. Shand succeeded Mr. Brown as Chief Engineer of the Pennsylvania Railroad Company, and as Chief Engineer of the Meadows Division, with the writer, who was Assistant Chief Engineer of the Pennsylvania Railroad Company, and had been closely associated with Mr. Brown at the time of the location of the line and its earlier period of construction. Mr. H. R. Leonard, Engineer of Bridges and Buildings, Pennsylvania Railroad Company, designed the Hackensack River Bridge, the superstructures of the other bridges, and the rail-locking device on the Hackensack River Drawbridge. The surveys and construction of the Meadows Division and of Manhattan Transfer were in charge of Mr. William C. Bowles, Engineer of Construction.

JAMES FORGIE

B.H.M.HEWETT

WM.LOWE BROWN

CHARLES M.JACOBS

B.F.CRESSON,JR.

F.LAVIS

H.F.D.BURKE

The North River Division

CHARLES M. JACOBS . *Chief Engineer*

JAMES FORGIE . *Chief Ass't Engineer*

B. H. M. HEWETT *Resident Engineer*

WM. LOWE BROWN *Resident Engineer*
River Tunnels

B. F. CRESSON, Jr. *Resident Engineer*
Terminal Station West

H. F. D. BURKE . *Resident Engineer*
River Tunnels

F. LAVIS . . *Resident Engineer*
Bergen Hill Tunnels

MONOGRAPH
by
B. H. M. HEWETT

THE NORTH RIVER DIVISION

Bergen Hill and North River Tunnels

ONE evening during the year 1906 two men were sitting together at the Engineers' Club in New York City. One, a native New Yorker, was a civil engineer; the other a stranger from the West. They were talking of the engineering work then in progress in the city. "What about these new Pennsylvania Railroad Tunnels?" the stranger said at last. "We hear some wonderful stories out our way about these tunnels, and I would like to find out something about them."

"Well," said the New Yorker, "let me give you an introduction to Mr. Charles M. Jacobs, who is the chief engineer of the tunnels under the North River. I am sure he will be glad to show you something of the work. I think you will get a good idea of what these tunnels are and how they are built; and assure you that it is a most interesting trip."

In the morning the visitor arrives at the office of the chief engineer at Fifth Avenue and Thirty-fourth Street, New York, and presents his letter of introduction. Mr. Jacobs welcomes his guest and tells him that it is perhaps worth while to point out the absolutely unprecedented problem which the Company had to solve in that it had to provide tunnels across the rivers surrounding the city which would be capable of carrying the fastest and heaviest main line passenger traffic, and thus the tunnels had to be of much larger and heavier construction than the small rapid transit tunnels which honeycomb this city. Not only that, but the bed of the Hudson River through which these tunnels had to pass consists of a mud which is extremely soft and contains about 33 per cent of water. The question of stability of tunnels through a material which seemed so entirely unsuitable for carrying heavy loads, was one of the most serious questions for which the engineers had to provide an answer in their plans. Mr. Jacobs explains that the tunnels have to pass through materials of every description, from the hardest rock in the Bergen Hill to the softest mud under the Hudson River, and that the visitor will find most varied methods are being used to deal with these varied conditions. In order to give him a rough idea of the amount of work to be done, the chief engineer tells him that there are about 1,100,000 cubic yards of excavation to be removed; that the weight of cast iron placed in the tunnels is 65,000 tons, with 2,500 tons of bolts; that 273,500 barrels of cement are needed to make the 200,000 cubic yards of concrete; that 906,000

pounds of dynamite will be used; and that the weight of the structural steel comes to 3,700,000 pounds.

Mr. Jacobs then introduces the visitor to his chief assistant engineer, Mr. James Forgie, whom he had brought over from London owing to his experience in work there similar to the Pennsylvania Railroad work, especially while an assistant of the late Mr. J. H. Greathead, who was really the pioneer of modern methods of tunneling by compressed air with shield, so that Mr. Forgie was most eminently fitted for his most onerous position.

Mr. Forgie now takes the visitor in hand, and before directing him to the work itself, explains some of the preliminaries that had to be done before contracts were let and the work begun. The visitor is told that before anything can be done in the way of making plans for such a piece of work, many borings have to be taken along the line of the proposed tunnels, so that an exact idea may be had of the ground that is to be met, these borings being taken not only along the line of the tunnels on dry land, but across the Hudson River by means of scows anchored in the stream. The borings are put down to and into bed rock, which in the middle of the river is over 300 feet below the surface of the water. Mr. Forgie also mentioned the long time taken in the careful designing of every detail, which occupied the years 1902 to 1904, and the letting of the contracts for the same. The work, the visitor learns, is divided into three main sub-divisions which had been let to the following contractors, all of New York City, and each one having had extensive experience in the carrying out of large and heavy construction work:

Bergen Hill Tunnels—William Bradley.

North River Tunnels—O'Rourke Engineering Construction Co.

Terminal Station, West—New York Contracting Co.

Mr. Forgie takes the visitor into the drafting room, where he sees a number of men busily engaged in designing of all kinds, in the recording of the works' progress, and in the hundred and one details to which a large work of this kind gives rise. Here he meets Mr. Paul Seurot, the office engineer, who has had charge of all this drafting work and under whose care the elaborate and careful contract drawings were made. As they walk through the office the visitor asks Mr. Forgie why it was that Mr. Cassatt chose Mr. Jacobs to be the chief engineer of such a work, and he is told that it was because of his unrivaled experience in the tunneling of the Hudson River. In the year 1892 his first introduction to the difficulties of tunneling in and around New York City was effected. In that year he began work on a tunnel to carry the gas mains of the East River Gas Company from Ravenswood, Long Island City, to Seventy-first Street, New York City, and passing below Blackwell's Island. This turned out to be a most formidable undertaking, as in place of the solid rock which was expected, the ground proved to be so rotten that it gave way completely and the tunnels became filled with mud and water. The contractors threw up their job and Mr. Jacobs finished it with his own forces under almost incredible difficulties, using an air pressure of fifty pounds per square inch above the usual atmospheric pressure to hold the water out. This pressure has seldom been exceeded in tunnel work. He afterwards successfully finished the old Hudson Tunnel which was started in 1874 and which had emptied more pockets and ruined more hopes than any other tunnel has done in the past or is likely to do in the future. Mr. Jacobs was the first man to walk dry-shod below the Hudson River, which he did on March 11, 1904, and knew more of its qualities as a thing to be tunneled than any other living man. Mr. Forgie then gave the visitor letters of introduction to the resident engineers, and mentioned that in order to get the best possible talent no pains had been spared in searching for men who were best qualified by training and experience to look after each respective portion. Mr. Fred Lavis, in charge of the Bergen Hill work, had had a varied career in railroad work of all kinds in the Western States of the Union and in many parts of South America. On the river tunnel section the work had been divided into two residencies, with Mr. W. L. Brown in charge of the New York side and Mr. H. F. D. Burke in charge of the New Jersey end. Mr. Brown had come direct from the great Assouan Dam on the Nile, Egypt, and previous to that had been in charge of tunnel work in London. Mr. Burke had come direct from India, where he was engineer for the State of Bharatput in that country and had previously had charge of tunnel work in London as well as experience on the construction of the Uganda Railway in Africa. Mr. B. F. Cresson, Jr., who was in charge of the Terminal Station-West, has been associated with Mr. Jacobs and his partners for many years. The staff as a whole was chosen strictly with a view to its greatest efficiency, so that there was hardly a state in the Union or a country of Europe without at least one representative. After receiving the letters of introduction, the visitor walks to the river front at Thirty-second Street, where he finds the despatch boat *Victor*. The captain, after examining his credentials, proceeds across the river. A safe landing having been made on the opposite shore, near the foot of "King's Bluff," at Weehawken, the historic scene of the encounter between Alexander Hamilton and Aaron Burr, the captain details a boy to guide the visitor to the office of Mr. Fred Lavis, the resident engineer in charge of the Bergen Hill Tunnels. On learning that the visitor wishes to go into the tunnels, Mr. Lavis asks him whether he is familiar with the design of the tunnel, and when the visitor says

he is not, it is explained to him that through the Bergen Hill the work consists of two entirely distinct tunnels, each to carry a single line of track. He is told that the Bergen Hill consists for nearly its entire width of 5,940 feet of trap rock, which is an igneous, basaltic rock of extreme hardness and toughness. This rock is entirely self-supporting, but in order to give the tunnels the proper finish and to make them uniform with all the rest, they are lined with concrete and have a semi-circular arched roof and flat benches on either side containing vitrified earthenware ducts to enable the electric cables to be carried through the tunnels. The tunnels are quite straight and rise on a 1.3 per cent grade from Weehawken to the Portal at the Hackensack Meadows. The contract was let on March 2, 1906, to William Bradley of New York.

The visitor is then provided with an overcoat and a waterproof hat, and accompanied by Mr. Lavis he steps out into the yard. One of the first things that strikes his attention is the enormous pile of iron castings stacked up along one side of the yard. Never having seen such castings before, he asks Mr. Lavis what they are and he is told they are the segments which form the lining of the tunnel passing underneath the Hudson River, which the visitor will enter later on. On the way to the shaft Mr. Lavis points out the storage yard for cement, of which a large quantity has to be kept on hand for use at any moment. The visitor then finds he is at the edge of the Weehawken shaft itself. Mr. Lavis tells him that the first important piece of construction was that of this shaft, which was built during the time when the drawings and specifications themselves were being prepared. This was done in order that time might be saved, so that when the contractors for the tunnels themselves were obtained the necessary shafts would be found ready waiting for them and the time of making them would thereby be saved. The work on Weehawken shaft was started on June 11, 1903, the contractors being the United Engineering and Contracting Co. The shaft, which is on the line of the tunnel, so that it forms a piece of "open cut" at this point, is 76 feet deep, 56 feet wide at the bottom, 100 feet wide at the top, 116 feet long at the bottom and 154 feet long at the top. There were 55,000 cubic yards of excavation taken out and 10,000 cubic yards of concrete put in. The shaft was finished September 1, 1904, on which date the contractors on the tunnels stepped into possession and began their work.

The two men then stepped into a small elevator or "cage" and were lowered rapidly to the bottom of the shaft. The visitor now finds himself in front of the entrance to the Bergen Hill Tunnels, looking westward.

Inside the tunnel a busy scene presents itself. Cars filled with rock drawn by mules pass in an endless procession, while from the far end of the tunnel comes a confused noise of hammering and escaping air. Before reaching the face Mr. Lavis stops the visitor and explains briefly to him the method used in driving a tunnel of this kind, so that when he gets to the "face" he will be in a better position to understand what he sees going on. Every piece of rock has to be taken out by means of drilling and blasting, and in this case as is usual in American tunnels, the excavation is done as follows:

A small tunnel, called a "heading," is driven in advance on the center line of the finished tunnel and at the top. The driving of the heading goes on continuously until it meets the heading driven from the opposite end. The rest of the excavation is called the "bench," and the excavation of the bench proceeds also all the time but is kept about fifty feet behind the face of the heading. All drilling is done by power drills driven by compressed air. Those in the heading are supported on columns which are screwed or wedged tightly between the roof and the floor of the heading, and each column supports two, three or four drills. The drills are started and holes ten feet deep drilled all over the face of the heading; when these holes are finished each is loaded with dynamite, the dynamite exploded, and the rock thrown in small pieces back into the tunnel. The drilling for the bench is done in a similar manner, except that the drills are mounted on tripods instead of on columns, and the holes are drilled vertically into the top of the bench—which is really the floor of the heading—instead of horizontally as in the case of the holes in the heading. As far as the rest of the routine is concerned, it is the same. It is generally found that a good deal more drilling and blasting has to be done after the heading and bench excavation is done, in order to trim the rock out to the full size. To help in the disposal of the broken rock a small steam shovel is used.

They now arrive at the face, where the actual work of excavation is proceeding. Two or three heavy columns are wedged between the floor and the roof, and on these columns rock drills driven by compressed air are pounding the rock with a deafening noise. The roar of escaping air fills up the spaces between the blows of the drills. As in all work of an engineering nature, the general impression is that of confusion, noise and dirt. Mr. Lavis knows what the visitor does not, that into every operation that is being performed, careful thought has been put, so that the greatest amount of work may be done with the least expenditure of money and time. Presently Mr. Lavis motions to the visitor—for the noise is so great that it is impossible to make one's self heard—that it is time to retire, as the holes have been drilled and are about to be loaded and fired. He scrambles down the rock pile, the drills are removed from the columns and hurried down the slope, followed by the columns themselves, and the rubber hose is taken away. Then the "powderman" comes up with his dangerous burden; the sticks of dynamite with wires attached to the caps, are inserted in the holes and tamped down with paper tubes of sand above them; the wires are connected with the battery, which is kept 300 feet or more away from the face. The electric lights are carried back to the same distance, every man in the tunnel goes back behind the battery; the powderman takes one last look around to see that everything is all right. He then gives the long-drawn warning shout of "Fire!" and presses the key of the battery. The visitor has been warned to put his fingers in his ears. A tremendous explosion shakes the entire tunnel, and dense clouds of thick acrid smoke and dust fill the air. Some of the men now carry a pipe as near the face as they can get and the compressed air is turned on through it, so that the fumes are blown away as quickly as possible. After the air has been blown into the heading for some

twenty or thirty minutes, it is possible for one or two men to go up into the heading and carefully test the rock, picking down all loose pieces and preparing for a fresh attack. The columns are carried up the pile of debris; the drills follow, and with the columns are set up again; the air connections are made, and once more the drills are pounding at the rock and the "muckers" have hurled themselves on the huge pile of freshly shattered rock awaiting their labors; the mules resume their ceaseless journeys to and fro; and another ten-foot step has been taken in the piercing of the Bergen Hill.

Mr. Lavis tells the visitor that the average advance per attack is about 8½ feet, the average time for each attack about 36 hours, the average advance per 24 hours was about 5 feet; that the depth of the drill holes was 10 feet and the diameter of the holes, 2¾ inches. He tells him that on the Bergen Hill Tunnels the average number of men employed per day is 450, and that they are worked on two shifts of ten hours each. The best week's work in the trap work has been 803 cubic yards, equal to 41.8 lineal feet of full section of tunnel, or an average of six lineal feet of full section per day. The best month's work has been 145 feet of heading in trap rock.

Of course work of this kind requires a very considerable plant on the surface, and the contractor installed most of his plant at the Hackensack Portal. There are two pairs of Stirling boilers with a total capacity of 2,000 horse-power and eight air-compressors of the Rand straight-line steam-driven type, with a normal capacity of 1,250 cubic feet of free air per minute. About 50 tons of bituminous coal are burned and about 12,000 cubic feet of water used in the 24 hours.

The visitor was anxious to know how the cement lining is placed inside the rough rock which was all he could see, and so Mr. Lavis described to him that the general sequence of laying concrete lining is as follows:

The concrete is first placed in the foundations up to the elevation of the bottom of the conduit lines; then follow the walls—called "sand walls"—on which the waterproofing is laid, and which come outside the main lines of the tunnel. The vitrified conduits for electric cables are then put in place; the bench walls, or covering for the conduits, are then placed; and last of all the arch. The lining of these tunnels consists wholly of concrete, which is formed of a mixture of cement, sand and broken stone. These ingredients are mixed in the proper proportions, water is added, and the semi-liquid concrete is filled in behind the moulds or "forms," usually made of wood. The forms are left in place until the concrete is "set" or hardened, when they are moved ahead and the operation is repeated. The visitor is told that on this contract the concrete is mixed in "Hains" mixers, by which the materials are allowed to drop successively through hoppers so that they arrive at the bottom in an intimately mixed condition. The concrete was hauled to the point of work by locomotives. For the purpose of putting in the concrete, the contractor, William Bradley, made a sub-contract with Messrs. King, Rice & Ganey.

Mr. Lavis tells his guest that the heading which they have visited is being driven to meet a similar one which is drawing near from the western side of the hill.

They have now arrived at the shaft again, and the

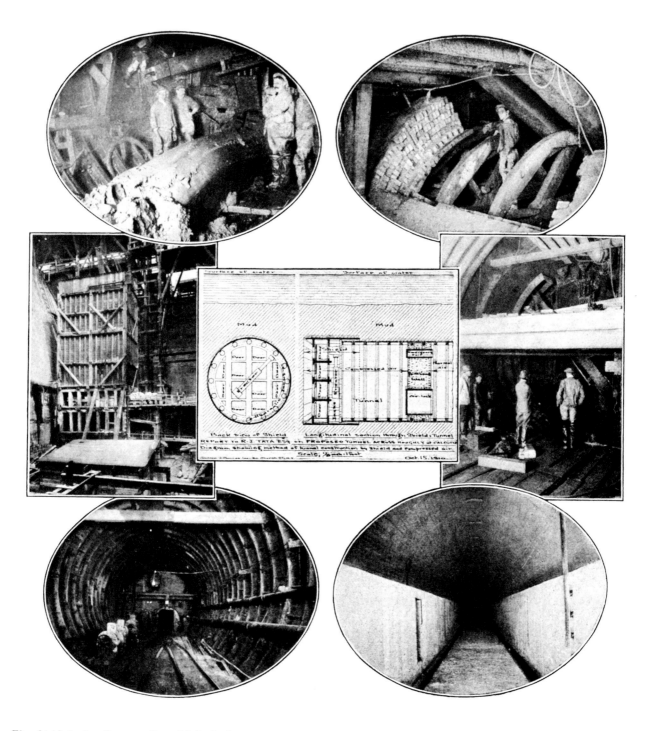

The shield during the operation of "shoving" or going ahead with one of its bulkhead doors open, allowing the mud or silt to squeeze through this door into the tunnel.

Interior view of one end of the Weehawken Shaft. The high box-like structure on the left comprises the sand and stone bins for the concrete mixer which is below.

General view of a shield-driven tube tunnel during construction and before concrete lining is put in. The cross timbers at the top support the upper or emergency platform which leads from the shield to the emergency lock in the bulkhead wall.

Brick arch in process of being built in tunnels under Thirty-second Street, New York City.

Putting in a side segment in the shield-driven tunnel. The shield is to be seen ahead of the heavy cross timber. The man in the top part of the shield is in charge of the hydraulic valves which control the pushing jacks and the erector. The erector is seen lifting a segment into position.

View through one of the completed Bergen Hill Tunnels, showing length of 1⅛ miles of tunnel looking from the Weehawken Shaft towards the western portal on the Hackensack Meadows, ready for traffic.

visitor notices opposite him and leading in an easterly direction, two more tunnels precisely similar to that in which he has just been. Mr. Lavis explains that he is to visit those tunnels, and informs him that they are part of the North River Residency and are under the supervision of other resident engineers, Mr. W. L. Brown and Mr. H. F. D. Burke. Mr. Lavis then despatches his visitor to the *Victor*, which carries him to the New York side.

He has no difficulty in finding the Manhattan field office, as he again sees the now familiar piles of iron castings, and the "head house" towering above the mouth of the shaft. He makes his way upstairs to the office and finds Messrs. Burke and Brown discussing a lunch which includes tunnel coffee, which is always a prominent feature in work of this kind, as the doctors claim it is the best antidote for the ill effects of compressed air work.

Mr. Brown suggests that before going down into the tunnel it would be well to have a look at the general plans, and to see the kind of work done in the office. From the plans the visitor learns the reason for the enormous piles of iron castings he sees on every hand. He sees that the tunnel which crosses under the Hudson River consists of two separate tubes, each one to contain one line of track. Each tube is 23 feet in external and 21 feet 2 inches in internal diameter, and is built of cast iron segments forming "rings," each 2 feet 6 inches in length; these rings are bolted together segment to segment and ring to ring, thus forming a strong watertight barrier against the mud and water in which they are buried. Inside the cast iron tube is placed the concrete lining, very similar to that used in the Bergen Hill Tunnels. The visitor was greatly interested in the gauges in the resident engineers' room, which showed continuously a record of the air pressure in the tunnels, the revolutions of the air compressors, and every other detail enabling them to be in constant touch with the work. In turn he then visits the cement laboratory, where most careful tests are constantly in progress as to the quality and soundness of the cement used on the work, as well as the quality of the bricks and the efficiency of the waterproofing and other materials that are built into the tunnel, in order to make sure that they are in accordance with the specifications; the drafting-room, where a number of young men are plotting on plans the progress made, and making record drawings of every part of the work exactly as it is built; and the photographer's room, where are seen the elaborate arrangements for photographing every stage of the work as a matter of record, and where samples of compressed air are analyzed daily to assure the requisite degree of purity being maintained.

In the inspectors' room they find a gang of young engineers who have just come up from duty in the tunnel where they carefully watch every stage of the work and make records which may serve to show what every operation is costing. The "alignment corps" room is devoted to the use of the men who are charged with the difficult work of furnishing the lines and levels to which the tunnel has to be built, so that the work started from one side of the river may meet exactly that which is built from the other side. By this time he is quite astounded by the multifarious duties with which the field engineers are charged, and he asks how large a staff it is necessary to maintain, and is informed that on the river tunnel section the staff reporting, through the residents, to Mr. Jacobs as chief engineer numbers about one hundred men, most of them engineers of various kinds, and that this organization, which is purely for supervisory purposes, is entirely distinct from the contractor's organization, that is, from the men who actually do the work in the tunnels. Mr. Brown and Mr. Burke now ask the visitor whether he wishes to go below, and when he says "Yes," they tell him it is first necessary to pass a medical examination. This, of course, sounds rather alarming to the visitor, but he is assured that unless a man is suffering from an extremely weak heart there is no danger in a short visit in compressed air; and they now hand the visitor over to one of the assistant engineers, who is to act as his guide underground. This young man is a type of the many who are to be seen above ground and below. His get-up suggests efficiency rather than a striving after a Beau Brummel effect, and his old felt hat, flannel shirt and khaki trousers tucked into tall boots, show many signs of honorable conflict with Mother Earth. The guide conducts him downstairs to the contractor's offices. Here they are fortunate to meet Mr. George B. Fry, general superintendent of the contractors, O'Rourke Engineering Construction Co., who on hearing that the visitor has come with a letter of introduction from Mr. Jacobs, shows him the arrangements made for the comfort and convenience of the men. These are unusually complete. Every man is provided with a steel locker so that he may make a complete change of clothes before going below. Drying rooms are provided, so that his wet tunnel clothes may be thoroughly dried before he puts them on again. Hot and cold baths are at his disposal, as well as hot coffee in liberal quantities. In fact he is looked after in every way. The visitor is then taken into the doctor's office and examined by Dr. A. J. Loomis, who has had an unrivaled experience in this kind of work, having been with Mr. Jacobs ever since the undertaking of the Hudson River tunnels, now known as the "McAdoo tubes." Armed with a clean bill of health from the doctor, the visitor is now taken upstairs again, and all is in readiness for his descent into the North River Tunnels. He is now provided with rubber hat, coat and boots, all of them several sizes too large, and led through a covered passage towards the shaft itself. He steps into a small elevator or "cage" and is shot rapidly down to the bottom of the shaft. His guide tells him that the depth of this shaft is 55 feet, and the size 22 feet by 32 feet in plan. It is placed on the north side of the tunnel line, so that the bottom of the shaft is connected with the tunnels by a cross passage. Work on this shaft was begun on June 10, 1903, and finished on December 11, 1903. The contractor was the same organization that built the Weehawken Shaft, namely the United Engineering & Contracting Co. of New York. At this point he begins to wish he had never embarked on such a hazardous expedition. There is a great deal of water dripping, a great deal of darkness, what appears to him a great deal of noise and confusion, and visions of extremely dirty-looking men hurry in every direction. He goes forward and finds he is in the tunnel itself, a line of electric lights marking its direction. A little further on he finds a wall built entirely across the tunnel. In this wall are three massive iron doors. His guide goes up to the wall, opens a valve, so that air escapes with a roar, waits a few moments, and when the escape of air stops, pushes open one of the doors, motioning the guest into a small iron compartment provided with a narrow bench on one side. He then shuts the door, turns another valve, and immediately a loud hissing sound fills the entire compartment. By this time the visitor is reminded forcibly of Mr. Dante's well-known remark on hope and is in such a state of mind that he would be willing to give all he has to find himself once more in sunlight. After allowing the compressed air—for such it is that is now filling the compartment—to flow in for a few seconds, the guide shuts it off and asks the visitor whether he is feeling any discomfort about his ears, and finding he is tells him to pinch his nose, shut his mouth, and attempt to blow through his ears. The guest carries out these complicated instructions to the best of his ability and finds the pain disappearing. This pain is caused by the fact that the pressure on the outside of the eardrum is greater than that on the inside, because the delicate and complicated ear passages do not allow a ready adjustment of pressure between the inside and the outside, and this process is used to permit the passages to take up the equilibrium of pressure. The guide now turns on the air-pressure again slowly, the temperature rising rapidly all the time, and finally, when the air pressure inside the "lock"—for such is the name, derived from the locks on a canal which raise water from one level to another instead of air pressure in this case, of the little chamber in which they are—is equal to the pressure inside the tunnel itself, the inner door can be opened and the guest steps into the working chamber of the tunnel. What he sees now is a regular succession of rings of cast iron forming a gigantic tube, with two lines of narrow-gauge tracks laid on a timber floor, and an overhead platform supported by timbers laid across the tunnel above him. On one side cars containing cast iron segments run down the track in the direction in which he is walking, while other cars loaded with black semi-liquid mud are constantly met being pulled up on the other track by means of an endless rope.

The guide now stops and describes the method by which a tunnel of this kind is actually built. The iron shell is put in place by means of a "shield," which is an ingenious tool which both protects the work under construction and also assists in the building of the iron shell. The tunneling shield consists essentially of a cylinder slightly larger in diameter than the tube or tunnel it is intended to build. The front end of this cylindrical shield is provided with a bulkhead or diaphragm, in which are doors that may be opened or closed at will. Behind this bulkhead a number of hydraulic jacks are arranged in such a way that by their thrust against the last erected ring of iron lining, the entire shield is pushed forward. The hinder end of the shield is simply a continuation of the cylinder which forms the front end, and this portion or "tail" always overlaps the last few feet of the built-up iron shell. It is clear that when the doors in the bulkhead are closed the tunnel is protected from an inrush of either water or

ground, and the openings in this bulkhead may be so regulated that control is maintained over the material passed through. After a ring of iron lining has been erected within the shield, excavation is carried out ahead. When enough excavation has been taken out the hydraulic jacks are thrust out, thus pushing the shield ahead. Another ring of iron is erected within the tail, for which purpose an hydraulic swinging arm called the "erector" is mounted on the shield itself. Excavation is again carried on, and the whole cycle of operations repeated, thus gaining a length equal to the width of one ring every time the jacks are moved forward. This method of construction can be followed in almost any kind of ground which can possibly be met and it is especially valuable in dealing with soft, wet ground, in which the open system of tunneling operates at enormous difficulty and cost.

The visitor is not yet clear as to the exact function or need of compressed air in which the work is carried on, so his guide explains that in passing through ground charged with water the shield is assisted by compressed air; that is to say, temporary bulkhead walls containing the "airlocks" are built across the tunnel behind the shield, and air compressed to the degree necessary to overcome either entirely or partly the "head" under which the water in the ground lies, is forced into the entire length of tunnel lying beyond the walls. This converts the ground from an unstable into a stable material by driving out the water from it and simplifies enormously all the methods of handling it.

They walk further through the tunnel and the visitor now finds himself in the midst of a very busy scene. Some thirty or forty men are hard at work, and in the dim light it will take him some time to make out any concerted action or method in their manner of working, but after a time he will see that the operations they are performing are somewhat of the following order. We will suppose he has arrived at the shield just after the jacks have been forced out, so that the men are ready to build up an entire ring of iron lining. A flat car containing two segments is run as close to the shield as possible; an iron chain is attached to the end of the revolving "erector" and hooked on to one of the segments. This erector is then revolved, the segment pulled off the car and allowed to drop with a loud crash into the bottom of the "tail" of the shield. Five or six men immediately jump down into the bottom with bolts and bolt this segment to the corresponding segment in the last erected ring. When this is done the chain is hooked to the other segment on the car, and this segment is then dropped into position and bolted up to the first one and also to the last erected ring. Another car containing two more segments has meanwhile been brought forward. They are in turn picked up by the revolving erector and one is placed on each side above the two first put in. This process is repeated over and over again until all the segments had been erected. The last segment to be put in place is the narrow "key" segment. The whole gang then tightens up bolts, and the shield is ready to be shoved ahead again.

A man climbs up into one of the top compartments of the shield; four more men detach themselves from the group, each armed with a foot rule. One climbs up into the top of the shield, another takes his place on

CHIEF ENGINEER OF THE NORTH RIVER DIVISION AND STAFF

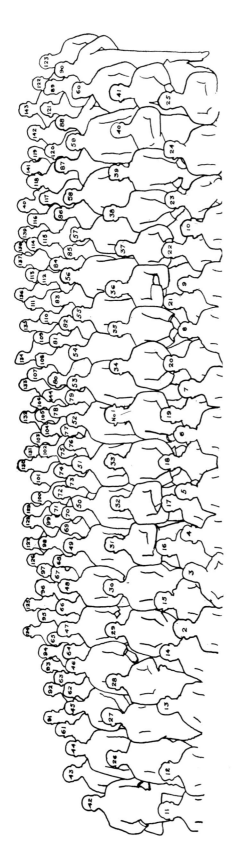

NORTH RIVER DIVISION STAFF

1. Charles M. Jacobs.
2. D. O'Connor.
3. J. L. Hessner.
4. L. Y. Frost.
5. B. J. Dunne.
6. Wm. Feney.
7. J. Gefvert.
8. J. Gourlay.
9. E. Sneed.
10. W. J. Gordon.
11. A. Koenig.
12. D. V. Cummins.
13. J. L. Scudor.
14. J. Hansbury.
15. J. Connolly.
16. J. E. Alexander.
17. J. Goerz.
18. J. F. Ferguson.
19. A. S. Hay.
20. H. S. Craven.
21. W. Taylor.
22. S. H. Coombe.
23. J. J. Kelly.
24. A. Miskell.
25. H. D. Bastow.
26. H. I. Wild.
27. W. H. Lyon.
28. I. R. Taft.
29. E. Y. Allen.

30. F. Lavis.
31. H. F. D. Burke.
32. B. H. M. Hewett.
33. James Forgie.
34. A. J. Loomis.
35. B. F. Cresson, Jr.
36. Wm. L. Brown.
37. J. C. Naegeley.
38. J. Soderberg.
39. H. E. Boardman.
40. J. F. Rodenbough.
41. H. U. Hitchcock.
42. A. Gregson.
43. H. Meeker.
44. A. S. Webb.
45. J. B. Ancher.
46. W. W. Baker.
47. H. W. Hegeman.
48. R. T. Robinson.
49. J. F. Sullivan.
50. Geo. Andrew.
51. P. F. Dietrich.
52. W. B. Johnstone.
53. M. Ketchum.
54. A. W. Gill.
55. E. R. Peckens.
56. C. F. Thomas.
57. F. A. Hitchcock.
58. E. A. Saunders.

59. G. Taylor.
60. S. F. Michael.
61. C. J. Dore.
62. L. Jenkins.
63. N. Maynard.
64. T. A. Skelly.
65. F. Kiernan.
66. H. E. Lindholm.
67. C. Frost.
68. J. A. Beck.
69. F. P. Nickerson.
70. R. L. Reynolds.
71. M. D. Case.
72. R. M. Beck.
73. L. E. Firth.
74. W. A. Winter.
75. P. B. McMahon.
76. A. F. Treadcroft.
77. J. A. Birch.
78. A. L. Heyer, Jr.
79. T. D. Penrice.
80. A. E. Price.
81. A. F. Combes.
82. N. C. McNeil.
83. G. D. Long.
84. H. C. Kirkwood.
85. J. D. Richardson.
86. T. B. Whitney.
87. C. Richardson.

88. J. S. Butler.
89. B. F. Colmer.
90. I. F. Druar.
91. K. M. Cameron.
92. S. L. Webb.
93. F. A. McDonald.
94. G. T. Whelton.
95. H. F. Thomas.
96. A. W. Heisler.
97. A. Culver.
98. W. A. Sanders.
99. J. J. Davidson.
100. R. A. Case.
101. R. Seweizer.
102. F. Beck.
103. F. Banville.
104. T. C. Caddigan.
105. C. P. Gehling.
106. H. F. Reynolds.
107. F. Kerr.
108. W. A. Bartley.
109. B. C. Gillette.
110. T. B. Brogan.
111. R. S. Campbell.
112. H. S. Palmer.
113. W. P. Katz.
114. W. Strache.
115. G. J. Greene.
116. G. T. Haldeman.

117. L. Patterson.
118. Victor Meek.
119. R. H. Robson.
120. C. G. Barry.
121. J. B. Joseph.
122. Paul Lingle.
123. C. C. English.
124. P. J. O'Brien.
125. H. Duberstein.
126. R. B. Wolff.
127. F. W. Swanson.
128. R. Von Brunn.
129. J. C. Stephens.
130. J. P. Conkling.
131. F. M. W. Conkling.
132. O. A. Conklin.
133. P. Hogan.
134. F. E. Pareis.
135. C. R. Shafer.
136. F. Odone.
137. H. G. Wallace.
138. W. Cusack.
139. D. B. McAllister.
140. N. D. Brainard.
141. J. J. Leonard.
142. L. M. Palmer.
143. G. V. McShane.
144. D. F. Yard.

the right-hand side, a third on the left, while the fourth stands at the bottom. The foreman stands on the bottom platform of the tunnel in such a position that he can see each of the men with the foot rules. The man who climbed up into the top compartment is the man who controls the hydraulic valves by which the pressure is admitted to the jacks and by the regulation of which the shield is guided. The foreman knows whether his shield has a tendency to the right or to the left, or to get above or below where it should be; and by regulating the distance which each jack is moved forward he can drive his shield in the same way as the steersman of a ship can control her course by the use of a rudder. As the man in charge of the valves admits the hydraulic pressure twenty-four jacks move out, with their total pressure of 3,400 tons, and the shield goes ahead. The foreman watches closely the readings on the four foot-rules, and as a result of those readings he calls out repeatedly instructions to the man in charge of the valves to shut off this one, and to open that one, so that by the time the shield has been pushed through the soft mud for the required distance for two feet six inches in order to permit of the erection of one more ring, he knows that it has traveled on the line and on the grade which he desires. Sometimes while the shield is being pushed forward, all of the doors in the front of the shield are closed tight, so that it pushes its way bodily through the soft ground and none whatever is brought into the tunnel. Usually, however, there is at least one door of the shield open, as this much facilitates its pushing. The mud streams in through this door in a semi-liquid mass like an enormous sausage. While the shield is going forward and mud is flowing into the tunnel, cars are run up as near as possible on both tracks, and men who are not actually engaged in the shoving of the shield, shovel the mud into the cars as it pours through the shield. By the time the shield has advanced its stroke of two feet six inches, half of the mud that was brought in has been usually cleared away. After the shield has stopped, the rest of the mud is filled into the cars and taken out of the tunnel, and by that time cars of iron lining have been brought down, and things are once more ready for the erection of another ring of iron lining. It will be seen at once that the entire operation is one that is repeated over and over again, so that men become more and more skilful. When the work first started five and six hours were spent in erecting one ring, while towards the latter end of the work the same operation has been done in thirty minutes. The visitor begins to realize that every ring is like every other ring, and that the whole skill of the operation consists in steering the heavy shield, weighing 200 tons, through the semi-liquid mud exactly on the course laid out by the engineers.

While they stand watching the work a couple of young engineers are seen going over all the bolts, seeing that they are properly tightened and that all the work is well done. The visitor hears voices on the platform above his head and makes out another party of three or four. "Here comes the alignment bunch," says the guide, and they see that this new lot of men have instruments with them and are engaged in seeing that the last ring of iron is in its proper place. An instrument is turned on the ring, a graduated staff is held against it, the instrument is read, two men with lighted candles in hand and a steel tape clamber over the ring and measure it in every way. Calculations are made in a book, a consultation is held with the foreman and detailed instructions as to the position of the last ring and the precautions to be observed in the next "shove" of the shield are written on a bulletin hanging in a box at the side of the tunnel. His guide impressed upon him that what he had seen was typical of tunnel work in compressed air in the ground underlying the Hudson River itself and forming by far the greater part of the ground through which the shields on the North River Division are driven. As a matter of fact, however, these shields, before they arrive at the actual Hudson River silt, were called upon to pass through every conceivable kind of ground from the hardest rock to the worst kind of filled ground; gravel, clay, boulders, wooden piles and rip-rap all had to be dealt with, and the method of attack had to be modified in each case to suit the particular conditions. When in rock, blasting had to be done just as in the case of the Bergen Hill Tunnel, and great care had to be taken to prevent flying rock from unduly damaging the shield, which in this case followed behind the excavation and was simply pushed into the hole made by the blasting. As the rock surface dropped lower and lower towards the river, another condition was met, in which the lower part of the shield was in rock and the upper part in soft ground. This was a still worse condition of affairs, as it was not possible to shove the shield bodily through the soft ground, as was done in the sub-river portion, but the entire roof had to be timbered heavily to support the soft ground, while the rock in the bottom was excavated by drilling and blasting. On the Weehawken side the tunnels passed through a long stretch of coarse gravel containing water under a heavy pressure. The gravel was of such an open character that as fast as the compressed air was blown in, it escaped through the ground in front of the shield, and although a very large margin had been allowed for emergencies, the compressed air plant was inadequate to supply the requisite amount of air for both the tunnels, so that they had to be advanced one at a time, and even then for a period of two months the entire compressed air plant was worked at its maximum capacity without stopping for a single moment day or night. On the Weehawken side the tunnels also passed underneath a heavy warehouse, built many years ago and supported on an enormous number of long piles. As the shield passed beneath this warehouse the piles had to be cut, and this operation was an extremely delicate and hazardous one.

On the New York side the bulkhead wall forming the margin of the river consisted of a pile-supported crib-work with a mass of rip-rap thrown down around the piles. This formed a very awkward combination for the shield, as the loose rip-rap, consisting of stones about the size of a man's head and larger, formed an entirely open passage for the compressed air, so that the escaping air produced heavy geysers or "blows." These continued to such an extent that the mud covering above the tunnels was completely blown off at this point, and when soundings were made to determine what depth of mud was above the tunnels it was found that the sounding lead was striking directly on the top of the

Building concrete side wall of land tunnels, showing waterproofing at right.

Part of locker room for contractor's compressed air tunnel force.

The operation of caulking the joints of the iron-lined tunnel below the Hudson River; tightening up bolts, hammering the caulking mixture of sal-ammoniac and iron borings into the joints and putting the caulking mixture in the joints preparatory to hammering it in.

A type of the timbering used in the Bergen Hill Tunnels in the sandstone near the Weehawken Shaft before reaching the "trap" rock of which the Bergen Hill is composed.

Making a boring into bed rock from the tunnel below the Hudson River. This water is coming from a depth of 200 feet below the tunnel, and is pouring in in enormous quantities.

Putting in the top segment. This is called the "key," and is the last put in. The erector is seen supporting the key, which is being thrust up into the space prepared for it.

New York rock tunnels during progress of concrete and brick work. This view shows some of the timbering used in a section built by the "cut and cover" method.

iron lining. In order to stop this "blow" it was necessary to throw about 30,000 bags of clay above the tunnels before the blow could be checked. However, notwithstanding these troublesome incidents, which were all expected and provided for, owing to the careful borings and test pits sunk before the work was started, the shields were successfully driven until those that were started from the New York side met those traveling eastward from the New Jersey side. The visitor was anxious to know how tunnels are started from the opposite sides of a high mountain or deep river and brought together so exactly, when those working in the tunnel cannot see which way they are going. His guide tells him that it is difficult to explain this part of the work shortly and yet clearly, but in the case of the tunnel engineer it forms by no means the least of the troubles he has to get over. The principle is that of triangulation and instrumental work similar to that used by the navigator who starts from one port and finally brings his ship to anchor at another half the world away. This survey work is done on the surface before the tunnels are started and then transferred below ground by way of the shaft. The period during which the two tunnels are approaching one another is always an anxious one for those responsible for that part of the work, and they are apt to suffer severely from an aggravated form of nightmare at that time. In the case of these tunnels a very accurate junction was made and the two shields came together, rim to rim, like two tumblers placed edge to edge. The guide told the visitor that the first piece of traffic to pass through the tunnel was a box of cigars pushed through a small hole in the ground from New York to New Jersey between the two shields before they actually met.

The visitor then meets "Paddy" Fitzgerald, the best practical shield man alive in New York. He has worked on most of the important tunnels around the city, and what he does not know about tunneling is not worth knowing. Every man in this tunnel works the better for knowing that he has "Paddy" Fitzgerald behind him, and if anything goes wrong you may be quite sure he will be found in the middle of the mess, and also that he will not go away until all difficulty or danger is past.

On their way back to the lock the visitor notices another piece of work in progress which the strangeness of everything had prevented him seeing before. A scaffolding was in place around the tunnel so arranged that traffic through it was not impeded, and a crew of husky negroes was engaged in scraping out the joints of the iron lining, taking off, replacing and screwing up bolts, and hammering some substance into the joints they had just cleaned. An overpowering smell of ammonia hung over the tunnel at this point, and two inspectors were minutely examining every bolt and every inch of joint and marking them with mysterious signs in chalk upon the iron. In reply to the visitor's question the guide tells him that this is the operation which makes the tunnel proof against mud and water. In order to illustrate the function of the iron lining he takes up a wrench and removes a bolt from the lining; instantly there is a spurt of water followed by mud which squirts across the tunnel and then settled down into a steady stream squeezing through the bolt hole

and forming a sausage-like mass just like that which came in through the shield door, but on a smaller scale.

He tells the visitor that the duty of these tubes is to provide in the first instance a dam against the water and mud in which they are embedded, and for this purpose it is necessary that they be made perfectly water-tight, since the tube is built up of segments bolted together, the entire inside surface of the tunnel is cut up by a number of horizontal and circumferential joints, with an enormous number of bolts holding the segments together. As the tunnel is originally built, water comes in through all the joints and also through many of the bolt holes, and the next operation is to stem this water out so that the interior of the tube may be perfectly dry. In the case of the joints this is done by driving into them a mixture of sal-ammoniac and iron borings, which forms what is called a "rust-joint." This mixture is driven into the joint with caulking tools, similar to the caulking of the seams of a wooden ship, and in a slightly damp condition, and after it has been in place for a short time it hardens and expands into a dense rusty mass of iron which effectually keeps the water out. In the case of the bolts, every bolt has to be taken out and rings of rope-yarn dipped in red lead and oil placed under the head and nut, after which the bolt is screwed up tight again. This whole operation is an extremely monotonous one and one that must be watched and inspected with the most minute care, as the slightest piece of careless workmanship results in a leak that may be very difficult to detect and may cause an enormous amount of work to set right. It is also a very unpleasant part of the work as the whole tunnel becomes filled with ammonia gas, which in compressed air is very trying to those breathing it.

The visitor was anxious to know whether this iron tube will not eventually become attacked by rust and decay, being in contact with wet earth. He is told that this is impossible because no oxygen is present on the outside of the tube, so that rusting cannot occur. As a further safeguard against decay every segment is dipped, during manufacture and while it is still hot, in a pitch solution, which when cool forms a hard enamel coating over the cast iron. Cases have been known where samples have been drilled out of a tunnel thirty-eight years old and the iron found to be just as good and fresh as the day it was put in. Where a tunnel is in rock and is not, therefore, closely surrounded by earth, "grout"—consisting of a mixture of sand, cement and water—is blown by compressed air into the space between the ground and the outside of the tube, filling every crevice and when set hard forming a perfectly tight coating outside the lining.

The guide tells him that the iron tube being completed and the joints made water-tight, the next operation is the putting in of the concrete lining. This follows the general form of the concrete lining of the Bergen Hill Tunnel, and the operation in its main features follows that adopted there. From a construction point of view the chief feature is the fact that, to give greater security to the tunnels in soft ground, the concrete is heavily reinforced with twisted steel bars, which are placed in some cases circumferentially in the lining and in other cases longitudinally. These bars greatly increase the strength of the concrete, and the principle adopted in

Preparing to put in bottom segment of a ring of tunnel lining. The segment is seen near the front behind the stooping men.

Snapshot of a blast in the Terminal Station West excavation. Cheap house rent could be obtained in the vicinity during the progress of this part of the work.

The bottom segment is being lowered into place. The man in front of the segment is Mr. P. Fitzgerald, the Tunnel Superintendent; the man with hands in pockets, to his right, is Mr. H. F. D. Burke, the Resident Engineer.

Another type of timbering in the New York rock tunnels. This shows the method used where the roof was in soft ground. Note the wide span of the excavation.

Type of timbering used in the New York rock tunnels between the end of the shield-driven tunnels and the Terminal Station.

Completed tunnel east of state line under river.

the design was that the iron tube itself without the concrete lining is strong enough to carry the traffic, while the concrete lining without the iron lining is also strong enough. The concrete lining is carried out from both ends of the tunnel, the mixers being placed at the shaft at each end, and the concrete carried down to the point of work, so that the concrete lining comes to a junction in the middle of the river as the original iron tubes did.

The concrete work is divided into the following stages: first, the bottom concrete is put in; next follows the "duct bench," that is the concrete in which the vitrified earthenware ducts to hold the electric cables are embedded; third, the arch is put in; fourth, the ducts are laid on the duct-bench; fifth and last, the concrete covering the ducts and forming the "side benches" or walking platforms for the trackmen's use, is run the entire length of the tunnel. Before the concrete is placed the interior of the iron tubes is thoroughly washed, scraped with wire brushes, and cleaned of every particle of dirt. All the forms are carefully built of timber and made to run on tracks so that they can be readily moved forward with as little delay as possible. The concreting is carried on in lengths of about twenty feet at a time and the forms are left in place for about forty-eight hours so as to allow the concrete to become thoroughly set.

Several cross passages are built between the pair of tubes, so that ready access may be had from one to another; these passages are ordinarily closed by steel doors, so that each tube is entirely separate in order to help the ventilation. On the vertical sides of the bench refuge niches are placed at twenty-five-foot intervals for the use of the trackmen, and there are also ladders at short intervals on the face of the bench to allow the trackmen to get up from the track level to the top of the bench.

Passing out as they entered, with the lock door closed behind them the visitor drew a sigh of relief to think that he had passed through this experience in compressed air unscathed. His guide then explained purely from a layman's point of view what the dangers and discomforts really were. In the first place the danger from compressed air does not occur at the time of entering into it, nor during the period one is in it, but rather after one has come out; that is to say, a man enters the lock, and provided his ear passages are not blocked, he feels no discomfort at all, nor any sensation beyond the rise in temperature. While in the compressed air he feels as merry as a cricket, and in fact usually better than he does outside. He feels as though he could work more, and his general sensation is one of well-being. When, however, he has come out, that is the time he must take care. The generally accepted idea about compressed air sickness seems to be that the blood and organs and tissues of the body absorb, by reason of the pressure to which they are subjected, bubbles of nitrogen gas from the air. When a man passes from compressed air to normal air the tissues lying near the surface give off these bubbles of nitrogen gas readily, while the deep-seated organs such as the heart, kidneys, spinal column, etc., may retain this gas under pressure after he has come out into the normal air. This gas exerts pressure on the nerves and nerve centers, thereby causing

intense pain, and it is the doubled-up and distorted positions which this intense agony causes the sufferer to assume, that have given rise to the tunnel man's name of "bends" for this complaint. When this pressure is present on the spinal column, unconsciousness may occur, and these cases of coma are the most dangerous ones with which the doctor is called upon to deal. A man in a state of coma from compressed air is a man in an extremely serious condition, and it may take all the doctor's skill and patience to pull him round, and even though the life is saved, partial or complete paralysis of limbs or organs may result. In some cases the paralysis disappears after perhaps several years, while in some cases it is permanent. It is for this reason that extremely slow decompression is such a vital thing to observe, as it allows the bubbles to disperse, and if decompression takes place in two stages still better results are obtained. That is to say, supposing there is a pressure of twenty-five pounds per square inch above normal at the shield, there would be two airlock bulkhead walls in the tunnel separated by a distance of 400 or 500 yards. Men would pass from the twenty-five-pound pressure into one of say five or ten pounds, then walk the distance between the two airlock walls, and then pass from this to normal pressure. The walking exercise between the two locks tends to assist in displacing the minute bubbles of nitrogen gas from the deep-seated organs, so that when decompression is completed in the second stage there is found to be very much less likelihood of trouble occurring. The visitor was interested in these details, and asked what means were used to cure men who were unlucky enough to be attacked by this peculiar complaint. His guide replied that the great stand-by was the medical or "hospital" lock, which is now provided at every compressed air work of importance. This medical lock consists of a lock exactly the same as those used in the tunnel, except that it is divided into two compartments. The treatment consists in taking the patient into the lock, raising the pressure to two-thirds of that in which he was working at the shield, and then allowing the pressure to lower itself very slowly, say at the rate of about fifteen pounds an hour. These hospital locks are provided with mattresses, thermometers, pressure gauges, clocks and everything to enable the doctor to keep a careful watch on the patient, and the double compartment is for the purpose of allowing the doctor to enter and leave the lock in order to visit his patient at any time. Another rule is that the higher the pressure, the shorter the length of stay in the compressed air; thus, for an ordinary pressure of about twenty-five pounds above normal, six to eight hours is not too long for a man in perfect health provided he comes out slowly; but in pressures of forty pounds per square inch, very much shorter shifts have to be observed, such as three hours in, two hours out, and three hours in, or some such combination. All workers in compressed air have to observe certain simple rules of health, such as never to enter the compressed air on an empty stomach, not to use intoxicating liquors, to put on extra clothing when coming out, to get seven hours' sleep every day, to avoid sudden chills, and not to take cold baths on coming heated from the tunnels.

The visitor could not understand, with the ground so soft as he saw it to be, how it is the tunnels do not sink

Tenth Avenue Portal.

Making a boring into bed rock from the tunnel below the Hudson River. This water is coming from a depth of 200 feet below the tunnel, and is pouring in in enormous quantities.

The tunnel shield in place. The shoving jacks are ranged in a circle round the outer edge.

Part of New York rock tunnels with lining completed.

Driving a rock heading in the Bergen Hill Tunnels. The drills are seen in place and the men tending them.

View below Ninth Avenue after most of the excavation had been done.

indefinitely within it. His guide replied that though they are lighter than the mud through which they pass, and therefore not certain to tend to settle at all, this question is one that has occupied a great deal of thought on the part of the engineers, and to guard against this possibility it was originally intended that the tunnels should be supported by large cast iron "screw piles" put down through the bottom of the tunnel at intervals of fifteen feet until they reached ground that was much firmer than that through which the tunnels themselves passed. In order to be perfectly certain whether these piles were necessary, a large number of borings were made through the bottom of the tunnel in order to get still more precise knowledge of the conditions of the ground below the tunnel than was given by the preliminary borings, and to see exactly what kind of material the piles would have to penetrate if they were necessary. These borings were of great interest to geologists, as they were the first that had ever been taken down to bed-rock across the Hudson River in New York City. They disclosed the fact that bed-rock in the middle of the river is about 215 feet below the bottom of the tunnel, or about 300 feet below the surface of the water. At the point where the tunnel crosses the water is about fifty-five feet deep on the average, and the top of the tunnel is about twenty-five feet below the bed of the river. The borings taken through the bottom of the tunnel were attended by very great difficulty, as just above the rock comes a layer of gravel charged with water at a head of 300 feet, so that to bore through this material brought enormous volumes of water into the tunnel.

A long series of experiments was made after the iron tubes had been put into place. These experiments lasted for eighteen months, and were of the most minute and searching character. The result was that it was decided the tunnels were perfectly safe and stable without these supports, and consequently none was put in except the few used in the experiments. Further, careful and minute measurements were made and are being made on the stability of the structure, and these have amply confirmed the results of the experiments made during construction.

The pair, returning eastward, had now reached the foot of the Manhattan Shaft by which they had descended, and the visitor saw ahead of him more tunnels of a type that reminded him strongly of the Bergen Hill Tunnels which he had first visited on the New Jersey side. There was, however, the difference that instead of the general absence of timbering which he had seen there, there was a complicated mass of timbering supporting the roof in what appeared to him a state of haphazard confusion. His guide explained to him that he was in a section of rock tunnel connecting the shield-driven tunnel with the "open cut" work of the Terminal Station yard, and that if he cared to do so, there was an opportunity of actually seeing some concrete lining work in progress.

His guide told him that whereas in the case of the Bergen Hill Tunnels there were two separate tunnels driven independently and running side by side through the hill, in this case, although each track was in a separate compartment, the width of the street in which the tunnels had to lie was not great enough for this separate method of construction, thus necessitating an excava-

tion wide enough for two tracks, and the building of a dividing wall between them when the permanent lining of the tunnel was put in. This made a very wide span for the excavation—some sixty to seventy feet.

The visitor was curious to know why the rock on the Bergen Hill Tunnel required no timbering while that where he then was seemed to need so much. The guide explained that the New York rock is of a kind known as mica schist, which is very friable, and likely to fall in large masses unless properly supported, and that moreover a good deal of the tunnel in which he then stood was partly in rock and partly in sand and gravel, which with the greater span previously described, made it still more necessary to support the roof. In fact, this soft ground roof made so much trouble that it was found better to build the tunnel for a considerable length in Thirty-second Street by "cut and cover" method, that is, by excavating from the surface down over the entire width and length of the tunnel and building the lining in the excavation thus formed and then filling in earth above, in fact following the same method that was used in the general construction of the present New York subway. The methods of excavation by drilling and blasting the rock are similar to those used at Bergen Hill.

Presently they arrived at the point where the concrete lining is being put in. From this part of the work he could only carry away with him a bewildering recollection of large cars being hauled into the tunnels filled with wet, sloppy-looking concrete which looked as though it could never harden into the massive stone-like material which it afterwards became. On arrival at its destination this was being shoveled into place behind timber moulds or "forms." It was explained to him that, speaking generally, the first thing to do was to put in the bottom concrete forming the foundation for the whole tunnel, then to form the bed for the vitrified ducts to carry the electric cables, after which the ducts themselves were laid; then to lay the concrete for the side benches and the middle wall, and finally the arches, which here are of brick work.

The visitor was now brought up the shaft, and their way through the office lay through the engine-room where he could see, as it were, the heart which pumped the life-blood into the curious underground organism which he had been exploring. He was taken first to the boiler-room, and here he saw stokers shoveling coal into the hungry jaws of the three 500 horse-power Sterling boilers. The next things he saw were the three air compressors built by the Ingersoll-Sergeant Drill Company to supply air to the working chambers of the tube tunnels. His guide told him that when these air compressors were running at 125 revolutions per minute each machine had a capacity of 264,000 cubic feet of free air per hour. He showed the visitor how the air was cooled by water-jackets through which a constant supply of cold water was pumped before the air was sent down to the tunnels. He showed him how the air supply was taken from above the power-house roof in order to have it as pure as possible, and added that in the cold weather it could be taken from within the power-house itself. His attention was next drawn to the high pressure air compressor also built by the Ingersoll-Sergeant Drill Company, and used to supply the

The shield during the operation of "shoving" or going ahead with one of its bulkhead doors open, allowing the mud or silt to squeeze through this door into the tunnel.

Two shields which have met in the middle of the river, having been driven from opposite sides. The shields have been partly dismantled, and only the outer shells or skins remain.

Back view of a "bulkhead wall," i.e. the wall which holds the air pressure inside a tunnel being built with the aid of compressed air. Towards the left are steps leading to a platform which gives access to the top air-lock or the "emergency lock."

General view of a shield-driven tube tunnel during construction and before concrete lining is put in. The cross timbers at the top support the upper or emergency platform which leads from the shield to the emergency lock in the bulkhead wall.

Terminal Station West during construction, looking west from Ninth Avenue elevated railway.

General view of Weehawken Shaft and part of the yard. The building on the left of the picture to the right of the tall derrick is the Power House for the River Tunnels. The one to the right of that and below the three stacks contains the Resident Engineers' offices.

View through one of the completed Bergen Hill Tunnels, showing length of 1⅛ miles of tunnel looking from the Weehawken Shaft towards the western portal on the Hackensack Meadows, ready for traffic.

high-pressure air for the drills and all other machines driven by compressed air, including the work of grouting. The capacity of this machine was 66,000 cubic feet of free air per hour, when running at eighty-five revolutions per minute. There were also three powerful hydraulic pumps built by the George F. Blake Mfg. Co. for the supply of water power for working the tunnel shields. Usually one of these pumps was required for each shield, thus leaving one in reserve. These pumps were designed to work up to pressures of 6,000 pounds per square inch, and the ordinary pressure actually used was about 4,500 pounds per square inch. He saw the electric generators made by the General Electric Company of Schenectady, which were used to supply electric lighting for the tunnels and works. He also saw the workshops, with their lathes, presses, drills and every conceivable appliance for repairing machines and tools; blacksmith's shops; and store rooms, with multitudinous spare parts all neatly stored away in compartments. When the guide told him that this entire plant was duplicated on the other side of the river he was not surprised when he heard the contractors had had to pay out for plant alone on the New York and New Jersey sides the sum of $700,000 in prime cost, and that the cost of operating each of these plants came to about $3,500 per month.

Returning, after a much-needed wash, the visitor took his leave and departed with his letter of introduction to Mr. Cresson, the resident engineer of the last remaining section of the work, the Terminal Station West.

Mr. Cresson followed the apparently inevitable custom of resident engineers in advising a look at the plans before going out on the ground, and he showed him that the piece of work which he was looking after consisted of an open rock cut forming the westerly approach to the Terminal Station proper. The area covered by the work is about six and three-tenth acres, and included about 503,000 cubic yards of excavation, nearly all rock, 18,000 cubic yards of concrete, and about 660 tons of steel work. Mr. Cresson told him that before work was started all the area was covered with building except the portion occupied by Thirty-second Street, which east of Tenth Avenue was purchased by the Company, together with the rest of the property, and closed to the public. The first building to be removed was No. 463 West Thirty-second Street, which was taken down during 1905. Contracts for wrecking the buildings were awarded to the George W. Jump Company and the Rheinfrank House Wrecking Company. House-wrecking work was begun on May 1, 1906, and finished on August 27, 1907. About 5,000,-000 bricks and 6,000 truck loads of timber, iron fixtures, etc., were removed.

The contract for carrying out the work of excavation and concrete retaining walls was given to the New York Contracting Co., Pennsylvania Terminal, on April 28, 1906. Work was begun on the east side of Ninth Avenue on May 11, 1906. Drilling was begun on the east side of Ninth Avenue on May 21, 1906, and the first blast was fired on May 24, 1906. The rock was a fair sample of New York gneiss. The average depth of the excavation from the surface to the bottom was about fifty-eight feet, and the sides of the excavation are lined with concrete acting as retaining walls. After the visitor had a fair idea of what the work involved, Mr. Cresson invited him to go out on the ground. They therefore walked down to Tenth Avenue, and there standing above the portals of the Thirty-second Street Tunnels coming from the Hudson River, in which he had lately been, and looking eastward, he got a comprehensive view of the entire work. Looking as they did from this elevation, they could see a huge channel cut through the rock and resembling the idea he had formed of the Panama Canal under construction in the "Culebra Cut," minus the water, and instead of the tropical jungle on either side, tall tenement houses, with a liberal display of family laundry waving in the breeze in the narrow back yards. Small but extremely busy steam locomotives were running hither and thither, each with a string of battered-looking cars containing lumps of rock of all shapes and sizes. Derricks scattered at intervals were engaged in lifting the shattered rock and stacking it on the cars. The steady pounding of innumerable rock drills was heard, and the drillers and drills could be seen perching in almost inaccessible positions along the sides of the cut. In one place he saw heavy wooden forms firmly braced against one side of the excavation, and the work of depositing concrete behind these forms was in full progress. Mr. Cresson described to him the elaborate arrangements that were made behind the concrete wall to carry off the water, and told him that behind the form were numerous drains which would be built into the wall in order that no water pressure should come on the wall itself. The visitor noticed a length of wall from which the forms had been removed, and remarked on its beautifully smooth and uniformly white appearance. Mr. Cresson explained to him that this appearance was obtained only by the exercise of a great deal of care, both in the form itself and in the treatment of the wall after the forms were removed. The form is allowed to remain in place for eighteen or twenty-four hours, depending on the weather. As soon as the form had been removed a scaffold was erected against the face of the wall, which was whetted and thoroughly rubbed, first with a wooden float and then with a cement brick, until the surface was as smooth and uniform as he saw it.

Mr. Cresson informed the visitor that the chief engineering difficulty in connection with his work was that in and under Ninth Avenue. Here not only the Avenue itself, with all its pedestrian, vehicular and surface railroad traffic had to be supported and maintained without interference to the traffic, together with a number of large sewers, water mains, gas mains, and such public utilities, but also the elevated railroad with its constantly passing trains. All this meant that very great care had to be taken in order that no damage whatever should occur. No blasting was done near the supports of the elevated railroad while trains were passing over the structure, and occasionally trains were stopped during a heavy or uncertain blast. Watchmen were kept on duty day and night, and log mats and timber protection were used for the girders and columns of the permanent viaduct. The method of underpinning Ninth Avenue was, generally speaking, as follows:

The first stage was to cut down the east side of the Avenue about twenty feet. Beams and supporting posts were placed under the surface railroad tracks, and cross girders and temporary shoring girders placed under the elevated railroad; next structural steel I-beams were placed under the surface railroad tracks and the elevated railroad carried on temporary shoring girders, while heavy cross girders were placed at intervals below the supports for the elevated railroad, these cross girders being supported by four concrete piers resting on the surface of the unexcavated rock. The twenty-four-inch water main was supported by a timber cradle and the sewage carried through a temporary pipe. Next, the elevated railroad was carried on supports under the columns, the temporary shoring girders removed, and the permanent supports resting on the heavy cross girders put in place. The surface railroad tracks were carried on supports wedged up from the heavy cross girders, and the east and west sides of the avenue were excavated down to the final depth. Five rows of the permanent steel roof girders were then placed on each side of the avenue and supports erected on these, on which the ends of the heavy steel cross girders were placed. The two outside concrete piers supporting the cross girders were removed and the sixth row of the permanent steel roof girders placed below. The ends of the cross girders now rested on the permanent steel roof below, and the forty-eight-inch cast iron sewer replacing the original brick one was carried on brackets at the ends of the cross girders. This left only a narrow core of rock below the middle of the avenue, and as everything was then supported independently of this core of rock, the excavation could be completed. With this explanation in mind the visitor was rather better able to understand the operations he saw going on before him at Ninth Avenue.

That same evening our visitor, now feeling rather tired, found himself again at the club, and again met his friend the New Yorker, who asked him whether he had yet seen anything of the tunnels, and if so what his impressions were. The Westerner described his trip, and in conclusion said: "Not only have I seen a vast amount of work in progress, but I feel that behind this there is a still vaster amount which I have not seen. I have seen only the finished product being put in place. Before this stage is reached, many men have spent years in work—presidents and directors in anxious calculations, engineers in making, abandoning and remaking hundreds of plans, miners in mining ore and coal, iron workers in fashioning this ore into castings and steel. Men have made cement, machinery, bricks, tools, shields, and a thousand other things in order that the men I have seen can carry out the work.

"I realize now that directors' schemes and engineers' plans mean absolutely nothing, unless men can be found who will enter the tunnel and transmute these ideas into facts, and it seems to me that these men carry on a trade that is most romantic and one that brings them together with the feeling all uncommon and skilled trades inspire. In the depths and darkness men experience to the full the 'industrial equivalent of war' about which I have heard, and here, where there is no winter, no summer, no day and no night, I think that the humblest mucker should receive a due share in the credit for the work in which he is as necessary a link as any director or engineer."

COMPLETION AND INSPECTION OF NORTH RIVER TUNNELS

ENGINEERS AND CONTRACTORS PLACING THE LAST SHOVEL OF CONCRETE IN NORTH RIVER TUNNELS, MAY 27, 1909

1. James Forgie, Chief Assistant Engineer.
2. John F. O'Rourke, President O'Rourke Eng. & Const. Co.
3. B. H. M. Hewett, General Resident Engineer.
4. Wm. Lowe Brown, Resident Engineer.
5. F. J. Gubelman, Vice-Prest. O'Rourke Eng. & Const. Co.
6. George B. Fry, Gen. Supt. O'Rourke Eng. & Const. Co.
7. Dr. A. J. Loomis, Chief Medical Officer.

AUTOMOBILE PARTY MAKING FINAL INSPECTION OF THE PENNSYLVANIA RAILROAD'S NORTH RIVER TUNNELS.

FROM LEFT TO RIGHT:

First seat: F. J. Gubelman, Vice-Pres. O'Rourke Eng. & Con. Co.; Geo. B. Fry, Genl. Supt. O'Rourke Eng. & Con. Co.

Second seat: Jno. F. O'Rourke, President O'Rourke Eng. & Con. Co.; Jas. Forgie, Chief Asst. Engr., North River Division.

Third seat: A. J. County, Asst. to 2nd V.P., Pennsylvania Railroad; Chas. M. Jacobs, Chief Engineer, North River Division; Samuel Rea, Sec.- and Vice-Prest., Pennsylvania Railroad.

Electric Traction and Station Construction

GEORGE GIBBS . . *Chief Engineer*

E. ROWLAND HILL *Ass't to Chief Engineer*

HUGH PATTISON *Sup't of Construction*

S. A. SPALDING . *Ass't Engineer, E. T.*

R. D. COMBES . *Structural Engineer*

C. G. EDWARDS *Ass't Sup't Construction*

E. J. BELL . *Sec'y to Chief Engineer*

MONOGRAPH
by
E. J. BELL

Condensed from Mr. Gibbs's paper for the Am. Soc. C. E.   Permission of
Mr. Gibbs and Am. Soc. C. E.

E. ROWLAND HILL

HUGH PATTISON

S. A. SPALDING

GEORGE GIBBS

R. D. COMBES

C. G. EDWARDS

E. J. BELL

ELECTRIC TRACTION AND STATION CONSTRUCTION

THE Pennsylvania Station is unprecedented among railway stations. It has a ground area of seven and one-half acres, which is about twice that of St. Peter's in Rome and one-third more than the area of the Palais de Justice, in Brussels (the latter being considered the largest building of the Nineteenth Century), and two and one-half times that of the New York Public Library. In length the station exceeds the Capitol at Washington. In contents, it measures about 40,000,000 cubic feet. It is designed wholly for railway purposes and for the comfort and convenience of passengers and its design has not been subordinated to the purpose of a hotel or office building. In consonance with its legitimate purpose, the aim has been to make the structure a monumental gateway to the largest city in the country.

GENERAL PLAN: A passenger terminal may be located either adjoining or over the tracks served. The former plan has generally been adopted heretofore, where land was cheap, and especially because of the necessity of large open spaces in order to dispose of the smoke and steam from locomotives. In large modern terminals, however, this plan has disadvantages in the costly property involved and in the enormous distances between the head-house facilities and the point where the passengers board the trains. Furthermore, with the advent of trains propelled by electric motors, it is entirely possible to utilize the basement of a station building for the tracks, and the levels immediately above for the facilities. Thus, when passengers arrive at the station, they are at the nearest point to the one at which they board the train. It is true that this arrangement involves different levels, and thus the use of stairs or lifts, but, in order that a station may be in the heart of a great modern city, the depression or elevation of the tracks is unavoidable, and stairs are a necessity, regardless of the location of the building.

The form of construction adopted for the Pennsylvania Station, therefore, is that of a bridge over the yard and platforms, the building having its main floor intermediate in level between the streets and the track platforms. The main station facilities are centrally located as regards the building itself, which may be entered from any one of the four sides, and also as regards the trains at the platforms underneath, so that the distances, which are necessarily considerable in a station of large capacity, are the least possible. It is believed that the unusual opportunities afforded for entrance and exit, and the separation of incoming and outgoing passengers on different levels, make this building unique among the large stations of the world in the distribution of crowds without delay or confusion. These numerous means of access, moreover, should prove an important factor in building up the section of the city surrounding it, not only from one but from all sides.

Because of the location of the passenger facilities on different levels, it is difficult to describe the arrangement of the building. In general, however, the station consists of a hollow rectangle with marginal buildings surrounding the plot from the street level upward; an intermediate building at the street level, starting from the middle of the Seventh Avenue façade, used for a main entrance and arcade, and continuing to its north and south axis, where it joins a high cross-structure containing the main waiting-room, with the floor one story below the street level. Immediately east of the main waiting-room and on both sides of the arcade, at the street level, are located the restaurant and lunch-room. The rectangular space between these latter, the arcade and the marginal building, are open courts, roofed over at the street level with glass skylights, for train-sheds and for driveways to the baggage-room under the arcade. These driveways communicate with the inclined interior streets, or drives, entered from the north and south ends of the Seventh Avenue front.

Continuing westward from the main waiting-room, and on the same level, there are two sub-waiting-rooms, and between these and the marginal buildings at the west end of the station, the space is occupied by the main concourse, a roofed-over structure of glass, containing the assembly space for outgoing passengers, prior to their admission to the stairways, leading down to the track platforms. Under this main concourse there is an exit concourse, narrower than the main one, and having stairways at either side from each platform for incoming passengers. Both these concourses connect at their respective levels with a two-deck passageway under Thirty-third Street, the entire length of the Station between Seventh and Eighth Avenues, and designed to connect with future rapid-transit subways in either of these avenues. At present this passageway is used for intercommunication with the Long Island section of the station, elsewhere referred to, and for an entrance and exit to Thirty-fourth Street.

The central vestibule of the Seventh Avenue façade may be considered as the main foot-passenger entrance, leading from which is the arcade, flanked by shops on either side; thence down one floor level by the main stairway to the main waiting-room, in which are the ticket-office and parcel-rooms, the baggage-checking booth, and other minor facilities. The waiting passenger may then proceed to the sub-waiting-rooms (smoking or non-smoking), where seats are provided; or, without retracing his steps, may enter the main concourse to the west, where the gates leading to the outgoing train platform stairs are located. Both the main waiting-room and the concourse may be entered from two side streets, and the latter from Eighth Avenue as well.

Carriage passengers enter the building at the south end of the Seventh Avenue front by a driveway leading down to the waiting-room and outgoing carriage passengers leave by a similar driveway at the north side of the building. These driveways are also used for the wagon delivery of baggage to and from the baggage-room.

To accommodate the large number of suburban and commutation passengers of the Long Island Railroad, a practically independent station, within the main station, has been provided. This is at the north side under and adjoining Thirty-third Street. It may be entered at the Seventh Avenue corner, by the driveway, by a stairway from Thirty-third Street, or by an entrance and exit from Thirty-fourth Street, midway between Seventh and Eighth Avenues. There is a separate waiting-room, with the usual facilities, a wide departure platform, and a concourse communicating with other platforms.

A description of the architectural motif of the design of the building prepared by Mr. W. Symmes Richardson, of Messrs. McKim, Mead and White, the member of that firm who was especially charged with working out this problem, will be found on page 77.

STATION FACILITIES: Of the more important operating features of the building, those involving engineering problems will be described in some detail. They were planned only after extended consideration, to utilize to the fullest available space in the building, with the greatest flexibility of operative methods, and for the future growth of business up to the capacity of the terminal as a whole.

OPERATING ARRANGEMENT: The station tracks are arranged for both through and stub-end operation. Through trains on both the Pennsylvania and Long Island Railroad are handled by electric locomotives; suburban service of the Long Island Railroad is handled by multiple-unit motor cars. There are eleven station platforms, serving twenty-one tracks, of the latter, sixteen (Nos. 1 to 16, inclusive, numbering from the south side) are normally assigned to the Pennsylvania Service. The remaining five tracks to the north (Nos. 17 to 21, inclusive) are assigned to the Long Island Service.

Pennsylvania Railroad trains—except certain short distance expresses from Philadelphia, and certain locals—after unloading, proceed through the Thirty-second Street and East River Tunnels to a large terminal yard in Long Island City, where they are turned, cleaned, and made up for the return trip. The short distance expresses are turned and stored in the station yard. All Long Island trains are at present cared for in the station yard; the expresses are switched into the north yard, and locals, after unloading, are tail-switched from the two tracks adjoining the incoming platform to the tracks adjoining the outgoing platforms. In case of necessity any platform may be used for either arriving or departing passengers. The Thirty-third Street tunnels are normally used for Long Island Railroad business exclu-

sively, these tunnels communicating with tracks Nos. 14 to 21 inclusive, but the Thirty-second Street tunnels may be used in emergencies, thus making all station tracks, except the southernmost four, available for Long Island Railroad service.

PLATFORMS: The original plan of the station contemplated following the usual American practice of making track platforms about nine inches high above the rails. Detailed development of the station facilities, however, indicated that low platforms are open to some serious objections, and a departure was decided on in the adoption of the English standard practice, making the platform flush with the car floor, a decision which may have a far-reaching effect on the future practice in other stations in America. The controlling reasons for the adoption of high platforms in the New York Station were:

(a) The greater ease in loading and unloading cars, an advantage which will be appreciated by passengers who are infirm, or who have hand baggage.

(b) The saving in time of loading and unloading trains. This will tend to prevent congestion on narrow platforms, and is an important factor in utilizing to the fullest the station facilities, especially in local excursion and commuter services.

(c) A saving of about four feet in the vertical lift between the platforms and the street; this is also an important advantage in a station depressed below the street level.

(d) The elimination of the dangerous practice of crossing tracks at grade, a consideration which applies to employees as well as to passengers, and has special force in a station where the view is obstructed by columns, etc.

(e) Incidentally, they permit the convenient use of hydraulic power for operating the elevators and lifts, giving space under the platforms for the machinery and piping; they also provide space for housing the signal and certain other electrical apparatus.

The usual objections against high platforms for steam railways did not have controlling weight, in the case of this terminal station, because of its location and the type of equipment adopted for other reasons, thus:

(a) The new steel cars used for all purposes have vestibules with side-doors arranged so that they can be opened without requiring the trap over the steps to be lifted, and the fascia over the doors is of sufficient height to permit passengers to walk out on the platform level.

(b) The difficulty of handling baggage to and from trucks at the cars is minimized by using a special truck, with its platform only 9 in. above the car floor.

(c) The arrangement of lifts and cross-trucking subways under the tracks makes it unnecessary to truck across the tracks at grade.

(d) The first cost of the high platforms was not excessive, because of the cheapening of other constructive features of the station, such as the lifts, stairways, piping, signals, etc.

There are eleven passenger platforms under the station, varying in width from 20 to 40 feet and in length from 750 to 1,170 feet. All are "island" platforms, having a track on each side. The total platform length adjacent to passenger tracks is 21,500 feet. In addition, there are "island" platforms west of the station and under the post-office which are used exclusively for mail car purposes. Space has also been assigned for two additional platforms at the south side of the yard near Ninth Avenue, for future requirements. The platforms are of reinforced concrete with edges set 3 feet, 10 inches above the top of the rail, and 5 feet, 3 inches from the center of the track. These standards allow a normal clearance of three inches from the side of the widest car, and place the top edge always somewhat below the car platform, due allowance being made for wear, loading and variation in equipment.

MR. GIBBS, CHIEF ENGINEER; MESSRS. MEAD AND WEBSTER OF McKIM, MEAD & WHITE; MR. STARRETT, PRES'T OF
GEO. A. FULLER CO. AND GROUP OF CO-WORKERS, ELECTRIC TRACTION AND STATION CONSTRUCTION

ELEVATORS AND LIFTS: The location of the building over the tracks, and the peculiar arrangement of the public spaces and the offices, as well as the great area covered, made the planning of the necessary system of vertical conveyors for passengers and freight a difficult matter. Service had to be provided for:

(1) Passenger elevators from the track platforms.
(2) Baggage lifts between the baggage room, the platforms, and the subways underneath.
(3) Office elevators from the street level to the floors above.
(4) Service elevators and dumbwaiters between the restaurants and the kitchen.
(5) Moving stairways (or escalators) from the concourse to the street.
(6) Lifts and conveyors for handling mail from the trucking subways to the main floor of the Post Office.

passengers from the exit concourse under Thirty-third Street to the street level midway between Seventh and Eighth Avenues. By this means passengers are landed without effort in a private street and near the Thirty-fourth Street cross-town surface car line.

The selection of a suitable operating means for the entire elevator and lift system was made the subject of much study. The great area to be covered (about twenty acres for the building and yard) indicated that electric distribution of power, rather than hydraulic, would be simpler and cheaper. In fact, in the case of low station platforms, as first intended, it seemed to be essential to adopt electric elevators, as there was, in places, no available room for the piping runs and pres-

ELEVATORS AND LIFTS

Elevators, etc.	No.	Size of Cars	Capacity in lbs.	Capacity in passengers per hour	Speed in ft. per minute	Lift in feet
Passenger elevators	11	5 x 10 ft.	2,500	750	200	17
Baggage lifts	21	7 x 15 ft.	7,500		100	28
Post-office lifts	4	6 x 15 ft.	7,500		100	52 to 70
Office elevators	10	5 x 5 ft. 10 in.	2,500		300	40 to 70
Dumb waiters	2	4 x 3 ft.	400		200	54
" "	4	2 x 2 ft.	100		200	37
Escalator	1	Stair 4 ft. wide		9,000	85	25

Water pressure used at hydraulic lifts, 270 pounds per square inch.

In general, it was determined that each platform should be provided with a passenger elevator operating between the train level and the exit concourse. It was not possible, because of the plan of the building, to operate these to the street level, nor could they be made of sufficient capacity, without sacrifice of platform space, to handle entire loads. The arrangement adopted gives one elevator for each platform, eleven in all. Only three of these run to the concourse level.

Because of the high platforms, baggage trucking cannot be done across the tracks at grade, therefore a very complete system of lifts has been provided between each platform and the baggage rooms above, as well as to a cross subway below. Each of the nine long station platforms has been equipped with two lifts, one from the outbound baggage-room on the west side of the building, and one from the inbound baggage-room on the east side. The two short Long Island platforms on the north side of the station have one lift each. The lifts, generally, have a travel of twenty-eight feet. Mail handling to the post-office required the installation of four lifts from the platforms to the building proper.

The use of escalators, or moving stairways, from the platforms to the concourse was considered, and, although space was provided for them in the building framing, it was decided to defer their installation until their actual operating necessity was demonstrated. If not needed, they would be objectionable, as they would transport passengers to the main instead of the exit concourse; thus they would cause a conflict of passenger movements, and defeat the chief advantage of the double concourse system. The condition at the north side of the station, however, where large commuter travel from the Long Island Railroad is cared for, is special, and at this point an escalator has been provided, leading

sure tanks required for a hydraulic system. In case of the baggage lifts, however, it was desired to secure the advantage of the hydraulic plunger type, because of the ease and accuracy of control, simplicity, and absence of machinery and counterweights over the platforms and tracks. Therefore, when high station platforms were adopted, it was found entirely practicable to use hydraulic baggage lifts and passenger elevators, placing all piping and apparatus in the space under the platforms.

The conditions were somewhat different with the office elevators and kitchen dumb-waiters, as their plungers would interfere with clearances over the tracks, and therefore electric elevators were adopted for these services.

Power for hydraulic lifts is furnished by pumps in the Service Plant, and current for the electric elevators is taken from the general traction power mains through a special switchboard connection in the Service Plant. The electric elevators, being over the platforms and tracks, required special safety precautions to arrest a falling car or counterweight; therefore, all elevator shafts were provided with air-cushion wells, from eight to ten feet deep, and Cruickshank arresters for the counterweights. Thorough tests were made of the efficiency of these devices on all elevators; for instance, a fully loaded car was cut loose at the top of a shaft, allowed to drop freely seventy feet into the cushion, and was brought to a stop without spilling water or breaking an egg in the car; the air pressure developed in the cushion was about sixteen pounds per square inch.

To provide against the possibility of a baggage truck breaking through a lift-gate at the platform level, there are collision-proof gates of steel plates and reinforcing angles at all entrances to the lift shafts. These gates are of the disappearing type, moving in slots in the hatchways below the platform level. They are partly counterweighted, and are operated by compressed air, controlled through levers on the car and from the outside. A gate can be opened only when a car is at rest at the landing; if a car leaves the landing while the gates are open, they will close automatically. Either gate for a car can be operated independently.

In order to obviate the necessity of having an attendant at each lift, a special apparatus was installed to operate the hydraulic starting mechanism through electric control. This consists of push-buttons, located at each landing and on the car itself, electric circuits to a controller-board, and an electrically-operated pilot-valve on the board, controlling the hydraulic valve mechanism proper of the lifts. A car can thus be called or sent to any landing automatically by pressing the button for that landing. The car cannot be operated by the push-button control if any hoistway gate is open, and when a car is at rest at a landing and the gate is open, the car-operating rope is locked against movement until the gate is closed; furthermore, after a button has been pushed to send, or to call the car, all other buttons are inoperative until the car has moved to, and comes to a stop at, the landing called. If a gate is opened while a car is moving, the car will stop at the next landing toward which it is moving. In addition to this automatic control, the lifts may be operated in the usual way by hand-ropes.

BAGGAGE HANDLING: The baggage facilities have been planned for as rapid service as consistent with the very large platform area served, and to avoid long-distance trucking on platforms, which are necessarily somewhat narrow and obstructed by building columns. Therefore, two baggage-rooms have been provided; one at the east side, adjoining the main waiting-room and the driveways, for handling to and from wagons, for checking, and for arriving baggage from trains; and one at the west side, adjoining Eighth Avenue, for delivery to trains. The east room contains all the usual facilities for weighing, checking and storage; offices for the operating force, and for the Transfer Company, and is the one to which the public has access. The west room is chiefly a passageway for reaching the various platform lifts. The two rooms have communication by a trucking passageway under Thirty-first Street and under the Seventh Avenue front of the building. The following data relate to baggage handling in terms of amount handled at present in summer; the ultimate capacity of the facilities provided is much greater, of course, than the figures given:

    Total quantity per 24 hours..... 6,025 pieces
    Storage capacity 6,000   "
    Length of run from east to west
      room ....1,350 ft.
    Time required to deliver truck
      load to car at west end of
      platform ....   8 min.
    Number of baggage scales   4
      Capacity, total ....20,000 lbs.
      Capacity, weighing 10,000   "

BAGGAGE TRUCKS: There are four kinds of baggage trucks for station uses. The special trucks, used for general baggage purposes, were designed and built by the Pennsylvania Railroad Motive Power Department, at Altoona, and are similar to those in use elsewhere on the road, except that they have drop frames, with floors flush with the track platforms, for greater convenience in loading from cars. These special trucks are automatic and trailing, both of the same construction, except that the former are equipped with electric motors and storage batteries. The battery is of twelve cells of 200 ampere-hours capacity, with a maximum discharge rate of fifty amperes. The batteries are re-charged at a stand in the Thirty-first Street baggage passageway, where hand cranes, charging racks, and electric connections, communicating with a switchboard in the Service Plant, have been placed. The charging current is twenty-five volts, and is supplied by small motor generators in the above plant, as a part of the auxiliary power system.

The following trucks are provided for different station purposes:

    Electric baggage trucks 25
    Trailer baggage trucks of the same type,
      without motors 25
    Mail handling trucks without motors 25
    Funeral trucks 6

MAIL HANDLING: In order to load and unload cars in the shortest possible time it was thought essential to develop a complete system of mail-handling machinery, consisting of chutes and horizontal conveyors for outgoing mail and horizontal conveyors and bucket lifts for incoming mail, together with vertical lifts for mail on trucks. This system is designed to reach not only the Post-office Building, but, through the trucking subways under the tracks, any part of the main station building. In general the system is as follows:

Incoming Mail: Mail in less than car-load lots or in combination cars is unloaded on trucks and conveyed to the Post-office by elevator. In the case of car-load lots or bulk mail the mail is unloaded manually and dumped into hoppers on the platform, whence the pouches are pushed automatically by compressed air rams on a belt conveyor located under the platform. This belt conveys the bags to a point where a tilting tray operates to transfer them automatically to a vertical bucket lift, which elevates them to the mezzanine floor of the Post-office, whence they are delivered through spiral chutes either to the receiving mail platform on the first floor or to the basement of the building.

Outgoing Mail: Mail in less than car-load lots is handled directly into the cars by manual unloading from trucks. Bulk and car-load mail is delivered automatically into the cars as follows: Mail from the working floor of the Post-office is delivered to belt conveyors, which are located over the platforms, through spiral chutes, single, double, triple or quadruple, as occasion requires, for simultaneous delivery from the various building floors. The conveyor belts are operated by electric motors at a speed of about 100 feet per minute, and included in their paths are self-propelled carriages operating as "trippers" and running on tracks in the housings enclosing the conveyors. These carriages may be run automatically to any desired position opposite the mail-car doors and operate to trip the mail pouch into a spout attached to the carriage and thence to the car door. The conveyor machinery was installed by the Lamson Belt Conveyor Company.

TRAIN INDICATORS: In the main concourse, at the head of the stairs to each track platform there are gates and illuminated signs describing the destination and the departure time of trains. There are forty-four of these indicators. They consist of cast iron columns, sixteen feet high, two at each gate. The top of each column is four sided, and contains mechanism for moving steel tapes opposite the openings on the four sides simultaneously; on these tapes the numerals from 1 to 10 are enameled. The mechanism is operated by a crank key through vertical rods and gearing from sockets near the bottom of the post; by turning this key the tapes may be set to indicate any desired departure time. The posts also carry a four-sided card box, in which destination signs are displayed; these are placed in a frame, operating in guides in the post, and raised into position by a hoisting drum mechanism.

TRAIN STARTING SYSTEM: As the distance between the gates on the main concourse and the trains at corresponding station platforms is considerable, it was necessary to have a system for quick communication between the gatemen, the conductor of the outgoing train and the train director in the signal cabin, in order to insure prompt control of the starting of trains at the scheduled time.

At the head of each platform stairway there is a push button and lamp indicator; and on each platform at four different points there are instruments containing a switch, a push button and a lamp indicator with another lamp above it. There is an instrument for the same function in the interlocking cabin controlling the train movement out of the station. All these devices are interconnected by electric wiring, and operate as follows: About one minute·before the train is to leave, the conductor inserts a key in the platform instrument, thus showing the number of the track to the train director, who then closes the circuit, thereby lighting lamps, indicating to both conductor and gateman that the route has been set for the departure of the train. When the gateman closes his gate at the train-leaving time, he pushes a button, extinguishing his indicating light and at the same time lighting the lamp above the platform instrument, which notifies the conductor that the gate is closed. When the passengers are aboard the train, the conductor operates a push-button circuit-breaker, extinguishing all lights and restoring the apparatus to normal.

CLOCK SYSTEM: Electrically operated and centrally-synchronized clocks have been provided throughout the station and yard.

The clocks are of three different types; motor-driven, impulse-driven, and primary or self-contained. The master-clock is equipped with a transmitter and circuit-closing device to transmit operating and synchronizing impulses to the other clocks, and besides being a close time-keeper, is corrected automatically once in each twenty-four hours from a signal sent out by the United States Naval Observatory, at Washington.

The motor-driven clock is the fifteen-foot dial instrument in the main waiting-room; its hands move forward slowly each half minute. The impulse clocks, comprising those in the public rooms, have a jump movement forward each quarter minute by impulses sent out from the master-clock through the medium of a transmitter.

The "primary" clocks in the offices have self-contained winding and operating mechanism, with a winding battery within the clock and arranged to be corrected hourly by impulses received from the master-clock. The primary clocks are synchronized in multiple, and the impulse clocks are operated in series.

A central storage battery of twelve cells, in duplicate, provides the necessary source of energy for operating the entire plant. Each battery is sufficient for one week's work, the recharging being done alternately.

Nearly all the clocks are lighted by reflection from the general illumination of the rooms, but those on the exterior of the building and in the main waiting-room are lighted by electric lamps in the clock cases. The casings of the clocks on the exterior of the building and in the public rooms were designed by the architects, and at each location harmonize with the general finish of the building.

PNEUMATIC TUBES: For the prompt dispatch of messages and small packages between the different buildings throughout the yard and the offices in the station building, a pneumatic-tube carrier system has been installed. It operates at an air pressure of from two to four pounds per square inch, the air supply being taken from the compressors in the Service Plant through reducing valves into low-pressure storage tanks, located at various points throughout the yard and building, and thence piped to the tube terminals.

The tubes are of brass, specially drawn, are of various sizes, and have long radius turns. Each run is of a single tube, having terminals at the ends to serve for either dispatching or receiving the carrier. The terminals are normally open, and, when the carrier is placed in the tube, the door at that end is closed and air automatically admitted. The door remains closed until the carrier reaches the opposite end of the line; there it trips a trigger which opens an electric circuit and de-energizes the electro-magnet which holds the door shut at the sending end.

The carriers are of leather, and of the required sizes to hold messages, baggage checks, packages of tickets, etc., depending on the service. The length of the tube runs varies from 150 to 1,000 feet, the total length of the system aggregating 7,000 feet.

The following are the lines of intercommunication established:

From the telegraph office on the second floor of the Eighth Avenue building 2¼ in. lines to each of the following:
Two Pullman offices in general waiting room;
Baggage Agent's office in baggage room;
Station Master's office at northwest corner of concourse;
Assistant Yard Master's office in yard under Post Office.
From the two telegraph offices in the general waiting room, 2½ in. lines to:
Each Pullman office in general waiting room.
From Assistant Yard Master's office in yard 2¼ in. line to Signal Cabin "A" in the yard.
From Signal Cabin "A" 2¼ in. line to Car Inspector's office in yard.
From the ticket stock room 5 in. lines to two general ticket offices in general waiting room.
From Assistant Baggage Master's booth in baggage room 4 in. line to two baggage checking desks in baggage room.

LIGHTING: Small lighting units, rather than powerful arc lamps, were adopted for use in the Station. This decision was reached, not only because of the good architectural effect and the agreeable quality of small

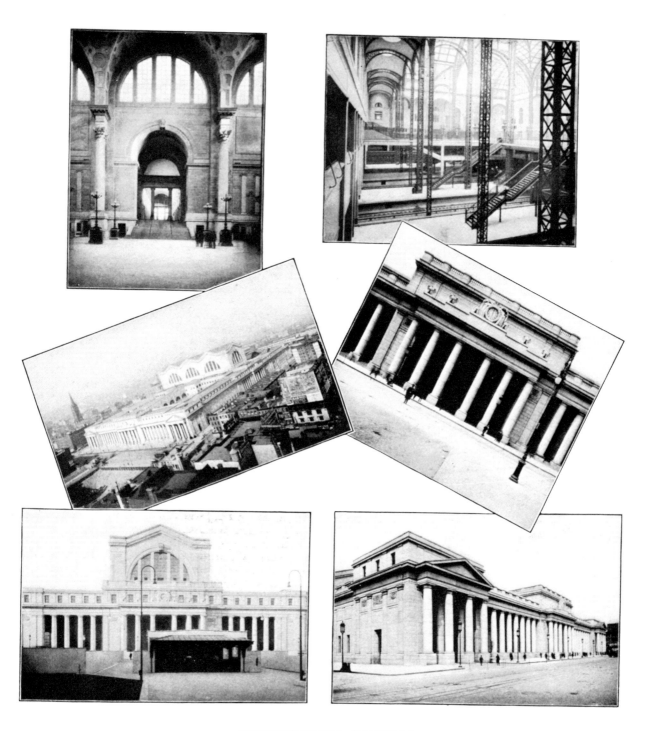

PENNSYLVANIA STATION

Main Waiting Room, looking east toward Arcade

Bird's-eye View

34th Street Entrance

Concourse, showing steps to platforms

Main Entrance

7th Avenue Façade

lights, but because of the effective diffusion secured from numerous sources of light. In general, the treatment adopted for different spaces is as follows:

The street lighting is by lanterns of moderate power, set on posts sixteen feet high and forty-five feet apart around the building; this system is used extensively in Europe, especially in Paris. The arcade is lighted by side brackets containing clusters of Nernst lamps. The public rooms, except the main waiting-room, are lighted by ceiling chandeliers, consisting of rings of Nernst lamps; the main waiting-room, because of its great height, is lighted near the floor only by two rows of cluster lamps on posts, with a limited amount of side-bracket lighting for wall illumination; the ceiling of this room is left in semi-obscurity, thus increasing the effect of height at night. The concourse, having its roof and floor largely of glass and ironwork, was a difficult space to light agreeably and effectively; after experiments with various kinds of lights, it was decided that rings of Nernst lamps around the columns, and ring chandeliers for the central spaces, gave the best effect.

For general illumination, the offices are equipped with ceiling lamps; local desk circuits, however, are provided in the base-boards of each room. The platforms are lighted by Nernst units about twenty feet apart and as high above the floor as local conditions permit. The intensity of the platform lighting, as will be noted from the list, is relatively low compared with other spaces, but is ample.

Electric current, used in the Station for lighting and motors, is distributed at the required voltages from a main switchboard in the Service Plant through cables to sub-switchboards, located at centers of the main divisions of the Station; from these boards it is further distributed to local boards in the smaller sections, or in individual rooms, and finally to the room switches in the offices, or to large groups of lights in the public rooms. All the larger public rooms are supplied with current from duplicate sets of feeders, one set of which is connected to an emergency bus in the Service Plant. The main feeders from the Service Plant are carried through the pipe subways under the tracks and in special pipe and wire shafts built in the Station building walls. The branch circuits are generally carried on top of the concrete floor arches and built into partitions. All feeders and sub-feeders are three-phase; branch circuits are single-phase. The lighting of public rooms is arranged so that half the lights are supplied by each of two feeders.

Miscellaneous power distribution is arranged in a similar manner, the power to the heating and ventilating motors throughout the building being distributed to the panels in these rooms from the sub-boards which are fed direct from the Service Plant.

Total number of lighting fixtures in
Station 21,000
Total equivalent combined candle-power
of lights in Station 335,000
Feet of conduit used 310,000
Feet of wire (No. 14 to 600,000 cir.
mils.) 690,000
Candle-power (mean hemispherical)
per square foot:
Main waiting-room 0.45

Other public rooms 0.60
Offices (general lighting) 1.25
Main concourse 0.35
Platforms 0.25

HEATING AND VENTILATING: Heating and ventilating are among the most important and complicated of the service requirements, and cover the heating of the main station as well as of the numerous buildings in the terminal yard, and the heating supply for cars standing in the yard, an area of about twenty-eight acres. The type of heating had a bearing not only on the kind and quantity of apparatus required but on the design and construction of the Station building itself, and therefore, the general heating scheme had to be determined prior to the construction of the building, and with an intimate acquaintance of the plans, in order that its service could be made to harmonize therewith.

The problem involved primarily the heating of a building having very large cubical contents, but especially one covering an unusually large ground area, and the fact that the building has no basement or cellar proper introduced special difficulties in installing large heating mains and radiating apparatus. The rooms in the building vary in size from the main waiting-room, 110 by 300 feet and 150 feet high, down to the usual dimensions of offices; and the occupancy covers the composite requirements of a railway station, a restaurant, and an office building. Many of the rooms are designed to house large numbers of people, some of the rooms have only indirect communication by windows with the outside atmosphere, and many are below the street level; therefore, it appeared desirable to use a forced-draft heating system, so that the air might be taken from suitable places and that proper ventilation could be had in summer as well as in winter, provided it could be installed and operated at a moderate cost as compared with other practicable methods.

To determine the best system of heating, all things considered, as applied to the local conditions, elaborate calculations and preliminary plans were made for various systems, as follows:

(a) Direct radiation in the various rooms, without forced ventilation.

(b) Indirect heating from pipe stacks located at central points, the warmed air being distributed through the ducts by forced draft.

(c) A combination of part direct and part indirect heating.

It appeared that portions of the Station, such as the waiting-rooms, kitchens, restaurants and toilets, where forced heating and ventilation were desirable, if not actually necessary, comprised at least two-thirds of the total area to be dealt with; and that if the indirect system should be used for places where it is essential, it could be extended to embrace the smaller spaces, such as the offices, without introducing prohibitive complication or without materially increasing the first cost of installation over that of the combined direct-indirect system. The conclusion was reached, therefore, that the indirect system with forced ventilation, both by draft and suction, should be adopted for all spaces except special isolated places, such as the baggage-rooms, which cannot be entirely closed by doors, and in cases of the small isolated buildings in the yard, where the direct system of radiation from pipes in the rooms should be used.

The next consideration was that of the medium of

PENNSYLVANIA STATION

33rd Street Carriage Driveway, looking east   Main Waiting Room, looking north

Train Platform and Stairways from Concourse   Exit Concourse, from north end

Main Waiting Room, from southwest corner

Main Concourse—General View

supplying the heat from a central point, the source of heat being the boilers in the Thirty-first Street Service Plant. It was concluded that low-pressure steam, either live or exhaust, conducted to the building through pipes, was impracticable, on account of the great area to be served, the very large dimensions of the pipe mains, pipe expansion troubles, and the lack of opportunity for draining properly the complicated system of return piping. Furthermore, exhaust steam thus used would cause excessive back pressure on the engines; live steam at high pressure would reduce the diameter of some of the pipes, but would still leave unsettled the question of proper drainage, and would make it difficult to control the pressure at widely separated points. The cost of operation would also be high, as no advantage could be taken of the economy to be gained by passing the steam first through the engines to produce light or power. The remaining method, namely, the use of water heated at a central point near the engines by exhaust steam from them, and distributed by pumping through a piping system to locally placed stacks in the building, appeared to be best. Such a system involves small piping only, is free from drainage troubles, is convenient for regulation, and gives the best quality of heat under varying weather conditions.

While, as above indicated, it was concluded that the water system of distributing heat was the only one filling the practical necessities of this particular case, an estimate was made of the comparative first cost of all systems, and it was found that the three available did not differ greatly in this respect, and that the indirect system with hot water could be installed at as low first cost as that of any other.

Comparison was made of the operating cost of both the direct and indirect systems, on the basis of both live and exhaust steam-heating means. It was found that the lowest operating cost would be obtained by using exhaust steam to heat water circulation with direct-heating radiators in the rooms. Forced ventilation, however, which as above stated was considered a necessity, would not entail a greatly increased operating cost by the use of indirect heating stacks, as the supply of exhaust steam would be ample for all except the severest weather.

Steam from the boilers in the Service Plant is passed through the various engines used for lighting, for air compressors, pumps, etc., and the exhaust is taken into tubular water heaters. Motor-driven centrifugal pumps circulate water through these heaters by the closed-pipe system into and through nine heating chambers in various parts of the Station building. From these the water returns to the circulating tanks and is used again. Connections are also made to the water heaters, so that live steam can be used when necessary. Through the heating stacks in the building fresh air is delivered from hoods on the roof, being drawn by fans and forced through a system of galvanized sheet-metal ducts into the various rooms of the building. In general, the warm air is admitted at or near the floor line and the foul air is drawn out by suction fans at or near the ceilings of the rooms. The design of the building is such that the heating stacks may be located in places where they occupy little valuable space, and the heating ducts are in most cases run in the ceilings of the rooms and passageways.

The total volume to be heated in the building is 10,-280,000 cubic feet, and it was estimated that to provide proper heating and ventilation under maximum conditions would require the circulation of 2,000,000 pounds of water per hour at a temperature of 200° Fahr., with a return temperature of 160°. The fans and local stacks used for transferring this heat have a capacity of 37,000,000 cubic feet of air per hour raised from zero to 130° Fahr., requiring about 77,000,000 thermal units.

The total loss for exposure, with the outside temperature at zero and the inside temperature at 70° Fahr., is about 30,000,000 B.t.u. per hour, and the air entering the rooms at such times is heated to about 120° Fahr., with a discharge velocity of about 300 feet per minute, an average drop of ten degrees is allowed for losses in the air ducts.

The heating surface in the nine heating chambers aggregates 76,500 square feet, made up of cast-iron cellular units in fifteen different stacks. Each of these stacks is provided with a motor-driven fan, the motor being belted to the fan pulleys, so that the fans may be driven either by single motors or in groups. The fans are multi-vane, and the motors are of the three-phase induction type, varying in horse-power from twenty to forty. The fan capacities vary from 15,000 to 75,000 cubic feet of air per minute. Screens are provided in the fan chambers for cleaning the air.

Galvanized iron ducts and exhaust fans are provided for ventilating purposes in addition to the heating fans. There are twenty-one different fans for the purpose, varying in capacity from 4,300 to 23,000 cubic feet of air per minute, with belted motors varying in capacity from two to ten horse-power. The total capacity of these ventilating fans is 43,000,000 cubic feet of air per hour, or sufficient to change the air in the different sections of the building from three to ten times per hour, depending on the occupancy of the particular space.

As the rooms used for different purposes communicate with one another, it was necessary, in designing this heating and ventilating system, to provide for suitable differential pressures in the rooms, in order that odors should not be communicated from one room to that adjoining; this is especially necessary in ventilating the kitchen and serving-rooms and also the various toilet-rooms. The pressure in these rooms, therefore, is maintained below that of those adjoining, so that the ventilation is into them rather than the reverse. The ventilating system of flues and fans, therefore, is divided into two sections, giving entirely separate ventilation for the kitchen and toilet-rooms.

In order to economize in the amount of heat required in the large public rooms in very cold weather, arrangements have been made to by-pass the discharge from the ventilating fans, either in part or entirely to the outside atmosphere, or to the heating stack chambers; thus the warmed air from the rooms may be used again in any proportion desired. The number of separate register openings required throughout the building to control the inlet and egress of air for heating and ventilating is 3,000.

PLUMBING: The plumbing comprises the extensive system of piping and apparatus for toilet-rooms and lavatories throughout the Station building and yard. In the various terminal buildings, fifty-eight separate toilets

PENNSYLVANIA STATION

Dining Room   Kitchen

Arcade, looking west

One of the Sub-Waiting Rooms

Lunch Room   Ladies' Retiring Room

have been installed. About one-third of these discharge directly into the sewers, and the remaining ones through ejectors. The capacity of the various toilets was determined by careful study of established practice for office buildings and public places. In the rooms of the Station alone, 864 fixtures have been provided, and a total of 932 throughout the entire area.

The main public toilets are noticeable for their size and completeness of arrangement. They are located immediately under the sub-waiting-rooms, on the level of the exit concourse, and are accessible by lobbies from the sub-waiting-rooms, and directly from the exit concourse. The men's toilet consists of a free room containing fifty-one closets, seventy-one urinals, and thirty-five wash-basins, and a pay toilet with twenty-nine closets and basins in separate enclosures. The women's toilet is similarly arranged, and contains one hundred free closets and thirty-three wash-basins, and a pay toilet of forty-four compartments having toilets and lavatories. The interior of these rooms is finished in marble floors and Carrara glass side-walls and partitions between fixtures.

All piping has been placed in galleries or compartments behind the fixtures, and all pipes are exposed for inspection and repair. This arrangement is somewhat unusual because of the limited vertical height between the floors and the waiting-rooms and the clearance over the track level, requiring that the fixtures have side outlets.

Water supply for the toilets is obtained from the pumps in the Service Plant; the flushing water is the waste from the jackets of the compressors and refrigerating plant. More than fifty-one miles of piping were used in the runs to the various plumbing fixtures.

The toilet-rooms which have their waste at a level below that of the city sewers in the adjoining streets and avenues required a special system for elevating and discharging the waste to the level of the sewers. The ejectors designed for this purpose use air at a pressure of from twenty-five to thirty pounds per square inch, operating automatically. They are located at twenty-two central points in niches in the subways under the tracks. Fourteen of the ejectors have a capacity of fifty gallons and eight of one hundred gallons per minute. Separate lines of pipe supply air from the compressors in the Service Plant to storage tanks near each group of ejectors; at these points reducing valves are placed to give the thirty-pound pressure required. Pipes from the ejectors are run through the subways to the nearest convenient points adjacent to columns of the building and viaducts, up which they are run to the street connections; the lift is generally from 40 to 70 feet.

COOLED DRINKING WATER: Pure drinking water of uniform temperature is distributed throughout the building by a separate system of piping. There are 158 special drinking fountains in the public rooms, the restaurant, the office and corridors. Water from the city mains is delivered to the Service Plant in Thirty-first Street, where it is filtered, cooled to 40° Fahr., and pumped to the fountains. In the public rooms the fountains are supplied with vending machines which dispense paraffined-paper drinking cups at one cent each.

WATCHMEN'S REGISTERS: A watchman patrols the building hourly, carrying a time register consisting of a "Newman" portable registering clock. He is required to record the time at stations by inserting in the clock a key kept in a special box at each station. There are key boxes at thirty-eight points in the building, and they are placed so as to require the watchman to pass through all important sections in making a round.

RESTAURANT: The dining and lunch-rooms each have a serving-room attached, with a kitchen, storerooms, refrigerator-rooms, offices and help quarters above. All these are thoroughly appointed with most modern apparatus throughout. The seating capacity of the dining-room is 500 persons, at 125 tables; of the lunch-room, 40 tables, or 160 persons, and 93 stools at the counters.

The refrigerator contract called for the installation of forty cold-storage rooms, the largest of which is 34 by 42 feet, containing about 12,000 cubic feet. The insulation is of compressed sheet-cork of the best grade; the inside walls are of Carrara glass, and the floors are of tile. The boxes are cooled by overhead brine pipes, receiving circulation from the refrigerating machines in the Service Plant. The temperature of these boxes varies from 8° to 38° Fahr., according to the purpose served; they were furnished by the Lorillard Refrigerator Co.

The kitchen contains twelve roasting ovens, three charcoal broilers, and three gas broilers, all erected under a hood fifty-four feet long. The pastry-room contains a gas range with ten ovens. The miscellaneous equipment includes electrical apparatus for meat-chopper, potato-parers, knife-cleaners, etc., and the service-rooms have electrically-operated dish-washing machines, steam tables, etc., etc.

In the serving pantries and behind the lunch counters cork flooring has been provided. In fact, wherever it is necessary for employees to have to stand, as in the ticket offices, cigar stands, elevators, etc., this flooring has been used to spare them fatigue. Eleven thousand square feet of cork flooring, furnished by David E. Kennedy, Inc., was used.

OFFICES: The Eighth Avenue front of the building, and eastward on the side streets to the concourse, contains the office section, on three floors. The first floor is devoted to the station master, locker-rooms, a hospital, the police department and funeral rooms. The second floor contains the offices of the general superintendent and the division superintendent and their staffs; the third floor contains the general offices of the Long Island Railroad. On the Seventh Avenue side there are two floors of offices, at present not fully assigned.

EMPLOYEES' CONVENIENCES: Part of the fourth floor has been fitted up for the housing and recreation of employees. The Thirty-first Street side contains sleeping-rooms, toilet and bathing facilities; the present capacity is 175 beds. The entire Eighth Avenue front has been fitted up for a Young Men's Christian Association, with an assembly hall, lecture-rooms, library and reading-room, billiard-room, bowling-alley, and gymnasium; there is also a large lavatory with shower-baths, and a locker-room. All the above have been completely furnished. Various small buildings have been provided at the track level, under the Station and in the yard, for toilets, locker and waiting-rooms, for employees on and off duty, or awaiting trains.

STATION SERVICE POWER PLANT: Aside from the traction requirements, there are numerous and important uses of power in various forms in a large Station, namely:

(a) Heating and lighting the Station and other buildings;

(b) Steam, compressed air, and water supply for cars;

(c) Air supply for the signal system, for tunnel drainage, pumping and sewage ejectors;

(d) Water supply for various purposes in the buildings, and for fire protection;

(e) Hydraulic power for elevators and lifts;

(f) Refrigeration for cold boxes in kitchens and restaurants, and for drinking water;

(g) Electric power for lighting buildings, tunnels and yards; stationary motors for elevators, heating and ventilating fans in building and tunnels, motors for pumping in yard and tunnels, power for car battery charging, operation of telephones, clock system, and other minor uses;

(h) Traction power for moving trains.

The character and location of the Station precluded the installation of machinery for providing these facilities in that building. But fortunately, a convenient location was available on relatively cheap property of the company on the south side of Thirty-first Street, about midway between Seventh and Eighth Avenues, and directly accessible under Thirty-first Street, to the Station and yard. The building erected on the plot has a frontage of 160 feet, a depth of 95 feet and a height of 86 feet above the curb, with a depth of 49 feet below. The building was designed of a height and character to harmonize with the Station building, with an endeavor to maintain the standards of the Station in all company constructions. The façade is of Stony Creek pink granite, similar in effect to that used for the Station exterior. The building construction is fireproof throughout, having steel framing, masonry walls, and concrete floors and roof. The machinery on the various floors, and the coal storage and stacks, required very heavy framing, 2,500 tons of steel having been used in the structure. The general plan divides the building by a fire wall vertically into two main parts, the west part being devoted to the machinery and boiler plant, and the east to the traction sub-station, offices and storerooms.

An idea of the equipment necessary to accomplish the requirements mentioned above may be obtained from the following concise statement which does not include any equipment for taking care of item (h):

Water tube boilers, 525 h.-p. each, ultimate capacity, ten boilers pressure, 200 lb. 5

Single acting, high speed, steam engines, 50 h.-p. each, driving Sirocco fans, for forced draft.... 2

Green fuel economizers 2

Water storage tanks, capacity 60,000 gal. 4

Coal conveyor, two pairs, capacity 120 tons per hour, 4

Coal skip hoist engine..................... 1

Ash conveyor, 50 tons per hour, motor driven, belted, 1

Garbage destructor 1

Boiler feed water heater, capacity, 6,500 gal. per hour from 70° to 200° Fahr. 1

Boiler feed pumps, duplex tandem, compound, steam driven 2

Hot well pumps, centrifugal, motor driven 2

1,000 k.w., 240 volt, 3 phase, 60 cycle, Westinghouse-Parsons steam driven, direct connected turbo generators (space for one additional) 2

2,000 cu. ft. per min. Nordberg, cross compound, Corliss, steam driven, air compressors, 100 lb. pressure, for signals and sewage ejectors...... 2

100 cu. ft. motor driven, air compressors, 125 lb. pressure, for brake testing.................... 2

Elevator pump, 1,500 gal. per min., 300 lb. pressure steam driven, for hydraulic baggage and passenger elevators 1

Elevator pump, 500 gal. per min., 300 lb. pressure, steam driven, for hydraulic baggage and passenger elevators 1

Compound steam-driven pump, 1,500 gal. per min., for baggage and passenger elevators.......... 1

Steam driven, Westinghouse, air brake pumps, for elevator system and for air cushion 2

Duplex, steam driven, Underwriter's fire pumps, capacity, 1,500 gal. per min. each................ 2

Motor driven, automatic, centrifugal pumps, for circulating cold water and water for flushing purposes, 3

Motor driven, centrifugal pumps, for hot water circulation to Station indirect heating system 3

Heater for Station indirect heating system 3

Heater, 635 gal. per hour, for hot water in Service Plant 1

Refrigerating plant, 40 ton ammonia compressors, engine driven 2

Brine pumps, motor driven, centrifugal 3

Motor-driven 1½ in. centrifugal pumps for circulating drinking water 2

750 k.w. single phase, 60 cycle, 11,000-420 volt, air blast transformers 3

500 k.w. single phase, 60 cycle, 11,000-246 volt, air blast transformers 3

150 k.w. 60-cycle, 11,000-2,200 volt, O.I.S.C. transformers for signals 2

100 k.w. 60-cycle, 11,000-220 volt, O.I.S.C. transformers for signals 2

80 k.w. 110-220 volt, motor generator sets for car battery charging 2

40 k.w. 110 volt, motor-driven exciters 2

25 k.w. 35 volt, motor generator sets, for baggage truck charging 2

55-cell storage battery, for emergency excitation.... 1

On the third floor of the Service Plant there is an instruction room and office, 6,200 square feet in area, containing apparatus to illustrate the construction and methods of operation of the special devices of the signal system, electrical equipment of the division, etc. These include complete working parts of the devices in question, with sectional models showing their internal construction. The systems illustrated are:

Block and interlocking signals,
Automatic train stop,
Car and locomotive air brakes,
Electrical control apparatus of locomotives and cars,
Tunnel alarm and telephone boxes,
Third rail construction and switching apparatus,
Apparatus for testing sight and hearing.

STATION YARD: The main Station Yard is between Seventh and Tenth Avenues, Thirty-first to Thirty-third Streets, including the sub-surface of these avenues and streets, and the surface as well as the sub-surface of Thirty-second Street, from Seventh to Tenth Avenues. The net area of the main yard is about twenty-seven acres and was excavated throughout to a depth of from forty to fifty feet below the original surface. The two easterly blocks, including the bed of Thirty-second Street, are occupied by the main Station building and west of Eighth Avenue a plot 400 by 400 feet has been sold to the United States Government for a general Post-office Building, now in process of erection.

The summit of the yard is 530 feet west of Seventh Avenue, from which point the grade falls east and west to the tunnel portals. From Tenth Avenue the grade rises eastward at the rate of 1.923 per cent to a point midway between Ninth and Tenth Avenues, thence at the rate of .4 per cent to the summit, and falls at the same rate to the crosstown tunnels.

The main approach tracks from the west fan out from the tunnel portals at Tenth Avenue to six running tracks, three for each direction to the main switch leads at Ninth Avenue, thence by double ladders, one to the north and one to the south, into twenty-one platform tracks covering the full width of the yard. At the east end all except five of the tracks are gathered into two groups, one leading to the tunnels on Thirty-third Street and the other to those under Thirty-third Street. The five southernmost tracks have stub ends and terminate at Seventh Avenue to lead in future to two tunnels under Thirty-first Street.

The Station Yard is not intended to provide unlimited car storage, but considerable space for this purpose is available in the corners formed by the rectangular configuration of the lot and the rectangular extension west of Ninth Avenue and 181 cars may be stored.

The tracks are generally spaced at thirty-one-foot centers, where platforms are between, and at fifteen-foot centers otherwise, to allow for the placing of building column supports. The total length of tracks in the Station Yard is about sixteen miles, of which three miles are adjacent to platforms.

The minimum overhead clearance in the yard between top of rail and girders is 16 feet, 2 inches, the same as the clearance in the tunnels. The maximum car equipment height is 14 feet, 9 inches over all, and fifteen feet over all for locomotives, leaving a net minimum clearance of 1 foot, 2 inches between equipment and permanent overhead structures. The overhead contact rail has a clearance of 15 feet, 4 inches from the under contact surface to the top of the track rail. The minimum clearance between sides of cars and columns between tracks is 1 foot, 6 inches, whether the cars are on tangents or curves, and the clearance for trucking on platforms is five feet, although in a few special instances it has been necessary to reduce this slightly. The clearance between edges of the high platforms and the sides of the cars is four inches.

In the yard area between Seventh and Ninth Avenues, a comprehensive system of subways has been constructed under the tracks for the following purposes:

Housing the various piping systems to the buildings and tracks, conveying steam, air and water. Proper and convenient maintenance required that all pipes should be readily accessible, which result could not be had by laying them in the ballast above the sub-grade; furthermore, because of the close spacing of the tracks and fact that this interspace in many places is occupied by columns there was no opportunity to lay out a practical pipe system in the ballast, and the buildings above the tracks were without basements in which to construct such a system. The high station platforms and the arrangement of the building itself required provision for trucking baggage, mail and express matter from one platform to the others, and this could be accomplished best by cross-trucking subways under the tracks. In places this was the only method possible as some of the platforms are under the streets and the baggage-rooms could only be reached by underground means. Communication between the various buildings could not be conveniently had at the track level or above, and therefore a longitudinal trucking subway between them was necessary.

In the portion of the yard under and west of signal cabin "A," at the intersection of the main track ladder, some accessible space was required for the large quantity of signal apparatus. This space was provided by constructing a basement for the building below the tracks, and a longitudinal subway, for the conduits and instruments; from this subway all connections were conveniently made for the switches and all apparatus was placed within easy reach.

The subways, therefore, while expensive to construct, furnished a valuable and comprehensive means for intercommunication for many important facilities without interfering in any way with the scheme of tracks or train operation, or requiring important modifications in the buildings themselves.

The layout of subways include a main longitudinal system from Seventh to Ninth Avenue used in part for pipeways, in part for trucking purposes, and generally for both. This longitudinal system is intersected by cross-galleries consisting of baggage-trucking subways at each end of the Long Island platforms at the north side of the yard, a main cross-trucking subway immediately under the outgoing baggage-room in the Station building and communicating with all lifts, and four cross-pipe subways approximately 400 feet apart, to cover the entire yard.

SUNNYSIDE YARD: While the yard is a stub-end one, as regards its location at the end of the division, it is double-end as regards train movements; this is accomplished by providing two loop tracks from the tunnels around the yard to its further end. Trains arriving from the New York Terminal, therefore, may enter the yard in the reverse direction and be ready to return to the station in the same head-end order, as generally required, thus minimizing the shifting and turning of special cars on a table. Furthermore, conflicting movements at the throat of the yard are avoided. It is important to note that the tunnel tracks from the New York Station are operated as two double-track lines, one (the Thirty-third Street tunnels) normally for Long Island Railroad trains; and the other (the Thirty-second Street tunnels) for movements to and from Sunnyside Yard. The Long Island Railroad trains, from the tunnels and from Long Island City, pass through the yard at a higher level than the yard tracks, and without grade crossings of any kind. A short distance east of the yard there is a jump-over connection and junction with the proposed New York Connecting Railway. The main freight connections of the Long Island Railroad to Long Island City pass around the yard to the north,

Tenth Avenue Tunnel Portal

Pennsylvania Station Yard—Main Signal Cabin
east of Ninth Avenue

Hackensack or Bergen Hill Tunnel Portal

Sunnyside Yard—Signal Bridge east of Honeywell
Street Viaduct

Sunnyside Yard—General View

Pennsylvania Station Yard—Main Signal Cabin east
of Ninth Avenue

Sunnyside Yard—Signal Bridge east of Bridge
Approach Viaduct

and cross the yard approach by overhead bridges near the tunnel portals.

The main, or south, yard has an ultimate capacity for 861 cars, and the supplemental, or north, yard has a capacity of 526 cars. The service buildings are between the north and south yards.

The south yard, which is used for cleaning and making up trains, is provided with platforms between tracks for trucking purposes, and a complete piping system for air, water and steam, as well as conduits and wiring for charging train lighting batteries, all having connections for each car on each track. All tracks in both north and south yards are equipped with third rail, so that electric motive power is available throughout for shifting trains.

PIPING: The piping and wiring systems are installed in a permanent accessible manner. Thus, from the boiler-house and auxiliary power sub-station a cross-pipe tunnel 603 feet long has been run at right angles to the main yard tracks, with openings to the inter-track spaces. Branching from this tunnel are concrete trenches, one between each alternate track, running the entire length of the tracks. In the walls of the tunnel and trenches are installed conduits for the battery charging wires, the system being centrally operated from the sub-station, the tunnels and trenches also contain pipe for air, water and steam. The trenches provide drainage for surface water and connect to the yard sewer system at suitable points.

WATER SUPPLY: A complete local water supply is derived from wells sunk within the yard area, furnishing sufficient water for all the requirements of the yard, up to 1,000,000 gallons per day and in addition, the requirements of the Long Island City power-house, the total being about 2,000,000 gallons per day. There are two wells, each about thirty feet deep. They are operated by direct suction through pipes to the pumps in the basement of the boiler-house.

YARD LIGHTING: The general illumination of the yard is effected by forty-one 3,000 candle-power flaming arc lamps of the long-burning type. These are mounted on steel poles from 200 to 350 feet apart, having special reference to important local points. Direct current at 110 volts is supplied to the lamps from the battery-charging motor-generator sets in the auxiliary sub-station.

YARD BUILDINGS: The following yard buildings have been provided:
(a) Sand house,
(b) Carpet shed,
(c) Commissary,
(d) Storehouse,
(e) Battery-repair house,
(f) Boiler house and auxiliary power sub-station,
(g) Oil house,
(h) Engine house and inspection shed,
(i) Wheel shed.

TUNNEL FACILITIES

LIGHTING: The tunnels are lighted continuously by a power entirely independent of the traction system. Each tunnel, moreover, has two circuits which are independent of each other and are fed from separate transformers and switching panels. The primary source of the lighting current is the sixty-cycle generators used for the general auxiliary power system, and located in the Long Island Power House and also in the Thirty-first Street Service Plant.

The lighting circuits are run in pipe conduits on the tunnel walls above the benches, and on one side of the tunnel serve as a hand rail. The lamps are of the Tungsten type, of twenty-five watt rating, twenty candle-power, and operate at thirty-three volts, being connected eight in series on a 252-volt circuit. They are fifty feet apart, on each side of the tunnel, and staggered so as to give a lamp for each twenty-five feet of the tunnel length. The lamps are seven feet above the tunnel side benches, and have enameled steel reflectors to throw the light in the direction of the movement of trains. Arrangements are made at various points in the lighting circuits for the attachment of portable extension connections for lamps to be used in repair work on various apparatus in the tunnels. The control of the current is from switchboards in the auxiliary power sub-stations in the shafts.

VENTILATION: Satisfactory ventilation for the tunnels was considered to be of great importance, as it was desired that, not only should the tunnels be safe under all emergency conditions, but that they should at no time be objectionable to passengers. Two general conditions were to be provided for; first, purity of the air, in normal operation; and second, requisite ventilation for an indefinite period in case of stoppage of trains in the tunnel from accident or other cause. It was thought, and afterward verified by trial, that the piston action of the trains when in motion would be an effective means of changing the air, as each tube contains only one track, and is isolated from the adjoining tube and open at each end to the free air. Where piston action has proved insufficient, as in the case of the deep tubes in London, it would seem to be because of the lack of sufficient free opening to the atmosphere, especially at the ends, and because of the by-passing of the air from one tube to another at stations. A special ventilating system, therefore, is needed only to provide air to a stalled train in an emergency, or to dissipate smoke and fumes from an electric arc, the possibility of which conditions was thought of sufficient importance to warrant the installation of a very complete forced-draft ventilating plant. It was determined that the air in the cars should not be allowed to contain more than eight parts of carbon dioxide per 10,000, requiring thirty cubic feet of fresh air per minute to each passenger. To insure this quantity of fresh air in the cars, it was thought advisable to furnish more, namely, fifty cubic feet per passenger per minute in the tunnels and the fan equipment was designed to meet this requirement, having due regard to emergency conditions and the occasional irregular spacing of trains. The quantity of air required per section of tunnel on this basis is about 60,000 cubic feet per minute, which will completely change the contents of the tubes three times per hour.

Plans for producing the requisite ventilation by exhaust, by pressure, or by a combination of both, were considered. The system found best adapted to the local conditions was patterned after the one used on the Norfolk & Western Railway and elsewhere. It is a forced-draft system in which a constant and uniform current of air is induced in the tunnel by forcing, in the direc-

Long Island City Power House—General View

Pennsylvania Station Service Plant

Electric Locomotive and Steel Car Train

Long Island City Power House—Turbine Room

Electric Locomotive, showing motors and running gear

tion of the traffic, the required volume of air into the portal. A divided nozzle, in the form of a tapering flue, is placed on each bench-wall for this purpose. This method requires no obstructing flues in the tunnels themselves, the nozzles being at the portals only, a consideration of great importance in keeping the side benches free for walkways. The arrangement of tunnels and shaft openings required in all fourteen sets of ventilating apparatus at different points.

The blowers are of the multi-vane, "Sirocco" type, belt-driven by induction-type electric motors, and the speed of the fan can be adjusted, by cone pulleys, from normal to 70 per cent or 40 per cent of normal, as required.

From tests made in the tunnels, with and without the fans running, it is apparent that, under normal conditions, the piston action of the trains can be relied on to give satisfactory ventilation. Records show that in the East River tunnels the air is changed every forty minutes by the passage of trains during non-rush hours, and every fifteen minutes during rush hours.

The average velocity of the air in the East River tunnels, due to the action of the fans alone, is about eight miles per hour. This is increased by the passage of trains to more than thirty miles per hour, the latter figure, of course, depending on the number of cars in the train and the speed.

It is evident, therefore, that in regular operation, the fans need not be run, and provision has been made to start and stop them, as required, from two central points, the power house for the East River tunnels, and the Service Plant for the North River tunnels.

TUNNEL ALARM SYSTEM: The tunnels are equipped with a special safety device which has two functions, one to cut off the current in a given section of the third rail, and the other to send a fire alarm call. The system consists of a series of alarm boxes, set about 800 feet apart. Each box is numbered and contains two levers, colored blue and red, respectively. The blue lever is marked "Power" and when pulled trips the circuit breakers controlling the third rail section adjacent to the box, thus cutting off the power and at the same time sending a call of two rounds of the alarm box number to the connected indicators. The red lever is marked "Fire" and when pulled performs the same function as the power lever, but sends in two additional rounds of the box number.

The box mechanism is operated by clockwork, set in motion by the winding of a spring when the lever is pulled, the clockwork actuates electric contacts in the circuits, controls an auxiliary tripper to the section circuit breaker, and spells the box number on the station indicators. Each box is provided with an interference magnet which prevents sending in an alarm from another box if one box on the circuit is in operation. Current for actuating the alarm circuits is obtained from storage batteries in the various sub-stations.

There are sixteen local or "Power" alarm circuits, corresponding to the section-controlling breakers, and there are three general or "Fire" alarm circuits, connected to switchboards in the power house at Long Island City, the Service Plant in Thirty-first Street, and the traction sub-station at the Hackensack Portals of the tunnels.

LONG ISLAND CITY POWER STATION

The power for operating the terminal division and the electrified zone of the Long Island Railroad is generated in a power station in Long Island City opposite Thirty-fourth Street, New York. This plant has been in operation since 1905 when the Atlantic Avenue branch of the Long Island Railroad was electrified.

The building is a steel frame structure with brick curtain walls and is of fireproof construction. The coal is stored above the boiler room in pockets having a capacity of 5,200 tons. There are four stacks carried from the base independently of the house, each of which is 233 feet high above the grates of the upper tier of boilers, or 275 feet from the base, with an interior diameter of seventeen feet. They are of steel, brick lined at the top.

The coal supply is hoisted in two-ton self-loading buckets from scows to a hoisting tower which is connected with the power-house by a bridge 500 feet long and 107 feet above the dock. These buckets travel at the rate of 1,000 feet per minute and deliver the coal to the crushing and weighing machinery in the tower, whence it is conveyed across the bridge in cars and deposited in the bunkers. This machinery unloads 150 tons per hour. The machinery for hoisting and trolleying the operation of the bucket was designed and built by the Robins Conveying Belt Company.

The machinery equipment of the power house, excluding that in the traction sub-station located in the building, may be concisely stated as follows:

Coal pocket at top of building; capacity, 5,200 tons.

Thirty-two 564-h.p. water-tube boilers, 200-lb. working pressure, 125° superheat. Space for sixteen additional 564-h.p. boilers.

Boilers equipped with 32 Type D, Roney stokers, 150 in. wide, twelve grates deep.

Two 8,000-k.w., 11,000-volt, 3-phase, 25-cycle, turbo-generators, and space for one additional for traction power.

Three 5,500-k.w., 11,000-volt, 3-phase, 25-cycle, turbo-generators, for traction power.

Two 3,000 k.w., 11,000-volt, 3-phase, 60-cycle, turbo-generators, for auxiliary power.

One 200-k.w., motor-driven exciter.

One 50-k.w., motor-driven exciter.

Two 200-k.w., turbine-driven exciters.

One 600-ampere-hour, storage battery of 110 cells.

One Tirrell regulator for 25-cycle generators.

One Tirrell regulator for 60-cycle generators.

Three 175-k.w., oil-cooled transformers.

Thirteen 1,200-ampere, 11,000-volt, Type C, oil circuit-breakers.

Thirty-nine 600-ampere, 1,000-volt, Type C, oil circuit-breakers.

SWITCHBOARD:

One bench-board, eight panels, for control of 25-cycle generators; and three panels for control of 60-cycle generators.

Six 25-cycle generator panels.

Two 60-cycle generator panels.

Two 25-cycle station panels.

One 60-cycle station panel.

STATISTICAL INFORMATION CONCERNING THE PENNSYLVANIA STATION

Building foundations begun	June 1, 1906
First steel column erected	May 27, 1907
First stone of masonry set	June 15, 1908
Finished exterior masonry	July 31, 1909
Building substantially completed	Aug. 1, 1910
Maximum number of men employed	4,240
Average number of men employed	1,800
Granite, exterior	490,000 cu. ft.
Granite, miscel. and in concourse	60,000 " "
Marble, interior	24,000 " "
Travertine	71,580 " "
Artificial stone	11,600 sq. yd.
Concrete fireproofing, cinder	243,000 cu. ft.
Concrete fireproofing, stone	720,000 " "
Granolithic floors	310,000 sq. ft.
Marble floors	85,000 " "
Cork floors	11,000 " "
Maple floors	147,000 " "
Terrazzo floors	10,000 " "
Vault lights	155,000 " "

Brickwork, all kinds	17,000,000 brick
Terra cotta furring and partitions	600,000 sq. ft.
Roofing, metal	300,000 " "
Roofing, tile	150,000 " "
Roofing, skylights	83,000 " "
Structural steel	27,000 tons
Ornamental iron	2,500 "
Glazing	80,000 sq. ft.
Plastering	85,400 " "
Painting (area)	2,800,000 " "
Cement	64,000 barrels
Length of building, east and west	789 ft.
" " " north and south	430 "
General height from sidewalk	76 "
Extreme " " "	153 "
Height, interior of waiting-room	150 "
" " " dining and lunch-rooms	32 "
" " " sub-waiting-rooms	56 "
" of concourse	100 "
" " exit concourse	11 "

	Dimensions.	Area, in sq. ft.
Concourse court	340 by 210 ft.	71,400
Concourse floor	475 " 125 "	60,000
Exit concourse floor	480 " 60 "	28,800
Thirty-third St. passageway, Seventh to Eighth Ave	654 " 30 "	20,000
Main waiting-room floor	300 " 110 "	33,000
Arcade	220 " 40 "	8,800
East baggage-room (T-shaped) (total area)	246 " 90 "	34,000
West baggage-room	321 " 50 "	16,000
Train-sheds (two, dimensions each)	216 " 112 "	48,384
Standing room for cabs (exit side)		Capacity, 25
Lunch and dining-rooms (two each)	115 " 60 "	6,900
Sub-waiting-rooms (two each)	100 " 60 "	6,000
" " " total seating capacity		Persons, 700
Women's retiring-room	30 " 38 "	1,140
Seventh Avenue shops (two each)	100 " 35 "	3,500
Arcade shops (two sides each)	184 " 76 "	28,000
Barber shop	50 " 30 "	1,500
Waiting-room ticket offices	20 windows,	2,400
Carriage driveway, Thirty-third Street	552 by 45 "	24,840
" " Thirty-first Street	530 " 41 "	21,730
Sidewalks around building	2,650 " 30 to 40 ft.	90,000
Women's main toilets		3,140
Men's " "		3,600
Hospital Department		1,400
Police Department		827
Funeral-rooms		600
Parcel-room		2,780
Office space, first floor, west of waiting-room		15,850
" " second floor, west of waiting-room		20,270
" " third floor, west of waiting-room		31,500
" " Seventh Avenue, front, two floors		21,500
Y.M.C.A., attic floor		16,800
Bunk-rooms, attic floor		10,200
Unassigned space, attic floor		27,800
Kitchen and storerooms		15,000
Ticket offices, main waiting-room		2,344
" " Long Island section		2,870

	No.		No.
Passenger elevators to track platforms	11	News-stands	8
Baggage lifts	21	Bootblack stands	7
Stairways to track platforms	48	Clocks	44

Number of station tracks adjoining platforms	21
Length of platforms adjacent to passenger tracks	21,500 ft.
Total area of platforms	244,270 sq. ft.
Number of passenger platforms	11
" " mail "	2
" " express " (future)	4
Four passenger platforms, average ... 21 ft. wide,	900 ft. long
" " " " ... 21 " "	1,050 " "
Two " " " ... 16 " "	1,000 " "
One " " " (L.I., loading) ... 47 " "	745 " "
Two mail " "	375 " "
Longest platform (No. 6)	1,140 " "
Total length of future express platforms	1,600 " "
Mail cars standing at tracks adjacent to platforms	25 cars
Storage space in yard "A" (Pennsylvania turning yard)	34 "
" " " " "B" (Long Island express yard)	31 "
" " " " "C" (" " local ")	50 "
" " " " "D" (Pennsylvania turning yard)	40 "
Total yard storage capacity	181 "

Total excavation (place measurement) for the entire yard, all contracts included ... 2,200,000 cu. yd.		Number of viaduct columns	771
		Number of Station building columns	650
		Number of Post-office building columns	200
Excavation begun ... July, 1904		Number of columns for other structures	16
Viaduct erection started ... Oct., 1905		Total length of viaducts	5,985 ft.
Viaducts completed ... Jan., 1910		Weight of structural steel in viaducts	23,500 tons

GENERAL INFORMATION CONCERNING THE NEW YORK TUNNEL EXTENSION OF THE PENNSYLVANIA RAILROAD

Length of run, Manhattan Transfer to Pennsylvania Station	8.78 miles
Total length of Tunnel Extension Railway, Manhattan Transfer to Laurel Hill Avenue, Long Island	13.41 miles
Total length of single track tunnels	14.57 "
Length of Bergen Hill Tunnel Section,	6,050 ft.
Length of river section, North River tunnels	6,360 "
Length of land section, North River tunnels	982 "
Length of cross-town section, near Sixth Avenue to East River (average)	4,747 "
Length of river section, East River tunnels	3,949 "
Length of land section, Long Island City	3,847 "
Total distance, Hackensack tunnel portal to Long Island City tunnel portals (average)	5.58 miles
Sunnyside Yard:	
Third Street to Laurel Hill Avenue.	8,815 ft.
Extreme width	1,625 "
Area	192 acres
Length of yard tracks (present)	25.72 miles
Length of yard tracks (ultimate)	45.47 "
Manhattan Transfer Yard:	
Length	4,050 ft.
Width	250 "
Area	23 acres
Length of yard tracks	11.49 miles
Station Yard:	
Length, Tenth Ave. to Sixth Ave.	3,488 ft.
Width, net, at track level (Thirty-	

first to Thirty-third Streets)	509 ft.
Area	28.3 acres
Length of tracks	15.62 miles
Pennsylvania Station:	
Length, east and west	789 ft.
Length, north and south	430 "
Area (of building at street level)	7.5 acres
Total trackage of Terminal Railroad, present	94.57 miles
Total main line trackage	44.0 "
Initial daily train service, P.R.R. trains in and out	150
Initial daily train service, L.I.R.R. trains in and out	200
Summer schedule, 1911, P.R.R. service, in and out	200
Summer schedule, 1911, L.I.R.R. service, in and out	250
Maximum daily capacity of station, based on maximum hourly capacity.	1,160 trains
Number of electric locomotives for 1911 service	33
Number of buildings required for all purposes	64
One traction power house, capacity	40,000 k.w.
Four traction sub-stations, total capac.,	24,000 "
One service power house, initial boiler capacity	2,625 h.p.
Total weight of structural steel used for entire Terminal Railroad construction	80,350 tons
Approximate total quantity of cement used for entire Terminal Railroad construction	1,942,000 bbls.
Excavation, including that for tunnels.	6,936,673 cu. yd.

THE ARCHITECTURAL MOTIF OF THE PENNSYLVANIA STATION

By W. SYMMES RICHARDSON, of McKim, Mead & White

IN designing the Pennsylvania Station, an attempt has been made, not only to secure operating efficiency for one of the largest railway stations in the world, but also to obtain an outward appearance expressive of its use, and of a monumental character. The problem involved was unusual, as the tracks are situated so far below the surface of the street that it was not possible to adopt any of the types of station buildings familiar in modern architecture. The exposed train-shed, with its large semicircular ends of glass, has become, during the last century, a form recognized by the layman as the railway type, and such features at the ends of the avenues of our modern cities suggest a great terminal, even to a stranger, when seen for the first time. Of such a character are the Gare de l'Est, the Gare Montparnasse, and the Gare du Nord, in Paris, the stations at Frankfort and Dresden, and, in fact, most of the principal stations of Continental Europe, as well as the splendid train-sheds of the Pennsylvania Railroad Company in Jersey City and Philadelphia.

Not only did the architects desire to give an adequate railway expression to the exterior, but they recognized the equal importance of giving the building the appearance of a monumental gateway and entrance to one of the great metropolitan cities of the world. This idea, in their opinion, has not always received the recognition which it deserves in the solution of problems of this character.

For inspiration, the great buildings of ancient Rome were carefully studied, and particularly such buildings as the Baths of Caracalla, of Titus, and of Diocletian, and the Basilica of Constantine, which are the greatest examples in architectural history of large roofed-in areas adapted to assemblages of people. Moreover, the conditions of modern American life, in which undertakings of great magnitude and scale are carried through, involving interests in all parts of the world, are more nearly akin to the life of the Roman Empire than that of any other known civilization. It seemed, therefore, fitting and appropriate in every way that the type of architecture adopted should be a development from Roman models, and while the building is of necessity, on account of the requirements of its uses, different from any building known to have been previously built, its inspiration can be directly traced to the great buildings of the Roman Empire.

To obtain the largest possible expression, simple materials have been used throughout. The exterior being entirely of granite, all unnecessary detail of ornamentation was omitted, and it has been hoped, considering the variegated character and style of the modern architecture of American cities, that in this way the monumental mass and scale of the building has been maintained in relation to its surroundings. The design is of Roman Doric, surrounded by an attic, with a colonnade along the Seventh Avenue front, and with colonnades on the other sides marking the principal entrances. To avoid monotony of effect in a building of such unusual frontage, the attic is broken into pavilions of varying heights, marking the important entrances. In the center of the rectangle, and dominating the entire structure, rises the wall of the main waiting-room, the largest room of its kind in existence. This wall is treated as a background to the buildings facing the street, and is broken simply by eight large semicircular openings of glass, each nearly seventy-five feet in diameter, which light the room and give to the building, when seen from a distance, something of the railway character above referred to. Apart from the practical consideration of obtaining adequately roofed-in areas, this room was primarily created to give the exterior of the building as distinctive a railway expression as was possible, considering the limitations of the problem.

At the north and south ends of the Seventh Avenue front are porticos leading to inclined descending driveways, forming entrances for carriages, which pass between the columns in the same way as in the Brandenburg Gate in Berlin, through which a great part of the traffic enters that city.

The official foot entrance to the station is in the center of the Seventh Avenue front, opposite West Thirty-second Street. This leads directly to the general waiting-room, in the center of the building, through an arcade, somewhat similar in scale and idea to the famous arcades of Milan and Naples, Italy. The main waiting-room is comparable in dimensions to the nave of St. Peter's Cathedral, in Rome. At the entrance to the waiting-room is a stairway forty feet wide, at the side of which is a niche containing the statue of the late A. J. Cassatt, president of the Pennsylvania Railroad, and the dominant personality in the tunnel and station project. The motif of the waiting-room design was suggested by the great halls of the baths of ancient Rome, above referred to, and consists of eight Corinthian columns, seven feet in diameter and sixty feet high, standing on pedestals, and supporting the coffered vaulted ceiling. At the north and south ends of the rooms are colonnades of single Ionic columns, thirty-one feet high, directly approached by bridges over the carriage driveways, from the central entrances on West Thirty-first and West Thirty-third Streets, and from which ample staircases lead to the floor of the room. The sub-waiting-rooms, opening into the retiring-rooms, are proportioned to the magnitude of the central room. The connecting openings are made as large as possible, and frequently are of screens of clear glass of great dimension, permitting comprehensive perspective views, not only of splendid architectural effect, but of great assistance as a guide to the movements of the traveling public. For the interior, the architects have selected a Roman travertine stone, brought from the quarries near Tivoli, Italy. Of this stone, the exterior of the Colosseum, the Tomb of Hadrian (now the castle of St. Angelo), the Quirinal Palace, the Cathedral of St. Peter's, and nearly all the churches and most of the palaces of Rome are built. Considered purely from the structural standpoint, it is one of the finest building stones known, but its selection for this building, for which it has been imported into this country for the first time, was due principally to its beautiful, warm, sunny color, and its tendency to take a polish and improve in appearance by contact and use rather than to absorb dirt, as is the case with so many of the limestones in common use both here and abroad. The stone, moreover, has a very interesting visible structure, which, in a building of such large dimensions, tends to give a more robust character and texture than it is possible to obtain in most other materials. A color motif has been given to the room by the insertion of conventionalized maps in the six large panels below the lunette windows; these maps were painted by Mr. Jules Guerin.

The concourse itself forms a courtyard with granite walls, enclosed by an iron and glass roof, forming intersecting barrel arches surrounded on three sides by tile domes against the walls of the building. The structural steelwork here is of an open latticed design, without ornament, the architectural effect being obtained by a careful study of the proportions and form of the structural members required. Here the architects have attempted to give to the structural steel a straightforward and adequate architectural expression, and while the design is quite different from anything yet built, it is suggestive in many ways of the train-sheds in the famous stations at Frankfort and Dresden, Germany. On the easterly side of the concourse is the continuous façade of the waiting-room, with semicircular openings, comparable in extent and scale to the Boston Public Library.

The design, fabrication, and erection of the concourse roof introduced novel problems. It was the desire of the architects to give the structural steel a dignified expression of design, and also to obtain an appropriate transition between the purely architectural lines and structural materials of the general waiting-room and adjoining rooms and the purely utilitarian and structural treatment of the railway operating features of the yards, such as the tracks, viaducts, etc., that is to say, the leading by an easy and unconscious gradation of effect from the monumental side of the station to the utilitarian. To accomplish this result the main architectural lines of the concourse roof were first determined, namely, the location of the columns, arches, and domes, and the general height and breadth of the intersecting members; the steel engineer being then given the problem of designing a structure to conform to the architectural lines outlined, the detail being a question of good proportion and adjustment from both points of view. The type and scale of lattice work, as well as the lines and sizes of the arches, notably the variation in depth between the spring and top lines of the arches, as well as varying widths between the diagonal ribs and the vault lines, was suggested to the engineer to obtain a variety of effect and to avoid the monotony which would result in the assembling of arches of similar forms and dimensions. To obtain the expression of these architectural features in steel, necessitated the use of an excess of material over what would be required by ordinary trussing to cover the area in question, but the excess amount of material was considered justifiable to fulfill the motives above referred to. The design of this difficult piece of roofing was due to the joint efforts of the architects, Westinghouse, Church, Kerr and Company, and Messrs. Purdy and Henderson, engineers.

Throughout there has been a consistent and continuous effort to maintain a unity and simplicity of design, so that the structure will count as a whole of many inter-related parts of similar scale. Ornament has been very sparingly used, and there is no attempt at decorative art, except for the color effect of the maps in the main waiting-room. The interior of the building is practically a monotone, it being the idea of the architects that a building devoted to railway purposes should be made of permanent and durable materials of simple character and capable of the easiest maintenance. The light buff of the travertine stone has formed the keynote of the color scheme for the plaster walls and ceilings, the larger ceilings having a pigment in the plaster to give a permanent stain, so that the necessity and inconvenience of repainting is reduced to a minimum. In a few places where decorative sculpture is used, such as the clocks over the main entrances, the eagles and bas-relief panels adjacent, and the large keystones on the exterior of the general waiting-room and over the arches leading from this room to the arcade and concourse, the work was placed in the hands of Mr. A. A. Weinman, a sculptor of reputation, who has given to the ornament and figures a distinct individuality appropriate to the uses of the building.

The East River Division

ALFRED NOBLE . . *Chief Engineer*

C. L. HARRISON *Principal Ass't Engineer*

G. C. CLARKE . *Resident Engineer*

GEORGE LEIGHTON *Resident Engineer*

JAMES H. BRACE . *Resident Engineer*

FRANCIS MASON . *Resident Engineer*

S. H. WOODARD . *Resident Engineer*

L. H. BARKER . *Resident Engineer*

MONOGRAPH

by

JAMES H. BRACE

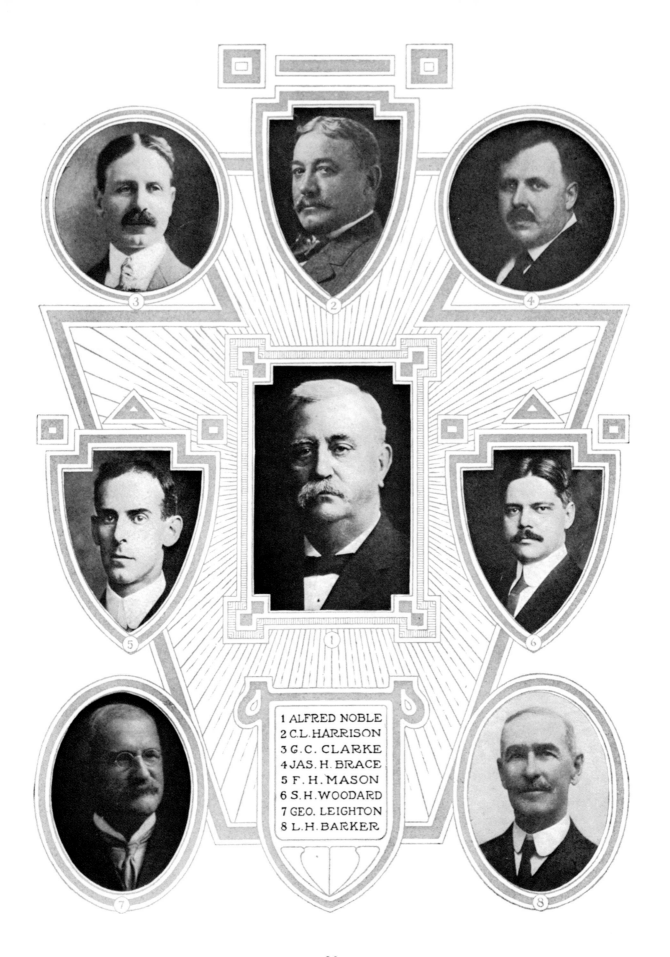

1 ALFRED NOBLE
2 C.L. HARRISON
3 G.C. CLARKE
4 JAS. H. BRACE
5 F. H. MASON
6 S. H. WOODARD
7 GEO. LEIGHTON
8 L. H. BARKER

THE EAST RIVER DIVISION

Manhattan Crosstown and East River Tunnels and Sunnyside Yard

THE East River Tunnels consist of four tubes, each a little over two miles long and each containing a single track extending under the Island of Manhattan and the East River from Seventh Avenue to near Van Alst Avenue in Long Island City. They start at the east end of the Terminal Building fifty feet below the street surface, and run parallel from Seventh Avenue to Second Avenue; two, A and B, under Thirty-third Street and the other two, C and D, under Thirty-second Street. From Second Avenue they converge until they enter the approaches to Sunnyside Yard at Van Alst Avenue. A and B are used by the Long Island Railroad for passenger traffic. C and D are used by the Pennsylvania Railroad for hauling empty trains to and from the station to their extensive terminal yards in Iong Island City. As it is the practice on the Pennsylvania Railroad to number tracks from south to north, the designation of these tunnels has for operating purposes been changed from A, B, C and D to 4, 3, 2 and 1, respectively.

For convenience in describing the work, we will divide the route of the tunnels into three sections, each differing from the other in physical features and consequently in method of construction. The first section from the station to the East River; the second section, the East River; and the third, the approaches and terminal yards in Long Island City.

The second section because of the unique engineering features and the dangers involved, alike occupied the minds of the engineers and appealed to the imagination of the layman. To understand the difficulties, one must form an idea of the banks and bed of the river.

Imagine two ridges of rock about two hundred feet high running north and south three-fourths of a mile apart. Between these and parallel to them, a third ridge, with a flat, irregular crest about fifty feet lower in elevation than the former. The slopes of the side ridges are covered and the valley between filled to a height slightly above the middle ridge with boulders, gravel and sand. The surface of this irregular covering of earth forms the bed and banks of the East River. The greatest depth of water, about sixty feet, is between the Manhattan and middle ridges. On the Long Island City side, the corresponding depth is about forty feet, while near the middle there is only about thirty feet of water. The determination by means of borings of the nature of the materials underlying the river was the first work of the engineers. After careful study of the results and balancing the advantages of the different depths, the vertical position of the tunnel was finally fixed so that the tunnels are entirely in rock near each bank of the river, entirely in earth when they cross

the two valleys, and with the bottom in rock and the top in earth across the greater portion of the central ridge. This difference in the material to be penetrated, together with the fact that the top of the tunnel was sometimes in sand while the bottom was in rock, constituted the chief difficulty of the river section. In order that construction might progress as rapidly as possible, work was started simultaneously from each side of the river toward the middle. The bottoms of the tunnels on the Manhattan side were ninety feet below the surface of the ground and on the Long Island City side, seventy-five feet. To gain access to the tunnels it was necessary to sink openings or shafts down to the level of the former. Two shafts, one over each pair of tunnels, were sunk on each side of the river. These shafts also served for carrying on the work both west of First Avenue and east of Front Street on the land sections. At the shaft sites on both sides of the river there was from thirty-five to forty feet of wet earth over the rock and, in fact, one of the shafts at Long Island City had to be started in eight feet of water in a slip connecting with the river. The caisson method was adopted for sinking through the earth and the rock also, if necessary, with provision for the use of compressed air if found desirable. On the Manhattan side it was found to be possible to sink the caissons under normal air pressure to solid rock, but on the Long Island City side it was necessary to use compressed air for the full depth. The river tunnels were also driven by compressed air in connection with shields.

Although these methods are well known to engineers, a brief description may be of interest to the public, whose misapprehension of them is evident from the recent remark of a well-known business man that, while it was more convenient for him to take the Long Island train from the new station to his home, he still used the ferry because he had a weak heart and felt sure he could not stand the compressed air. This impression is doubtless fostered by the peculiar sensation imparted to the ear drums when a rapidly moving train enters any tunnel or closely confined space. Before the train enters the tunnel the air within is under the same pressure as that outside, but the train acts as a piston, either pushing the air ahead, causing a slight vacuum or forcing it backward along the side of the train, increasing momentarily the pressure. Either of these conditions will cause the effect noted.

The following simple experiment illustrates the working of a caisson:

Take an ordinary glass tumbler, invert it and press it into a basin of water. Note that the water rises inside the glass but stands at a lower level than that outside.

This is due to the fact that the air inside has been compressed and exerts a greater pressure on the water inside the edge than does the ordinary atmosphere outside the glass. If we could further increase the air pressure inside the glass, we could force the water downward to the level of the edge of the glass. This is exactly what is done with a caisson, but instead of a glass we have a large box or cylinder made of steel or wood open at the lower end, called the cutting edge, which corresponds to the edge of the glass but with the roof of the working chamber, which represents the bottom of the glass, placed well down toward the cutting edge. This change in the position of the roof makes the cylinder more stable and less liable to topple over. Through the roof pipes are placed which connect with an air compressor. When work is going on the latter forces air of the desired pressure into the chamber. Access is provided to the working chamber by a lock, the essential parts of which are a small chamber in the roof of the caisson with a door at each end both opening downward or toward the air with higher pressure. Two valves, one at each end, are required, one opening into the compressed air chamber and the other into the open air. These valves are similar to those on an ordinary steam radiator. A person wishing to pass into the working chamber enters the lock, closes the door and valve at the open-air end, opens the valve connecting with the working chamber and allows the high-pressure air to enter the lock slowly. When the pressure of the air in the lock is equal to that in the working chamber, the door leading into the latter can be opened. To go out into the open air the process is simply reversed. To make doors air-tight when closed they are equipped with rubber gaskets. When the outer door is closed it is only necessary to hold the door tight until the pressure in the lock increases slightly above that on the outside. When this difference has reached one pound the pressure on a door 4 feet by 3 feet is 1728 pounds. That everyone does not realize what this means is illustrated by the following incident.

A city policeman had made himself slightly officious around the work at the Manhattan end and was not particularly liked. One evening he announced that he was going through the lock. An inspector went along to see that no harm came to him but did not offer the usual advice given to novices. The policeman pushed the outer door shut. As there was no catch he held it while the inspector admitted the high-pressure air through the valve. As the pressure rose to two or three pounds the policeman's ear drums began to hurt and he decided he had had enough. He made a dash for the door and began pulling to try and open it, but by this time it would have taken several tons' pull. He was very much mystified and concluded that the inspector was playing some trick on him. It was only by rapidly reducing the pressure in the lock to normal and thus releasing the door that the inspector saved himself from a clubbing. The officer declared he would never again try to enter the tunnels, but later when the operation had been explained to him this same policeman did go into the tunnel on the occasion of an accident and did good work.

After turning on the high-pressure air in the lock one was liable to have a stinging sensation in the ears. Physicians tell us that air is admitted behind the ear drums through small passages which may become blocked, especially when one has a cold in the head. When this is the case the compressed air does not readily reach the rear of the drum and the latter is pushed inward by the increased pressure on the outside. This causes the pain which can usually be relieved by swallowing, holding the nose and blowing or by twisting the jaw while the air pressure is increased very slowly. In bad cases, relief does not follow and cases of punctured ear drums are not infrequent. This is the only bad effect felt, however, while going under pressure and the only precaution required is to go in gradually. Men who are used to the work will frequently raise the pressure at the rate of twenty or thirty pounds per minute.

Returning to our description of shaft sinking. On starting work a pit is usually dug down to the ground water level. The caisson is erected in this pit with its lower edge below the water level. The air pressure within the caisson is then increased just enough to force out the water.

Excavation is begun around the cutting edge and the pit deepened, the caisson being gradually lowered to its final position. In the case of a shaft the bottom is then sealed with concrete and some form of waterproofing, with strength sufficient to resist the upward pressure of the water. After this, the roof of the working chamber may be removed, and the shaft is under normal air pressure. During the process of sinking a small amount of air escapes under the cutting edge.

In driving a tunnel with a shield the operations are analogous but much more difficult. We must now imagine our glass turned over on its side in the earth beneath the water and remember that the former is thoroughly saturated and runs almost as freely as water. We will further imagine that instead of the rim of the glass, we have a steel shell of a slightly greater diameter and telescoping for a short distance over the cylinder of the glass. We will then imagine the cylinder of glass replaced by a long tube made up of cast iron segments bolted together. The bottom of the glass or the roof of the working chamber in the case of the caisson replaced by one or more bulkheads or diaphragms of concrete and steel completely filling the tube for a length of several feet. Through these bulkheads are placed the air locks for the passage of men and materials and air pipes for maintaining the pressure. If the glass, after it has been submerged in the basin of water, is gradually turned on its side, the imprisoned air quickly escapes in a bubble. This is what happens in the tunnel. The air constantly escapes at the cutting edge of the shield, but not so freely through earth as through water. The air pressure forces the water back from the face of the shield and dries out the ground so that it can be worked. In bad ground the face is kept boarded as tightly as possible, all cracks puttied with soft clay and only small areas opened at a time to advance the excavation. On the inside of the rim of the East River shields and about midway of its length were attached twenty-seven hydraulic jacks having their line of thrust parallel to the line of the tunnel. The heads of the jacks bore against the face of the completed tube inside the shield. When the pressure was turned on to the jacks, the shield was forced forward, its cutting edge penetrating the material in front. The attempt was made to push the shield for

82

A segment of the iron lining being held in place by the erector and bolted in position.

"Guns" used to brace the face of the excavation when the shield was shoved. They consisted of two pieces of gas pipe which were allowed to telescope as the shield pressed forward.

A part of one of the enormous air compressing plants which made possible the execution of the undertaking.

A view in front of the shield looking toward it. It shows the cutting edge, working compartments and the forward side of the cross bulkhead.

A good idea of the methods employed in constructing the tunnels in open cut and also shows Tunnel "C" crossing Tunnel "B."

a distance of two and one-half feet each time, but this often had to be done in two or more operations. At the end of the shove the rear of the shield still enveloped the lining. The rams of the jacks were then drawn back into place and there was room to erect a new ring of cast-iron lining two and one-half feet long inside the shield.

When the face was entirely in loose material it was not practicable to dry it out much below the middle of the shield. After completing one shove preparations were at once made to move the face forward for the next. A few of the face boards were removed near the top. The sand was scooped out as far in advance of the shield as it would stand up without caving. Short lengths of plank were then inserted with one end resting on the top of the cutting edge and the forward end forced into the undisturbed material at the face. As soon as there was room, planks were also placed against the new face and braced against the shield and in this way, by careful work a cylindrical space sheathed with plank on the top and sides and in front was opened up in front of the shield down as far as the face was dry. Below this level the wet sand flowed back into the shield until stopped by the bulkhead about midway of its length. When everything was in readiness for a new shove the wet sand was shoveled out until it ran in faster than it could be handled. An attempt was then made to shove the shield forward. Although the jacks were capable of exerting a forward pressure of 5,150 tons on the shield, often it would move only a few inches. More of the wet material was then removed and the process repeated.

Compressed air was escaping from the face at all times. The quantity varied with the character of the material encountered, being great in coarse sand and almost nothing in clay. It also varied with the condition of the face and with the pressure maintained in the tunnels. It was this escaping air that caused the boiling so often seen at the surface from the Thirty-fourth Street ferries. It was, of course, desirable to keep the face dry as far down as possible but in attempting to do this the strain sometimes became too great on the overlying material when suddenly a great quantity of air would force its way to the surface of the river in a manner exactly similar to the bubble of air imprisoned in our glass. These sudden escapes of air were called blows and they frequently threw up a column of mud and water from ten to twenty feet above the surface of the river. These blows had the effect of at once reducing the pressure in the tunnels and, if they continued for a sufficient length of time, of flooding the tunnels. Fortunately this occurred on one occasion only. Usually a fall of pressure of from two to four pounds in the tunnel would restore the balance between the upward pressure of the air and the downward pressure of the water and sand. It was during a sudden severe blow like the one just described that occurred the much-talked-of adventure of the workman on the Rapid Transit Tunnel to Brooklyn. This man was working at the face when a blow took place and he was carried upward through the river bottom, appearing at the river surface, where he was picked up not much the worse for his experience. Nothing so exciting as this occurred on the Pennsylvania tunnels, although at one time a colored laborer attempting to escape during a blow from the face of the shield through one of the narrow openings in the bulkhead, was unable to pull himself through against the rush of air toward the face. After the excitement was over he resigned his job, informing his boss that the devil had caught him from behind and held him so firmly that he could not escape.

One of the English superintendents, who had been employed on a section of the Blackwall tunnel under the Thames, avers that he was standing at some distance from the shield when a blow occurred. As he was hurriedly making his way toward the front, he met a workman running in the opposite direction. Thinking he had been seized with panic, he grabbed him. The workman protested vigorously that his waistcoat containing a shilling had been carried away by the blow and that he was on his way to the surface to get it. It is stated that both were rescued at the surface of the ground. In any event a blow was rather an exciting experience for those in the tunnel at the time.

A dense fog would instantly fill the whole space and one literally could not see one's hand before one. This, together with the uncertainty as to whether the water would come in, was rather trying. After one or two experiences of the sort, the men almost without exception remained steady and at once commenced to check the loss of air by placing hay, bags or other material over the face where the loss was greatest. The valley on the Manhattan side of the river was largely filled with open sand and at one point there was only about eight feet between the bottom of the river and the top of the tunnel and it was thought best to deposit a blanket of clay over the line of tunnels. Permits were obtained from the United States Government to deposit the clay to a depth of about ten feet. Although this was of material benefit, the blanket was not of sufficient thickness to prevent almost continuous blow-outs, and as the necessity was apparent from time to time, the authorities allowed the blanket to be increased in thickness. This, together with the fact that the material toward the center of the river was more impervious, and that the men became more skilful, put a stop to serious loss of air after the first few months. Some of the most difficult work occurred where the tunnels were passing from an all-rock section to an all-earth section; that is, where the top of the tunnel was in sand and the bottom in rock. Here it was necessary to excavate the earth in front of the shield, thoroughly support it by temporary timbering, then drill and blast the rock at the bottom and smooth up its irregularities to grade with concrete, before the shield could be shoved into position.

The metal lining of the tunnels under the East River is similar to that of those under North River and consisted of a series of rings two and one-half feet in length measured along the axis of the tunnel. Each ring was composed of eleven segments, each measuring a little over six feet around the circumference of the circle, and a key one foot long. A good idea may be obtained of the segments by imagining an iron box six feet long, two and one-half feet wide and eleven inches deep on the outside with sides and bottom about one and one-half inches thick. Then conceive the ends of this box to be bent upward so that the back fits the curve of the outside of the tunnel. The sides and ends of the segments were planed smooth to make as tight a fit as possible

The Long Island portals of "B" and "D" Tunnels in the foreground and that of Tunnel "C" in the distance, through the viaduct. The portal of Tunnel "A" is behind the passenger train.

View in Sunnyside Yard, looking eastward. Tracks at the right and left of the one in the center of the picture lead to the loop which enters the Yard proper from the eastern end.

Track being placed at the Pennsylvania Station, New York City, east of Ninth Avenue.

The entrance to the south yard, Sunnyside Yard, and a view of the buildings between it and the north yard. The L.I.R.R. main line is at the extreme right.

Looking back toward the tunnels from one of the viaducts crossing the yard. The south side of the approach for the use of Long Island freight trains appears as a wall on the right of the picture.

The north side of the L.I.R.R. freight connection, showing the curved wall at the left.

and at the inner edges of the sides or flanges of the segments a groove extending one and one-half inches back from the edge and about one-quarter inch deep was cast. After the segments were erected in place the grooves came together, forming a recess over each joint one and one-half inches deep and one-half inch wide. In these recesses circular lead wires were forced and thoroughly caulked with pneumatic hammers, thus making the tunnel almost absolutely water tight. This work was done before the air pressure was removed from the tunnels. It was not feasible to form rust joints in these tunnels because the material through which they passed contained so much water. After the shields had met and the cast iron lining was completed across the river the air pressure was removed and the interior lining of concrete put in place.

A shield consisted of a steel cylinder 23 feet, 6¾ inches in diameter and 18 feet, 6 inches long that would just telescope over the outside of the iron lining. The front edge, known as the cutting edge, was heavily reinforced by a ring of cast steel. About midway of the length of the shields a very heavy circular girder was placed inside the steel shell. This girder was in turn braced by two horizontal and two vertical steel beams. The spaces between these beams and the circular girder and between the beams themselves were filled with steel plates, thus dividing the front part of the shield from the back by a steel partition. In front of this partition the shield was divided into nine compartments by two floors and two vertical partitions. The hydraulic jacks for shoving the shield were built into the circular girder with their rams projecting toward the rear. These jacks were twenty-seven in number, their pistons were nine inches in diameter and were built for a pressure of six thousand pounds per square inch. A visitor at the works once gave a vivid idea of this pressure by stating that it was equivalent to three tons weight on one's big toe. All the jacks were capable of exerting a forward push on the shield of five thousand, one hundred and fifty tons. When a shove had been completed the rear of the shield still overlapped the completed iron lining, while there was room to place a new ring within the circle of the shield. The segments, each of which weighed a little over a ton, were placed by means of two hydraulic erectors attached to the rear of the cross partition or bulkhead of the shield. These erectors consisted of a steel arm revolved at right angles to the line of the tunnel by a hydraulic ram working a rack engaging a gear on the axis of the arm. The arm was made of two lengths, one telescoping into the other in such a manner that the outer one could be extended by means of a second hydraulic ram attached to the arm itself. The arm of the erectors was then made fast to the plate and it was swung around the circle of the tunnel by the rack and pinioned into the desired position. The arm was then extended by means of the second ram and the segment bolted into position.

Through the back of each segment a hole was bored and fitted with a screw plug. After the shield had been shoved forward enough to clear each ring, the plug was removed and voids outside the lining were filled by forcing grout, or a thin mixture of cement, sand and water through the holes by means of a suitable machine.

A good way to get an idea of the routine work in the tunnels when the progress was at its best is to describe a trip of one of the comparatively few visitors who was admitted.

The visitor first applied to the chief engineer for a pass admitting him to the works. These were granted only to people who had some good reason for making the trip. The visitor was warned to bring with him his oldest suit of clothes and a complete change of underwear. Arriving at the Manhattan end, he was taken in charge by an inspector or engineer who took him to one of the contractor's physicians. There were several of these and one or more were in constant attendance, night and day. The physician put the visitor through a thorough physical examination. If he passed this successfully he was then given a permit to pass through the locks. He was next taken to the engineer's locker building, where he made a complete change of clothing, then to the top of the shaft and was lowered by means of a cage or mine hoist to the level of the tunnels, about one hundred feet below.

At the bottom of the shaft the visitor had to produce his pass from the doctor before he could get into the tunnels. Immediately in front of him, to the east of the shaft, was the first bulkhead, a concrete wall completely closing the tunnels. Projecting through this wall were three steel cylinders looking very much like ordinary steam boilers. These were seven feet in diameter and twenty-four feet long. They were the locks. Two of them were placed near the bottom of the tunnel and were ordinarily used for the passage of small mine cars containing the excavated material from the tunnel and admitting the segments of the iron lining and other necessary building materials. Above these and reached by means of an elevated platform was a third lock which was called the "emergency lock," but which was commonly used for access to workmen.

The material locks were in constant operation. Ordinarily the cars were shoved into the lock either from the inside or the outside of the bulkhead, according to the direction they were traveling. The operator on that end then signaled to the man at the opposite end, left the lock and closed his door. A very large valve was then opened and the air allowed to enter or escape from the lock. This it did with a roar resembling the escape of steam from a boiler. When there were no men in the locks the cars were locked through in from thirty seconds to a minute.

To a visitor with a vivid imagination the constant hammering on the doors by the operators for signaling purposes and the roar of the escaping air was somewhat terrifying when he thought that within a few minutes he would be shut up in one of these cylinders.

The visitor then entered the upper lock, after being cautioned by his companion how to relieve the pressure on his ear drums and the air was turned in very slowly. If he experienced no trouble, the air was admitted more rapidly. After a few minutes the inner door opened of its own accord.

From the lock he stepped out on a platform placed a little above the middle height of the tunnel. Leading away from this down the dimly lighted iron tube on the same level was a foot walk suspended on one side of

Construction of the three-track tunnels by the cut-and-cover method.

The outer or low-pressure side of the bulkhead. Only the two lower locks can be seen.

Sinking Long Island City shaft. Working chamber of caisson.

One of the steel buckets containing spoil from the tunnels being placed on a wagon which will carry it to the disposal pier. This saved handling the material so many times.

Construction of the so-called "twin-tunnels." The entire cross section was excavated and afterwards the core-wall of concrete was built separating the tunnels.

Timbering out in front of the shield.

the tube. Walking along this foot walk, he soon came to a depression and had to get down on all fours to crawl under a steel partition which shut off the upper half of the tunnel. This partition was known as a safety screen and was joined to the lining by an air-tight joint. In case of a sudden flooding of the tunnel the workmen would attempt to get behind the safety screen nearest the shield, where they would be safe for a time at least, as the screen would imprison the air behind it and when the water arose to the level of the lower edge no more air could escape. The men could then make their way along the elevated platform to the emergency lock and thence into the open air. A new safety screen was put in place about every two hundred feet so there was one always within a short distance of the shield. As one neared the working face he stepped from the suspended gangway on to staging which was supported on rollers a little below the mid-height of the tunnel. This staging was about sixty feet long and the full width of the tunnel. It had a second platform which was only about six feet below the top of the lining. An elevator was provided for hoisting material from the temporary work tracks at the bottom of the tunnel to the two platforms composing the stage. The lower platform carried the machines used for grouting outside the iron lining, while both platforms served as staging for erecting lining, tightening the bolts and for caulking the joints between the segments. The staging was provided with iron wheels which traveled on rails supported on brackets temporarily bolted to the iron lining. There was also a telephone booth on this stage which gave communication with the Power House, engineers' offices, and the city telephone system. The front end of the traveling platform was only three or four feet from the rear of the shield and as the shield was advanced it pulled the traveling platform along by means of a pulley between the two. On the traveling platform ordinarily three or four men would be seen engaged in grouting behind the lining. Immediately at the rear of the shield five or six more men would be seen erecting the ring within the walls of the shield.

As soon as our visitor entered the tunnel he noticed that the temperature increased remarkably. By the time he arrived at the traveling platform he was willing to leave all surplus clothing in the locker provided for the purpose. If the weather was at all warm the workmen managed to get along with very little clothing indeed. The visitor next stepped through one of the small openings in the partition of the shield and entered the working compartments. Here he found two or three men in each compartment who were carefully removing the sand from the face and shoveling it into chutes leading down to the bottom of the shield or into small muck cars. As they shoveled away the loose sand they promptly placed short pieces of board or timber in front of the excavation and braced them from the shield as already described. When a sufficient amount of material had been excavated from the face, the superintendent in charge called up the Power House on the telephone and the high-pressure water was turned into the pipe leading to the jacks at the rear of the shield. This water at times was under a pressure as high as six thousand pounds per square inch. When it was admitted to the jacks the cylinders and

rams moved slowly out and came to a bearing on the face of the last ring erected. The shield then began to move slowly forward. Just before the shove was made, the braces from the timbering at the face were replaced by what were commonly called guns, consisting of two pieces of gas pipe; one about three inches and the other about two and one-half inches in diameter, the smaller telescoping into the larger. At the end of the larger tube were three set screws bearing against the smaller tube. When the guns were put in place these set screws were tightened as much as possible and made a rigid brace of these two pipes. When the shove was started workmen stood beside the guns with wrenches and loosened up the set screws just enough to allow the inner tube to slide back slowly but still offering a good deal of support to the face. By careful work in this way the shove was often made without breaking up the timber face. There was a good deal of creaking and groaning from the shield and small quantities of sand were continually running through the cracks of the face timber. Boards would occasionally break and the face cave in, letting boulders and cobbles and large quantities of sand run into the shield. This would be accompanied by considerable loss of air and occasionally by a blowout. On one occasion one of the foremen standing on the edge of the upper platform was caught in the sand and knocked down to the bottom of the shield, where he struck head downward and was completely buried. As fast as the sand was removed more ran in and it was some hours before he could be reached.

These operations all took considerable time as at best only four or five shoves would be made in twenty-four hours and in bad ground it frequently occurred that a shove could not be made for several days. As a visitor was not permitted to stay in the air pressure for more than an hour he was lucky if he saw all the operations described.

Leaving the shield the visitor returned to the lock, walking along the temporary tracks laid on the wooden floor near the bottom of the tunnel. When the bulkhead was reached he was soaked with perspiration and very dirty. He resumed his heaviest garments and entered the lock. The door was closed and the valve to the outer air opened. The lock at once became full of fog and the air had a sudden chill.

No one was allowed to depress at a faster rate than two pounds per minute, so that if the pressure was thirty pounds above the normal it took fifteen minutes to get out of the lock. While in the lock one often felt languid and depressed. Ordinarily there was no other affect, though in some cases the novice became dizzy.

After arriving in the open air the visitor was hurried up the cage to the locker room, where he was given a cup of strong coffee. He then took a shower bath and resumed his street clothes. He was kept under observation by his companion for an hour or more and if no bad effects developed in that time it was considered safe to let him go about his business. If he was so unfortunate as to get the "bends," which in ordinary cases were severe pains in the arms and legs, he was hurried to the hospital lock, which closely resembled the locks by which admission was had to the tunnels, with the difference that there were two chambers, the inner one having a door at one end only. The outer chamber served as a

The safety screen was used to protect workmen and save the tunnels in case of a blow-out as when the water rose to the level of the lower edge it would form a cushion and the flow would be checked.

A section of the completed tunnel under Thirty-third Street. The light is streaming through from its "twin" through cross passages which connect the tunnels every fifty feet.

Just inside of the bulkhead looking back toward the normal air. The machine in the foreground is used to draw up by means of ropes the muck cars.

Staging from which grout is pumped outside the tunnel shell. This staging is also used for caulking joints, bolting, etc.

Shovel operated by compressed air shoveling muck into a specially designed steel bucket standing on a small car.

A rear view of one of the East River shields taken at the time it was started from the shaft. The completed ring within the tail of the shield is the first ring of the permanent lining; the incompleted rings were afterward removed.

lock to allow the attendants to pass in and out after the pressure had been raised in the inner chamber. The pressure was raised rapidly to about half that in the tunnel and the pains nearly always disappeared. The parts affected were then rubbed by the hospital orderly to relieve the soreness and in some cases a current from an electric battery was applied. Pressure was then reduced very slowly, taking forty or fifty minutes in the operation. Commonly the pains did not return, but the parts affected were sore for some hours. As far as the writer knows, no cases of bends occurred among visitors, but they were frequent with inspectors and workmen, who remained in the air for longer periods.

When the tunnel pressure was more than thirty-two pounds above normal, the inspectors remained in the tunnel for two hours, were relieved by other inspectors for two hours, after which they returned for a second period of two hours. The workmen similarly worked three hours per shift. This work was kept up continuously twenty-four hours per day and thirteen days out of fourteen, enough men being provided to keep the shifts full. Alternative Sundays were taken advantage of for repair work. The work was carried on continuously, not only to rush its completion, but because there was less liability to accident if progress was continuous.

During construction the bends and other bad effects of compressed air were a very real danger and took toll of the lives of those engaged in the work, besides seriously disabling some and causing others temporary but serious discomfort. Some of the incidents connected with air work may be of interest. The only trouble experienced on passing into compressed air is from the ears. While under pressure a mild exhilaration is often noticed and it sometimes cures dull headache. The temperature is high and perspiration very free. One of the curious effects may be observed by blowing out an ordinary candle. So long as the tiny spark at the end of the wick has not been snuffed out the candle can generally be brought to a full flame by passing it rapidly back and forth two or three times through the air. In fact, the flame will often start up by itself after the lapse of a minute or more and in some cases after the user had deposited the candle in his pocket. It was easy to start fires under pressure and in case of fire the tunnels were soon filled with a dense choking smoke that would rapidly cause suffocation. Two fatal fires occurred during the work. The first was in "C" tunnel soon after work had been started from the Manhattan end. Several men had been working on repairs one Sunday night and on leaving the tunnel early Monday morning they noticed that, contrary to orders, the watchman, the only man left in the tunnel, was smoking. About an hour later, when the regular day shift started to enter the tunnel and turned on the valve admitting the high-pressure air from the tunnel into the lock, the latter was almost immediately filled with smoke. These men gave up the attempt to enter and returned to the normal air. There was known to be about fifty pounds of dynamite stored on a platform just inside the bulkhead, which could, of course, be reached by the fire. After some delay the superintendent, one of the walking bosses, and several volunteers succeeded, by covering their faces with wet cloths, in withstanding the effects of the smoke long enough to pass through the lock. The

tunnel was full of smoke and no idea could be obtained of the location or extent of the fire. The walking boss, who knew where the dynamite was located, pluckily groped his way to it and removed the box. The party could not long withstand the smoke and had to lock out. The man who had rescued the dynamite fainted, but none suffered any serious results from the effects of the smoke. It is hard, however, to conceive a more severe test of courage than this. The city fire department was at hand but could do nothing. The only way to extinguish the fire was to flood the tunnel, and preparations were made to this end. Although the watchman inside was almost certainly dead, all were reluctant to let in the water until all doubt was removed. The same party again made the attempt to enter the tunnel and to their surprise found that the air was nearly clear of smoke. The watchman's pipe had set fire to a small amount of hay at one side of the tunnel and this and a few pieces of boards were all that was burned. The watchman wore rubber boots or shoes and the fire must have caught into these or the bottom of his trousers. He apparently started to run to the shield, where there was water to put out the fire, but before he had gone fifty feet he was overcome and fell on the temporary plank floor of the tunnel. When found his feet were entirely burned away to a point above the ankle. The rubber soles of his boots, however, still remained. The only signs of a fire anywhere in his vicinity were the charred soles of his shoes, the edges of his trousers and the burned flesh. The man was, of course, dead but in a few minutes conditions in the tunnel were normal and no sign of the fire could be seen.

Although when in bad ground the men were in constant apprehension of being flooded out, water in large quantities broke in on one occasion only during the entire work. On this occasion, two men who were working in the quicksand at the bottom of the shield could not free themselves quickly enough and were drowned. All the others made their way back of the safety screen and escaped. The tunnel was only two-thirds full of water at the face. In a short time men were busy stopping up the crevices through which the air was escaping and the pressure was gradually raised. In about twenty-four hours the water was forced out of the tunnel, the bodies of the victims recovered and work resumed. On several other occasions large quantities of earth were forced into and through the shield, partially filling the tunnel for some distance back and in one instance this flow proved very difficult to check.

Another incident that attracted a great deal of attention at the time was connected with the building of the tunnels westward from East Avenue toward the river. This portion of the tunnels, although a part of the work covered by the contract for the river tunnels, was in the main driven without the use of air or shields by working westward from a temporary shaft at East Avenue. During the early part of the work what was called a bottom heading or a small-sized tunnel, was driven along what would be the bottom of the completed tunnel. These headings were on a rapidly descending grade, but after reaching a point about 1,000 feet westward from the shaft, the contractor changed his method and ran the small headings upward on an incline to the top of the tunnel instead of the bottom. This left a low point or invert in the small tunnel. At this particular point the rock surface came below the top of the tunnel and the contractor started operations of enlargement by making an opening to one side of the main heading, working this in a spiral direction upward and backward from the bottom heading until he had a short section of tunnel leading toward the east and directly above the bottom heading. In order to supply the compressed air to run the drills for this portion of the work, pipes connected with the compressors in Front Street had been sunk through the Long Island Railroad yards. These pipes passed downward through the short section of tunnel just mentioned in the bottom heading.

Early one Monday morning a cave-in occurred under East Avenue which broke the sewer in the street and allowed a direct connection from the sewer into the tunnels. Unfortunately this sewer was below the level of high tide in Newtown Creek. During the high tide a great amount of water poured into the tunnels, filling the low point or invert well above the opening connected with the short section previously mentioned but not filling the upper tunnel. During Monday rumors were heard that two men who were on duty in the tunnels during the previous night were missing, but as this was not positively known no further attention was paid to it, for the men had had ample time to escape.

About five o'clock in the afternoon one of the employees in the Long Island Railroad yards reported that someone was apparently tapping on the pipes that came up through the ground. Investigation was at once made and it was determined that signals from the surface were answered from below. It was then evident that the two missing men were imprisoned in the upper heading, about sixty feet below the surface of the ground. Operations had already been started to install additional pumps to unwater the tunnel. The contractor now redoubled his efforts, but at best it was evident it would take many hours to release the men. Several of the workmen were in favor of digging a well directly downward and this they started to do on their own account. They worked with great energy relieving each other at frequent intervals. It soon became a race to see by which means the men could be reached first. Divers with helmets were called in, but as they were unfamiliar with the tunnel they did not accomplish much. At about one o'clock on Tuesday the water had been lowered enough so that one of the foremen, by swimming and diving under over-hanging timbers, reached the imprisoned men. A short time after he was able to bring them up.

At the same time the other party had succeeded in sinking their well to within about four feet of the heading.

The men, although frightened and hungry, were none the worse for their experience. They had evidently gone to sleep in the upper heading, which was warm and dry and did not discover the incoming water until their escape was cut off. The plight of the men had, of course, become public, and a great crowd, among which were a number of reporters and photographers, had gathered around the shaft. As the men were somewhat weak, it was thought best not to bring them to the surface at once, but the crowd would not be satisfied until they appeared. In order to get rid of the people the

contractor's manager selected two pale workmen from the bottom of the shaft and helped them up one at a time. Their pictures were eagerly taken and appeared in the papers the next day as those of the rescued men. The crowd dispersed and later on the real victims were brought up to the surface.

Probably the event of most interest to all concerned in building the tunnels was the meeting of the shields or in other words the junction under the river of the portion of the tunnel built from the two shores. To the engineers responsible for the alignment it would measure the degree of accuracy of their work for more than six years. For the contractor it would practically assure success and remove the last anxiety over one of the most hazardous works ever undertaken. To the working force it was the end toward which many of them had been striving for over four years under very trying conditions. There was keen rivalry to be the first to actually break through into the opposite heading. To the Railroad Company it meant that they had not spent millions of dollars in vain. True, there was much work still to be done, but it did not present any extraordinary features.

To provide as far as possible against accident, it was decided to make the junction in the hard material at the east edge of the central rock ridge rather than in the soft material of the easterly depression, where the shields would meet had the work continued uninterruptedly from both sides. The shields from the Manhattan side were the first to reach the point selected and tunnel driving from that side was stopped. It was known that it would be impossible to maintain exactly the same air pressure in the approaching headings and as the thickness of the dividing wall was decreased there was danger of its being blown out as well as of its being dug out without proper precaution by workmen over-zealous to be the first through. As a precaution a bulkhead of concrete and sand bags was built at the cutting edges of the Manhattan shields completely closing the face. To provide for a passage between the shields before the removal of the bulkhead a heavy timber door was built into it and securely locked. The door was to serve both as a precaution against accident and to allow the officials of the work to be the first to pass through. While the bulkhead was being built an eight-inch steel pipe was forced forward horizontally for about fifty feet toward the Long Island side. The primary purpose of the pipes was to allow the engineers to check the alignment before the shields actually met. They also served to equalize to some degree the air pressure in the approaching headings. The checks of the alignment showed no deviation in any of the tunnels of more than one-half inch for either line or grade. As soon as the Long Island shields reached the end of the pipes the workmen could talk with those on the Manhattan side and they were greatly excited for the remainder of the time until they could actually pass from one to the other.

Owing to the difference of pressure at the two shields, there was a strong air current through the pipes. The men in "D" tunnel, the first to meet, procured a toy train and placing it in the pipe, it was forced through at a high rate of speed. This was the first train to actually pass through the tunnels. The workmen in "B" tunnel, the second to meet, not to be outdone by those in "D," procured a rag doll representing a lady and sent it through the pipe in the same manner, heralding it as the first lady to make the trip. This doll was preserved, framed and presented by the contractors as a souvenir to the engineers in charge of this tunnel.

As soon as the force from the East encountered the concrete bulkhead, they could not be restrained and one of the men soon had a hole through the concrete large enough to be shoved through head first, and in this way the entire gang came through to the Manhattan end, where an impromptu celebration was held.

During the following day representatives of the Railroad Company and the contractor's officials made the trip through the door previously mentioned. As all the junctions were successfully made, no one begrudged the workmen the satisfaction of being the first to make the trip under the river from Long Island to Manhattan.

The tunnels from East Avenue in Long Island City to First Avenue in Manhattan were all included under one contract, which was awarded to S. Pearson & Son, Inc. As it was realized that this portion of the work would take the longest of any on the East River Division to complete, it was first to be put under contract. Actual construction was started May 17, 1904. Five years later to a day the work received its final inspection for acceptance by the Railroad Company. It required, on the Manhattan side, until October 5, 1905, to sink the shafts, erect the shields and bulkheads and place the first tunnel under air pressure. Owing to the greater difficulties encountered, the same stage in the work was not reached at Front Street, Long Island City, until June, 1906. An opening was made between the shields in "D" tunnel, the first to meet, on February 20, 1908, and in "A" tunnel, the last, on March 18, 1908. Air pressure was finally removed in July, 1908. The remainder of the time until completion was occupied in placing the interior lining of concrete.

The length of the tunnels between the river shafts was three thousand nine hundred feet and between East Avenue and Front Street, the terminal of the Long Island Railroad, two thousand feet. Their construction involved, among other things, the excavation of three hundred and ninety-eight thousand cubic yards of earth and rock, placing thirteen thousand four hundred tons of iron and steel caisson and tunnel lining and one hundred and twenty-nine thousand cubic yards of concrete masonry.

E. W. Moir was vice-president and Henry Japp, resident director for the contractors. Charles E. Fraser, Allan Moir, Arthur Manton and A. A. Johnson were superintendents of various portions of the work.

Alfred Noble was chief engineer for the Pennsylvania Railroad, Charles L. Harrison, principal assistant engineer; Silas H. Woodard, George Leighton, Francis Mason and James H. Brace, resident engineers.

The railroad timed the beginning of operations on the different portions of the work, so that they would all be finished about the same time. The next section to be taken up on the East River Division was the Crosstown Tunnels from the station at Seventh Avenue to the Shafts already described at First Avenue. For a short distance east of the station there are three tracks in both Thirty-second and Thirty-third Streets. For the remaining distance there are two tracks under each street.

Construction was carried on to the westward from the First Avenue Shafts and both east and west from temporary shafts on each street between Madison and Fourth Avenues and between Sixth and Seventh Avenues. A topographical map of this portion of the city made in 1865, before the natural surface of the ground had been changed to conform to the established street grades, showed that a stream crossed Thirty-third Street just west of Fifth Avenue, flowed eastward through a good-sized pond, covering most of the area between Fourth and Lexington Avenues, Thirty-first and Thirty-second Streets and then in a northeasterly direction into Kipps Bay. All surface indications of this stream have long since disappeared but the test borings showed that wherever the lines of the tunnels crossed this stream there was a considerable depression in the rock surface and the rock beneath was not as solid as in other places. As the tunnels were originally designed, their roofs came above the rock surface in this stream bed near Fifth Avenue. Except near the station and the above localities, the tunnels were excavated in sound rock. The three tracks near the station in each street are built in one wide tunnel which, together with its masonry side walls, occupies nearly the entire width of the street. It was first planned to construct this work entirely by tunneling, but it was soon found best to adopt the open-cut method familiar in subway building. That is, by excavating a trench downward from the surface, building the masonry side walls and roof arch and then refilling the street to its original level. Where there are only two tracks, the material, except in a few places, could be excavated for the full width and height. In placing the lining, a concrete wall was built between the two tracks as well as walls on each side. An arch was then built between each side wall and the center wall, forming a twin tunnel in each street.

When the rock surface was penetrated near Fifth Avenue, despite all precautions, considerable quantities of water and fine sand ran into the excavation from the old stream bed. This left a cavity above the temporary timber lining, which was gradually enlarged and by continual caving extended upward to the asphalt paving. One evening a coal wagon was being driven along Thirty-third Street when, without warning, the rear wheels dropped through the pavement. This was the first indication that the caving had reached the surface. The foundations of many of the large buildings in this vicinity were not carried down to rock and the situation was so serious that work had to be stopped in this locality for a time. Some changes that had been made in connection with the arrangement of the tracks in the station made it possible to lower the grade of the tunnels sufficiently so that the top was below the rock surface and by careful work this critical point was safely passed. One of the features of this work was the use of steam shovels for excavating the rock after it had been loosened by blasting.

The cross-town tunnels were built by the United Engineering and Contracting Company. D. L. Hough was president and Paul G. Brown, managing engineer.

The engineering organization for the Railroad Company was practically the same as that for the river tunnels. The contract for this work was made in May, 1905, and all tunnel work was completed in March, 1909.

The third and last section of the East River work, as outlined at the beginning of this article, may be divided into two parts and described separately.

First, what was known as Section "A" and "B," extending from East Avenue to Thomson Avenue, Long Island City, and Second, the Sunnyside Yard.

Sections "A" and "B" cover the part of the work where the line changes from an underground to a surface railroad. There is a marked contrast in the physical conditions at the two ends of the Pennsylvania Tunnel System. At the west end the tracks emerge into the open air through the steep slopes of the Bergen Hills, on the east side they rise gradually to the surface through ground that is little more than a tidal flat along Newtown Creek. Under the East River and also Manhattan, each pair of tunnels contain an east and west bound track, but for operating purposes it was desirable to have the two east-bound tracks together on the south at the entrance to Sunnyside Yard, and the two west-bound on the north. To accomplish this result, "C" tunnel, the west-bound and northerly one of the Thirty-second Street pair, was built on a more rapidly ascending grade from the center of the river eastward and it crosses "B" tunnel, the southerly or east-bound track of the Thirty-third Street pair within the limits of Sections "A" and "B." About three-fourths of the line in these sections consists of tunnel built in an open trench, which was afterward refilled. The other one-fourth is depressed track with invert and side walls of concrete masonry. Where the tracks come above the rock surface, the overlying material is very wet and soft and it was necessary to support the entire structure on piles and to waterproof the bottom and sides to prevent excessive leakage.

Much of this work is directly on the former location of the Long Island Railroad tracks leading to North Shore points. These tracks were temporarily shifted to the south, out of the way, but it was necessary to provide a permanent connection crossing the tunnel approaches between the tracks leading into the Long Island City station and the freight yards on the north along Hunters Point Avenue. This was accomplished by a viaduct and elevated approach. The construction of the concrete approach to this viaduct is very unusual. Ordinarily two retaining walls would have been built and the space between filled with earth. In this case, owing to the nature of the soil, there was grave danger that the retaining walls would be forced outward by the weight of the material between them. The structure as built consists of two side walls with cross walls tying them together at intervals of thirty-three feet and a top of concrete that forms the support of the tracks. By this construction there is no side pressure on the walls.

The contractors for Sections "A" and "B" were Naughton Company and Arthur McMullen. George W. McNulty was their secretary and manager and C. W. S. Wilson, their resident engineer.

They started work on June 4, 1907, and were practically completed December 1, 1909. For the Railroad Company, George C. Clarke was resident engineer.

The last section of the work, the Sunnyside Yard, extends from Thomson Avenue to Woodside Avenue in Long Island City. The length of the yard is eight thousand five hundred feet, its maximum width, one thousand six hundred and twenty-five feet and covers one hundred and ninety-two acres.

In the yards the cars are cleaned, stored and refitted ready for their next westward trip. The yard is divided by the store and supply buildings, power sub-station and boiler-house into two parts; the North Yard, where the multiple-unit or suburban trains are stored, and the South Yard, used for Pullman and dining-cars and day coaches.

The North Yard has forty-two tracks with a capacity of five hundred and twenty-six cars; the South Yard, forty-five tracks that can accommodate forty-five electric locomotives and five hundred and fifty-two cars. Provision has been made to increase the number of tracks in the South Yard by thirty-two, allowing three hundred and nine more cars to be stored.

In grading the site for the yards it was necessary to move three million cubic yards of earth. This was accomplished in the main by the use of steam shovels and construction trains. One of the main features of the work was the construction of viaducts across the yard on the lines of the principal street crossings. There are six of these viaducts, as well as two under-grade crossings for streets near the east end of the yard. There are also seven railroad bridges to avoid grade crossings on the various tracks of the yard. All the bridges are constructed of concrete and steel in the most substantial manner.

The construction and equipment of the buildings mentioned above are also a part of this work. Their foundations are of concrete and their superstructure is of brick and steel. To provide service pipes throughout the Pullman yard a pipe tunnel crossing the tracks at right angles and concrete pipe trenches between the tracks were constructed.

The contractor for the excavation and the greater portion of the masonry was the Degnon Realty and Terminal Improvement Company. Mr. Waldo C. Briggs was resident engineer for the contractor.

Excavation was started in December, 1906, and completed in the latter part of 1909. Track laying was completed about one year later. For this work, Louis H. Barker was resident engineer.

C. I. LEIPER
DIVISION ENGINEER

H. C. BIXLER
TRAIN MASTER

C. B. KEISER
MASTER MECHANIC

C. S. KRICK
SUPERINTENDENT

H. F. SPILLINGER
PASSENGER AGENT

J. V. B. DUER
FOREMAN OF MOTORMEN

C. W. GLENN JR.
CHIEF CLERK TO SUPERINTENDENT

THE OPERATION OF THE RAILROAD

AS the construction of the various sections of the railroad was completed they were turned over to the operating department. The division organization taking charge of the administration of the properties which have been described in the foregoing pages is similar to that elsewhere on the Pennsylvania Railroad and, in brief, is as follows:

At the head is the Superintendent, who is responsible for the efficient operation of the territory and instrumentalities under his jurisdiction and to carry out his multifarious duties he is provided with a staff of officials composed of:

The Division Engineer, who has charge of the maintenance and policing of roadbed and structures, which include track, station buildings, interlocking stations, bridges, etc.;

The Train Master, who has charge of the movement of traffic, the baggage and the telegraph and telephone departments. All trainmen, switchmen, towermen, signalmen and the station force are under his jurisdiction;

The Master Mechanic, who is responsible for the operation of the mechanical and electrical features of the line—which include several large power-houses, extensive transmission lines, the intricate plumbing of the station buildings, etc.—and of the maintenance of rolling stock. He supervises the use of material, fuel and stores and consults regarding the requirements and efficiency of locomotives with

The Foreman of Motormen, who instructs the men who handle the electric locomotives and multiple-unit cars as to the proper performance of their duties and the economical use of power. He also sees that the engines are in good working order and are properly equipped;

The Passenger Agent, who has charge of the sale of tickets and the elaborate accounts which have to be kept in connection therewith;

The Inspector of Police, who has charge of the protection of the property and maintains order on trains and in stations. He also protects passengers from annoyance from disorderly persons;

The Chief Clerk, who has charge of the administration of his office force and represents him in many matters.

This entire division organization is a part of a grand division, composed of several divisions, and is subservient thereto—the railroad being divided into six grand divisions.

The New York Connecting Railroad

THE New York Connecting Railroad which is only about six miles long—half of it being bridge and viaduct structures—is the "missing link" so far as the north and south railroad travel is concerned. For when this line which connects the New York, New Haven & Hartford Railroad and the Pennsylvania Railroad is completed there will be an unbroken raial line from Quebec to the southernmost extremity of Florida.

The line, which will have four tracks, commences in the Borough of Bronx, near One Hundred and Forty-second Street, and gradually rises until at Bronx Kill it will have about sixty-five feet clear height above the water. The water here separates the Bronx from Randall's Island and the bridge at this point will be of the so-called lift type, that is, each half of the bridge will revolve in a vertical plane and vessels may pass between. The pier in the middle of the Bronx Kill will separate the two channels for eastbound and westbound ships. At present these channels are shallow and can be used by only row boats and small launches but it is the intention of the War Department to dredge the channels to the same depth as the Harlem River, so that vessels will be able to pass from the Hudson River to the Ship Canal in the Harlem River and through the Bronx Kill bridge directly into Long Island Sound and vice versa.

Another bridge on this line spans Little Hell Gate, as the estuary between Ward's and Randall's Islands is called. The water at this point has a rock bottom, is shallow and cannot be used by large vessels. The bridge will be of the riveted truss type and will have five spans. From this point to the bridge over Hell Gate, the waterway between Ward's Island and Long Island, the line will be placed on a steel viaduct carried on masonry piers.

The arch bridge over the East River at Hell Gate is of the braced steel type and will cross the river in a single span 1017½ feet between the towers; the clearance at high water will be the same as that of the Brooklyn Bridge and the others over the East River, 135 feet. The abutments will have a base of granite masonry surmounted by towers of moulded concrete masonry which will support the largest and heaviest members ever fabricated in a bridge shop. This structural steel will be much heavier than that used in the Firth of Forth Bridge in Scotland, which has two spans of 1,700 feet each and carries two tracks 150 feet above the tide, and some of the members will weigh 185 tons. Ninety thousand tons of steel will have to be fabricated and four hundred forty thousand cubic yards of masonry laid.

Architecturally this imposing structure has been designed to form a monumental gateway to the East River from the North.

The line has no grade crossings and passenger trains using it will run via the Pennsylvania Station while the freight traffic is diverted to the Bay Ridge Improvement, whence it will be transferred to Greenville freight yard and continue south.

THE CITY OF NEW YORK

By DR. JOSEPH CACCAVAJO, Consulting Engineer and Statistician

LESS than three hundred years ago the first white settlers landed on Manhattan Island, and shortly thereafter purchased it from the Indians for the historic sum of $24.00. Needless to say, these forbears of ours little dreamed that any company of men would ever need to spend $150,000,000 or $200,000,000 for the right to land passengers on this selfsame island.

Just why the Pennsylvania Railroad Company felt called upon to enter upon this stupendous undertaking has been ably treated elsewhere in this book, but a study of the more than wonderful growth of the City of New York shows the wisdom of their judgment and daring, in assuming the responsibility of tunneling under the Hudson River, which separates New Jersey from the Borough of Manhattan, and the East River which separates that Borough from the Boroughs of Brooklyn and Queens on Long Island.

Nothing that has occurred since the creation is more wonderful than the growth of New York City. The tabulation published herewith, shows the growth in population in the three hundred and twenty-seven square miles within the city limits, with estimates based on every known factor of growth, carried forward to 1950. They show the wonderful progress New York City has made in the past, and what may reasonably be expected in the future.

While the figures may be startling in some respects, they represent many years of study and careful consideration of the conditions peculiar to each of the several parts of the city. Pessimists may say that no city in the world's history has ever reached such a population as the 19,500,000 which my estimates show for 1950, but the answer to this is that there has never before been such a city as New York.

Look back and find that less than three hundred years ago (in 1628) New York had a population of 270; in 1650 it was about 1,000; by 1700 it had increased 400%; another fifty years and almost another 400% increase is shown, and 1800 found almost 80,000 people, or an increase of over 500% in fifty years. The next fifty years marked an increase of much over 700% and between 1850 and 1900, an increase of over 400% is shown in spite of the handicap consequent to the Civil War.

The upper sections of Manhattan and the greater portion of the Bronx have been brought close to the most important business and financial sections of the city by the construction of the subway; the successful construction of tunnels under, and bridges over the East River eliminate forever that natural barrier which has retarded the development of the vast areas in Brooklyn and Queens; and taking into consideration the fact that long before 1950 there will undoubtedly be many new transit facilities extended to all parts of the city, even including the now much neglected Borough of Richmond, it does not seem to be unreasonable or irrational to predict a growth in population of between 400 and 500% during the first half of the present century.

From another standpoint, considering the growth of the city in population per acre, it also seems reasonable to say that an average of ninety-two persons to the acre in the Greater City, is a conservative estimate for 1950.

Within a few years, when there will be practically no residential population below 59th Street, Manhattan will have less than 5,000 acres available for residential purposes, which means an average of more than 500 persons to the acre.

There are hundreds of acres in Manhattan to-day with a population of more than 1,000 people, and in some sections of that borough there are nearly 2,000 to the acre. This is congestion; but there are thousands of acres covered with extremely large apartment houses of the better sort, where there are as many as 500 people to the acre that cannot be considered congested in the accepted sense of the term.

With an average of 500 people to the acre, New York City would have a population of nearly one hundred million. This is by no means a prognostication, but merely another illustration of the immense amount of territory lying within the present city limits.

Most people will agree that statistics are a nuisance and that comparisons are odious, but in order to prove that New York City is the Wonder City of the world, I am going to stretch a point and give some real facts, omitting figures as far as possible.

As regards population, New York City is the second largest city in the world; in fact, considering that the population of London as given in the census reports includes all the residents of a territory more than twice the area of this city, we would outnumber even London in population if we were not prohibited by State lines from including the territory in nearby New Jersey, which is a part of the Metropolitan District.

Mayor Gaynor is the chosen executive of a people more numerous than the combined population of the Kingdoms of Denmark and Norway, and a city larger by more than half-a-million than the entire United States when George Washington was President and New York City was the National Capital.

It has a greater population than the combined population of the following capital cities of Europe: Rome, Madrid, Copenhagen, Stockholm, Christiania, Munich, Bucharest, Athens, Lisbon, The Hague and Edinburgh, with Geneva, Venice, Havre, and Dublin added for good measure.

The twenty-two square miles of Manhattan Island contain a greater population than ten of our great states with an area of nearly 800,000 square miles; Brooklyn outnumbers in population Vermont, Idaho, Utah, Montana, Delaware and Wyoming combined. Its population is greater than that of St. Petersburg, and is twice the population of Hamburg or Budapest. The Bronx would rank as the tenth city in the United States, and Queens Borough the nineteenth. Richmond, the smallest borough in population, has more residents than the sovereign State of Nevada.

The population of Manhattan and the Bronx is larger than that of Paris; and the combined population of Liverpool, Manchester, Birmingham, Leeds, Sheffield, Bristol, Bradford, Nottingham, Portsmouth, Oldham, Croydon, Brighton, Norwich, Birkenhead and Plymouth, the fifteen largest English cities next to London is less than that of New York City.

Right here it might be well to call attention to the work which is required of the Police Department of the City of New York. Very few citizens appreciate the good work it is doing, for the problems that confront the police officials here are not duplicated in any other large city. Whole sections of Europe, Asia and Africa are literally transplanted within the city limits, and a walk through our streets brings one in contact with people of every creed and color, each with their own peculiar customs and widely different viewpoints of right and wrong. As like seeks like, so we find many of our foreign immigrants seeking their own kind, and in consequence there are localities where German, Italian, Russian, Hebrew, Hungarian, Chinese, Polish, Greek, Armenian, and other languages are even more common than our own tongue. We have daily and weekly newspapers published in every known language. The foreign population is so large that it is necessary to have warning notices in the street cars, parks and public places printed in several languages, and our Police Department includes special bureaus with officers acquainted with the languages and conditions in the various countries from which the majority of our foreign population comes.

The more we study conditions in New York, the more we realize what a wonderful city it is.

New York City has a population greater than the combined population of Berlin, Hamburg, Munich, Dresden, Nuremburg, and Stuttgart, and is the third largest German city in the world. There are more than half as many native born Germans in this city as there are in Hamburg, and those of German parentage are equal in number to more than half the population of Berlin.

The natives of Ireland in the city outnumber the residents of Dublin, and those of Irish parentage exceed the combined population of Belfast and Dublin.

The number of native born Russians in New York City entitles it to rank among the first Russian cities, and there are as many native born Italians here as there are in Venice, while those of Italian parentage nearly equal the population of Rome.

New York ranks high as an Austrian city, and natives of England, Scotland and Scandinavia and other countries are here in large numbers.

Most of the cities throughout the world can estimate their probable future increase in population from the vital statistics, but this is impossible here, where one of the greatest factors in our growth is the million or more immigrants who enter our port each year. Nearly 80% of all the immigrants coming to the United States enter this port, a very large percentage of them remaining here in the city. In three years almost two and one-half million immigrants from Russia, Italy, and Austria-Hungary arrived here in New York, and they continue to come on every ship.

The Public Service Commission has under its supervision within the city limits, eighty-two street railways, thirty-two steam railroads, one stage-coach company, twenty gas companies, fifteen electric companies, two electric conduit companies, three gas-electric companies, thirteen express companies and fifteen holding companies, a total of 183 corporations. In addition there are the elevated railroads of Manhattan and Brooklyn and the subway system. For the year ending June 30, 1911, the transportation lines in the city carried 1,600,-000,000 passengers, collecting from them in fares $77,-943,772. The difficulty of the transit problem may be partially appreciated after a study of these figures.

The citizens and the city paid a gas bill of $31,843,-272 and a bill for electric lighting, etc., of $25,382,823 last year. The grand total for transportation, gas and electricity exceeded $135,000,000.

The United States census reports show that the tremendous ferry traffic in New York Harbor constitutes about two-thirds of the entire ferry traffic in the United States, and that the commerce entering and clearing from this port is almost equal to the combined commerce of every other port of entry in the United States.

The reports of the Board of Education show that the number of pupils enrolled in the public schools of New York City is rapidly approaching 800,000. Counting those attending the private institutions and the parochial schools, the school children of the metropolis are close to 1,000,000 in number and are the most cosmopolitan assemblage in the world. In one school alone are represented twenty-nine different nationalities in a register of 2,000 pupils.

Nearly $40,000,000 was spent last year for educational purposes and to maintain the public school system, or more than the combined expenditures of Maine, New Hampshire, Vermont, Delaware, Maryland, Virginia, North Carolina, South Carolina, Georgia, Alabama, Florida, Mississippi, Louisiana and Montana. As a further comparison, Chicago spent $9,690,622, and Philadelphia, $6,038,158.

There were nearly 135,000 births within the city limits during 1911, a number almost equal to the combined population of the states of Wyoming and Nevada in 1900 and more than the entire population of such great cities as New Haven, Memphis, Scranton or Richmond. The births in the city exceeded in number the entire population of Long Island outside of the city ten years ago, and equaled almost one-third the present population of San Francisco.

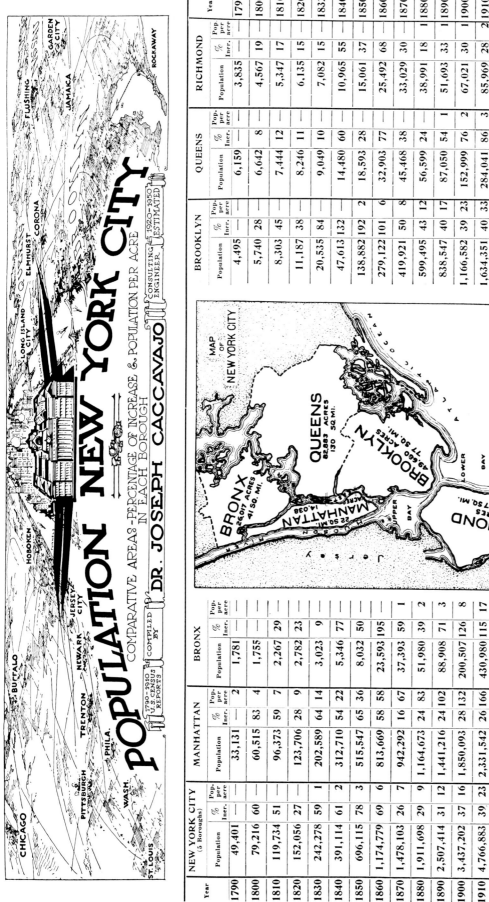

NEW YORK CITY (5 Boroughs)				MANHATTAN				BRONX			
Year	Population	% Incr.	Pop. per acre	Population	% Incr.	Pop. per acre	Population	% Incr.	Pop. per acre	Year
1790	49,401	—	—	33,131	—	2	1,781	—	—	1790
1800	79,216	60	—	60,515	83	4	1,755	—	—	1800
1810	119,734	51	—	96,373	59	7	2,267	29	—	1810
1820	152,056	27	—	123,706	28	9	2,782	23	—	1820
1830	242,278	59	1	202,589	64	14	3,023	9	—	1830
1840	391,114	61	2	312,710	54	22	5,346	77	—	1840
1850	696,115	78	3	515,547	65	36	8,032	50	—	1850
1860	1,174,779	69	6	813,669	58	58	23,503	195	1	1860
1870	1,478,103	26	7	942,292	16	67	37,393	59	2	1870
1880	1,911,698	29	9	1,164,673	24	83	51,980	39	3	1880
1890	2,507,414	31	12	1,441,216	24	102	88,908	71	8	1890
1900	3,437,202	37	16	1,850,093	28	132	200,507	126	17	1900
1910	4,766,883	39	23	2,331,542	26	166	430,980	115	36	1910
1920	7,000,000	47	34	2,500,000	7	178	950,000	120	61	1920
1930	9,800,000	40	47	2,500,000	—	178	1,600,000	70	92	1930
1940	13,700,000	40	65	2,250,000	10	160	2,400,000	50	125	1940
1950	19,250,000	40	92	2,000,000	11	142	3,250,000	35	125	1950

RICHMOND				QUEENS				BROOKLYN			
Year	Population	% Incr.	Pop. per acre	Population	% Incr.	Pop. per acre	Population	% Incr.	Pop. per acre	Year
1790	3,835	—	—	6,159	—	—	4,495	—	—	1790
1800	4,567	19	—	6,642	8	—	5,740	28	—	1800
1810	5,347	17	—	7,444	12	—	8,303	45	—	1810
1820	6,135	15	—	8,246	11	—	11,187	38	—	1820
1832	7,082	15	—	9,049	10	—	20,535	84	—	1832
1840	10,965	55	—	14,480	60	—	47,613	132	—	1840
1850	15,061	37	—	18,593	28	—	138,882	192	2	1850
1860	25,492	68	—	32,903	77	—	279,122	101	6	1860
1870	33,029	30	—	45,468	38	—	419,921	50	8	1870
1880	38,991	18	1	56,599	24	1	599,495	43	12	1880
1890	51,693	33	1	87,050	54	1	838,547	40	17	1890
1900	67,021	30	2	152,999	76	2	1,166,582	39	23	1900
1910	85,969	28	3	284,041	86	3	1,634,351	40	33	1910
1920	150,000	74	4	900,000	217	10	2,500,000	53	50	1920
1930	300,000	100	8	1,900,000	111	23	3,500,000	40	70	1930
1940	550,000	83	15	3,500,000	84	42	5,000,000	43	100	1940
1950	1,000,000	82	27	6,000,000	71	72	7,000,000	40	140	1950

The City of New York exceeds in population the combined population of these twelve States: Maine, New Hampshire, Vermont, Rhode Island, Delaware, Idaho, Montana, Nevada, Oregon, North Dakota, Utah and Wyoming.

There is a birth every four minutes, a death every seven minutes and a marriage every ten minutes within the city limits.

To keep pace with its wonderful increase in population, New York City spends hundreds of millions of dollars annually for building construction. Some idea of the immensity of the building industry in the city may be had from the fact that only twenty cities in the United States have a total assessed valuation of realty in excess of the amount which was added to New York City in building construction alone in 1911. The total amount of building construction in Chicago, the second city, was considerably less than one-half that of New York City.

During the past ten years the building construction in New York City amounted to $1,839,481,000, divided among the five boroughs as follows:

Borough.	No. of New Buildings.	Amt. Expended for New Bldgs. & Alterations.
Manhattan,	11,930	$966,654,000
Brooklyn,	67,148	463,156,000
Bronx,	15,123	257,273,000
Queens,	35,050	127,076,000
Richmond,	6,494	25,322,000

Not one city in the United States has a total assessed valuation of real estate equal to the amount which has been added to the value of New York City in brick, steel, stone and other building material alone during the past ten years.

The assessed valuation of real estate in Chicago is $603,000,000, which as the assessment is made on the basis of thirty-three per cent of the actual value instead of one hundred per cent, as in New York City, would indicate the total real value of property in Chicago is many millions less than the value of the buildings erected in New York City in ten years.

In addition to the strictly building construction, there are the great amounts expended for the stupendous public works, such as bridges subways and tunnels, streets, sewers, parks, docks and piers, water supply and other municipal improvements.

The assessed value of property in New York City for 1912 is $7,525,474,063, which is said to be greater than the combined valuation as given of all the states west of the Mississippi River.

To make provisions for the ever-increasing needs of the city and to guard against the possibilities of a water famine, the city of New York has gone into the Catskill Mountains for a new water supply and now has under construction the most gigantic water system ever conceived by man. It will cost in excess of $172,000,000 and next to the Panama Canal is probably the greatest individual engineering undertaking ever projected by any city or country in the world.

The greatest municipal building in the world is now nearing completion under the supervision of Commissioner Arthur J. O'Keeffe of the Department of Bridges, who has under his jurisdiction forty-five bridges over navigable streams varying from the smallest bridge in the outlying boroughs, valued at $5,000, to the largest structure crossing the East River, valued at $25,000,000. These forty-five bridges represent practically every known type of structure and with the new municipal building represent a total value of about $135,000,000.

Some idea of the size and wonderful capacity of the four great East River bridges may be had from the statement that the population of Buffalo, San Francisco, Cincinnati or Pittsburgh could be transported over the new Manhattan Bridge in two hours without overtaxing its facilities.

The total weight of trains, cars, vehicles and passengers passing over the four East River bridges in twenty-four hours is approximately 1,441,966,000 pounds, or 721,000 tons. The figures will be greatly increased when the Manhattan and Queensboro Bridges are used to their capacity.

The total weight of steel in the four East River bridges is 213,200 tons. The total length of wire in the Manhattan Bridge cables is 23,132 miles, and the total length of wire in the cables of the Brooklyn, Williamsburg and Manhattan bridges is 57,816 miles, or two and one-third times the circumference of the earth. The total length of line consisting of passenger trains, cars and vehicles passing over the East River bridges in twenty-four hours, if extended, would reach from New York City to Cincinnati, Ohio, a distance of 752 miles.

New York City has a water front 341 miles in length, there are 2,000 miles of sewers and over 2,500 miles of water mains; and if the streets of this city were put end to end they would extend far beyond San Francisco.

And this is "Little Old New York"—a city subjected to much unfair criticism; but for every one thing the most biased critic can find to condemn there are a thousand things worthy of commendation.

INDEX

The Contractors and Furnishers of Material

FOR THE

Pennsylvania Railroad Company, New York City Station and Approaches

1902-1910

SIGNAL CABIN "A" NEW YORK TERMINAL, PENNSYLVANIA RAILROAD

In the signal installation of the Pennsylvania Tunnel and Terminal Railroad, which is the largest single railway signal installation in the world, Kerite insulated wires and cables were used exclusively—on account of those qualities of safety, reliability and economy, which a half century of successful service has shown them to possess.

KERITE INSULATED WIRE & CABLE COMPANY

General Offices, 30 Church Street, New York   Western Office, Peoples Gas Building, Chicago

Lillibridge 80-102

The Story of the Escalator, or Moving Stairway, in the new Pennsylvania Station, which Transports 10,800 Passengers per hour from Train-Floor to Street-Level Quickly, Safely, Comfortably, and Without Physical Effort.

IN this age of tunnel, subway and elevated stations—this age of marvelous feats in transit problems that seem the limit of engineering science,—every contrivance or invention which saves time and contributes to the comfort and convenience of the public is a subject of more than passing interest.

One of the most wonderful, yet unpretentious equipments in this magnificent structure of stone and steel, is the little flight of stairs leading from train-floor to street-level of the Pennsylvania Station, on the Thirty-fourth Street side. This stairway—which outwardly is little different from ordinary stairways except instead of being stationary it is continually moving upward—is one of the most humane time and labor-saving inventions included in this station's showing of modern engineering marvels.

Technically, this stairway is called an Escalator—which is a coined word meaning "Moving Stairway." Instead of inconsiderately dumping its passengers far underground to laboriously and with great sacrifice of vitality, mental vigor, and loss of time drag themselves, their heavy baggage and bundles, up and down heart-straining, nerve-racking, energy-sapping, health-destroying stairs and inclines as prevail in other stations—the Pennsylvania Railroad Company has provided this modern invention—the Escalator or Moving Stairway—for transporting its passengers without physical effort from the underground to street level elevation.

If there is the slightest doubt as to its practicability or popularity a study of the illustration below will dispel it.

The Escalator in operation—everybody uses the Escalator, nobody climbs the old-time stairs

This illustration is made from an actual photograph without any alteration whatsoever and shows the Escalator in operation. It will be observed that nobody climbs the old-time stairs—everybody rides on the Escalator; ninety-eight per cent of the persons going out this exit use the Escalator instead of the old-time stairs adjoining it. The reason is obvious. The climbing of stairs is a laborious, energy-sapping, health-destroying hardship to everyone, an impossibility to many, especially the aged, the crippled and those afflicted with

asthmatic or heart trouble. The Escalator proves a great boon to all of them as it enables them to reach street-level quickly, safely, comfortably, and without physical effort.

A detailed description of this marvelous invention is highly interesting. In ordinary appearance the Escalator is little different from an ordinary stairway except that the first few steps at the bottom and top have less than the standard height. These steps vary in height until they diverge horizontally with the approach and landing level. The passenger walks onto the lower horizontal platform, where standing still he or she is carried forward and in a moment is slowly lifted on one of the uprising steps, which increases gradually until the step attains a uniform height of about eight inches. This uniformity is maintained until approaching the top landing where the height of the step is gradually decreased until it finally merges into the platform level. The speed is such that when the person walks onto the lower platform there is no effect on his or her equilibrium—and as the steps move upward equilibrium is as natural as though he or she were standing still—and upon reaching the upper level stepping onto the permanent flooring is as easy as ordinary walking.

There is not the least element of danger about an Escalator —everything is enclosed—no crevices or mechanism to catch one's person or wearing apparel.

Its passenger carrying capacity varies according to size from 3,600 to 10,800 persons per hour. This is far beyond the capacity of an ordinary elevator which, say seven feet square, may possibly handle 750 persons per hour. It will therefore be seen that the Escalator is the safest and most practical method of handling people en-masse, and for relieving congestion.

On nearly all railroads, transportation facilities and the caring for passengers after they have reached the cars are admirable and comfortable;—electric motors of one kind or another have replaced the steam locomotive and palatial steel coaches are provided, but in most cases getting to and from the train level when the tracks are depressed, or elevated, involves a great amount of heart-straining labor. This work is being done more and more resentfully every day that passes, for every passenger knows that Escalators or Moving Stairways, unquestionably successful and not prohibitively expensive to install and operate, exist for carrying people up and down these cruel hills.

The Pennsylvania Railroad Company have made a beginning in the matter by putting this Escalator, or Moving Stairway where it is much needed, and it is expected they will shortly install several more. In view of the advantages it seems incredible that more transportation companies have not, with wise foresight and judgment, equipped their stations with this great energy and labor-saving device, which through growing public demand must soon become universal.

Escalators or Moving Stairways have proved the key to progress where the quick, safe, and comfortable handling of large numbers of people is concerned, not only in the public service stations but also in the great stores and mills. Escalators have demonstrated that they are indispensable wherever they have been installed. Actual, every-day experience for over ten years has shown that Escalators have solved the difficult phase of the transportation problem.

The Otis Elevator Company, 17 Battery Place, New York City, with offices in all the principal cities of the world, are the patentees and manufacturers. They maintain an engineering department and will without obligation supply full information, show the way to best meet specific requirements, and submit estimate of installation cost. Write to them.

THE SIGNALS AND INTERLOCKING SYSTEM OF THE PENNSYLVANIA TERMINAL

Union Switch & Signal Company, Engineers and Constructors

TO the Signal Engineer, the Pennsylvania Terminal in New York, and its approaches, presented a set of conditions that have never been equalled in severity on this continent or in Europe. The scheme of protection by block signals and by interlocking begins with the yard at Manhattan Transfer, crosses the meadows and the Hackensack River, covers the tunnels and the main station yard on Manhattan Island, and finally includes the great storage yard in Long Island City, known as the Sunnyside Yard. The efficient operation of this Division demanded one broad and comprehensive plan of signaling and interlocking; but the great difficulty arose in the treatment of the main station yard itself. It became necessary to provide for the movement of a dense traffic, including passengers, mail and express matter, and including main line trains and suburban trains, arriving from and destined to points eastward, as well as westward, from the station. Some of these trains would run through, while tail switching would be necessary for others, and it was even necessary to provide storage yards for a limited number of cars. It was foreseen that it would be necessary to provide not only for great flexibility, but for great speed of operation in order to handle the dense and varied traffic that will use the station within a few years.

The main station yard is practically underground. The view is obstructed by a forest of columns carrying the overhead structures and also by various necessary structures in the yard itself. As is commonly the case in underground constructions, the clearances are limited. Finally, there was the complication of the pipes and conduits for all manner of power service, lighting and drainage.

These severe conditions and requirements have been met with remarkable completeness as to the protection provided and as to flexibility and speed of operation. No other great installation of signaling and interlocking is so thorough in all provisions for protecting movements of trains and yet so successful in avoiding delay to those movements.

The credit for this result is properly shared by certain engineers and officials of the Pennsylvania Railroad Company and of the Union Switch & Signal Company. On the part of the Pennsylvania Railroad Company, a sub-committee was appointed for the study and supervision of the plans and installation. This committee consisted of Mr. George Gibbs, Chief Engineer of Electric Traction, Chairman, and Messrs. A. H. Rudd, Signal Engineer; George D. Fowle, Consulting Signal Engineer, and C. S. Krick, Division Superintendent. This committee was for many months in constant relation with engineers of the Union Switch & Signal Company, and particularly with Mr. J. P. Coleman, Chief Engineer, who, during the period of design and construction, spent practically all of his time in the New York offices of the company. Broadly, the requirements were laid down by the Pennsylvania Railroad Company and the design of apparatus and circuits was by the Union Switch & Signal Company, subject to the constant control and supervision, and final approval of the officials of the Pennsylvania Railroad Company. The contract between the Pennsylvania and the Union Switch & Signal Company was of such a character as to give the greatest possible flexibility in engineering and in design and development of apparatus.

The preliminary work was much delayed by the business situation following the panic of 1907 with the result that finally it was necessary to do about two years' work in one year, and for months the Union Switch & Signal Company had a thousand men in the field in the actual installation work of this contract, besides the shop force engaged in the manufacture of apparatus, and a considerable engineering force that was employed up to the day of putting the installation into service. During a part of this period valuable assistance was rendered in the preparation of circuit plans by the Signal Engineer of the Pennsylvania Railroad and his office force and through their zealous co-operation the work in the field was expedited and the plant went into service on schedule time. Practically all of the field work was done in twelve months, during which time, also, an important part of the engineering work and of the manufacture was done. The speed and smoothness with which this work was carried out and the high efficiency of the apparatus since it was put into regular operation, are matters for congratulation for all of those concerned, both on the part of the Railroad Company and the Signal Company.

The installation itself represents the highest development of the signaling art, and combines several modern features, some of which had never before been largely used, and all of which have never before been assembled in one installation. These advances over customary prior practice comprise means for obtaining positive control of all signals of interlocking plants by actual position of switches over which they govern; the automatic control of signals by track conditions in advance of them and by the position of the next succeeding signal to which the impending train movement leads; the automatic locking of all switches in every route by the entrance of trains upon these routes, and the automatic release of switches in the rear of trains immediately the rear of a train passes clear of the fouling point of the track including the switch. They, further, involve means for giving visual indications to the operator of every act of a train in physically locking and releasing the levers controlling switch and signal operation; means for permitting the joint use of all tracks for traffic in either direction between adjacent towers by co-action of towermen and track conditions; the automatic announcement of trains in their approach to the terminal station through the various tunnels and the delineation of their movements from block to block through the tunnels by means of indicators in each tower adjacent to tunnel portals.

One striking departure from the usual practice, made in this installation, was the adoption of the Rudd and Rhea system of upper quadrant, three position signaling, which has very lately become standard on the Pennsylvania Railroad and on several other railroad systems. The three position signal, acting in the lower quadrant of the circle, has for some years been standard on the Pennsylvania lines west of Pittsburgh, but in the Rudd and Rhea system all of the indications are given in the upper right hand quadrant. In this system one signal blade displays indications in three positions, viz., horizontal, 45 degrees and 90 degrees, and thus performs the functions of two blades indicating in two positions each. The upper quadrant indication has long been used in Germany, but has only within a very few years been recognized as desirable in this country, but its use is now spreading fast.

It will be obvious that in the tunnels and in a large part of the terminal area, semaphore arms would be of little use and it was decided to employ light signals through the tunnels, and also in the station area, except for dwarf signals. This naturally resulted in the elimination of considerable signal mechanism as it was simply necessary to change the colors of the standard lights. Because of the difficulty of getting clearance for semaphore signals in the terminal area, and also in order to keep a uniform type of signal in that area, it was decided to use light signals even in considerable parts of the terminal area which are open to the daylight. In such places special lenses are used with lamps of high candle power, the lenses being hooded to screen them from the direct rays of the sun. This involved considerable experimentation to produce the best lens for the purpose, and the best arrangement, and in these experiments important assistance was rendered by Dr. Churchill of the Corning Glass Company. The results have been entirely satisfactory.

The ordinary light signals are equipped with 4 c. p. lamps, two in multiple for each lens. The current is shifted from lamp to lamp by relays which are energized or de-energized by the movement of the interlocking machine levers, or by the action of trains on the track circuits or by both. The track relays are worked by alternating current, while those controlled from the machine operate by direct current. Many of the relays of both the A. C. and D. C. types employ an unusual number of contacts, as many as eighteen frequently being used. Because of this peculiarity these relays are of a new and ingenious type, the contacts being actuated by a pneumatic cylinder, the valve of which is in turn actuated by an A. C. or D. C. magnet, according to the function of the relay.

In the tunnels, a track stop is used in connection with each block, the purpose of which is to apply the brakes if a home signal is over-run in the stop position. This stop is essentially the same as that designed and used heretofore by the Union Switch & Signal Company for the Boston Elevated, the Interborough Rapid Transit, the Hudson & Manhattan, Philadelphia Rapid Transit, and other installations. Because of the necessity of running the rolling stock used in the tunnels over

various lines of the Long Island Railroad, some improper operation of the stop valves has occurred from flying ballast, and other casual obstructions. To avoid this, Mr. E. R. Hill, Assistant to the Chief Engineer of Electric Traction, has recently devised a new form of valve and a special tripper arm for the track device, which, having been constructed by the Union Switch & Signal Company and the Westinghouse Air Brake Company, are being installed under his direction.

The alternating track circuit control is of the one rail or the two rail type, as conditions may justify. Through the interlockings, for example, it was found more practicable to use the one rail control because of the lesser difficulty it offered in getting close definition between the limits of the great number of short track sections there used, and here the ample capacity supplied by the large number of rails, for taking care of the return power current, makes it entirely practicable to use the one rail system. Outside of the interlocking territory, the two rail system is used; that is, both rails are employed for the return of the power current. The methods and apparatus for the employment of a distinctive current for signal control on electrically operated railroads, are now well known, and do not call for special description here.

The switches, automatic stops and semaphore signals throughout the entire installation, from the Manhattan Transfer to the Sunnyside Yard, and including those yards, are operated by the electro-pneumatic system. The interlockings are operated from eleven cabins, with a total of 516 working levers, four in the terminal area, four at the Sunnyside Yard, two at the Harrison Yard, and one at the Hackensack Draw. These operate a total of 1,185 operative functions, or an average of over two per lever, a higher average than can be obtained by any other system, and are as follows: 457 high signals, 187 dwarf signals, 267 single switches, 46 slip switches and 46 pairs of movable point frogs. There are also 104 automatic signals and 48 automatic stops besides the above. In one cabin in the terminal there are 900 relays, and the total in all of the cabins is 2,824. The total length of signal wire used was 8,-500,000 feet.

CLINTON POINT STONE COMPANY
115 Broadway, New York City

This Company furnished the crushed stone used in constructing the Pennsylvania Tunnels and Terminal. It owns and operates quarries for producing crushed trap rock at Rockland Lake, N.Y., and crushed blue stone at Stoneco, N.Y., and Verplanck Point, N.Y., all located upon the Hudson River.

It is interesting to note that the product from these quarries is shipped by water to all points between Albany, N.Y., and Tampa, Fla., the stone for the concrete work of the Florida East Coast Railway Company coming from its quarries at Stoneco.

The trap rock furnished by it is the standard quality used in all road work by the Boroughs of Manhattan, Brooklyn, Bronx, Queens and Richmond, and is also specified for much fireproof concrete work.

The location of the quarries upon the Hudson River provides means of transporting its product by water and secures for its customers the lowest possible freight rates.

It also manufactures a very high grade of carbonate of lime used by asphalt companies in surfacing roadways.

The capacity of its quarries is in excess of 5,000 cubic yards per day.

HARNESSING ELECTRICITY

Westinghouse Electric & Mfg. Co.

OF first importance in the project of the Pennsylvania extension into New York was the use of electricity. It was due only to the advance in the electrical art that this greatest corporate work of recent times was made possible. In no other way could the passage of trains under the river barriers of Manhattan Island be secured. The planning of this great achievement, its execution, and the remarkable smoothness of its operation from the very start reflect the greatest credit upon the engineers, upon the operating staff, and upon the manufacturers of the electrical apparatus.

The product of the Westinghouse interests is used exclusively in this electrification for:

First: The generation of power at the main power-house at Long Island City.

Second: The control and distribution to the various high-tension currents radiating from the power-house.

Third: The transformation of electric energy from the form in which it is generated to that suitable for application to the third rail by means of transformers, rotary converters and controlling apparatus located in the sub-stations.

Fourth: The extensive auxiliary uses, such as lighting, pumping, ventilating, operation of elevators, etc., distributed over the road at switching stations, shaft houses and tunnel vaults.

Fifth: The operation of the signals and track switches.

Sixth: The motive power, comprising electric locomotives and multiple unit trains.

The execution of the electrical contract called for the highest order of skill by the numerous electrical specialists of the staff of the Electric Company. Many of the problems were original and of greater magnitude than any previously undertaken, but these were advantageously solved and the resulting success of operation of all of the electrical apparatus is most gratifying.

EAST PITTSBURGH WORKS OF WESTINGHOUSE ELECTRIC & MFG. CO.

for the exclusive use of the great electric traction systems: of the Interborough Rapid Transit Co., both elevated and subway lines; the Brooklyn Rapid Transit Co., both surface and elevated lines; the Third Avenue Railroad Co., surface lines; the electrified steam lines of the Long Island Railroad, and for the New York Central electrification in New York.

Apparatus for the control of the power at the power-house, sub-stations and switching station is largely of the remote control type and incorporates many ingenious features especially adapted to this installation. Heavy switches connecting to the third rail are operated through a small pilot wire from the main power station miles away.

The electric locomotives are the most powerful ever built and, in fact, are not only the equivalent of the most powerful steam locomotives for hauling heavy loads but have also the high speed characteristics of passenger locomotives. To perform this work, by far the most powerful railway motors ever built are used, connection being made to the driving wheels of the locomotive by means of side rods. This type was decided on after most careful and elaborate investigation and tests, in order to secure the safest and most reliable form of drive to deliver the large amounts of power from the motors to the wheels.

An enormous amount of electric current, sufficient, in fact, for the requirement of one hundred trolley cars, is utilized by the motors of each locomotive, and this power is readily controlled from a small master switch, by the use of the unit switch control system. The efficiency of this control in service has been such that inspection is scheduled only at intervals of 2,500 miles of operation as compared with from one to two hundred miles between inspections for a steam locomotive. The variation of the field strength of the two motors by using field control, gives four efficient running positions and more efficient regulation than is commonly secured with four motors. The reliability and maintenance of the electrical apparatus has proven that a delay is practically unheard of and the cost of maintenance is remarkably low.

The Long Island Railroad, which is operating trains into the Pennsylvania Station, has to-day the largest mileage of electrified track of any steam railroad. The power supplied comes from the main power station at Long Island City, and it is interesting to note that all transformers, rotary converters and controlling apparatus, as well as the train equipments, are exclusively of Westinghouse manufacture. The same reliability of operation of the sub-stations and the same high

TRAIN EMERGING FROM NORTH RIVER TUNNELS, PENNSYLVANIA STATION, NEW YORK

The turbo-generators installed in the power-house were designed at a time when they were the largest in existence and it is further interesting to note that the Westinghouse Companies were the pioneers in turbine development in this country, and to them is particularly due the great advance in the electrical art which turbo-generator development has produced.

The rotary converters are of the same high standard of excellence as those furnished by the Westinghouse Company

efficiency of the Unit Switch Control was experienced from the beginning of operation in 1905 as has been obtained with the later apparatus.

By the successful consummation of such wonderful undertakings as these, the present state of the electrical art has become one in which all engineers take the greatest pride. The ease and despatch with which traffic is handled inspires all railroad men with the greatest confidence and conviction as to the superiority of electric operation.

The main line and other portions of the New York, New Haven and Hartford Railroad, operating with passenger, freight and switching electric locomotives; the Boston and Maine Railroad operating with electric locomotives through the Hoosac Tunnel, and the Grand Trunk Railroad operating with electric locomotives through the St. Clair Tunnel, all by the Single Phase System, are completely equipped from power-house to motive power with Westinghouse apparatus and the success obtained has been notable.

Abroad, the Società Italiana Westinghouse furnished all of the electrical apparatus, including the electric locomotives, for the electrification of the Giovi Line over the Appenine Mountains, where steam locomotives proved inadequate for the traffic. This noteworthy installation is what is termed the Three Phase System.

The accomplishment of great things can be traced to small beginnings. In 1886, when the use of electricity in this country was confined to very limited areas, Mr. George Westinghouse, who had long been active in mechanical development for railway uses, as evidenced by his air-brake system, became impressed with the possibilities of the wider and greater application of electricity. Upon the very elementary design of the alternating current transformer, he secured the development of a system of electric generation which made economic use possible over an extended area. This was the real beginning of the extensive uses to which electricity is put at the present time and in its progress, led to the inception and growth of the Westinghouse Electric and Manufacturing Company, which at present employs approximately 20,000 employees and has a productive capacity of $50,000,000 worth of electrical apparatus per annum.

IRON WORK

IN a work as extensive and complex as the Pennsylvania Railroad's New York improvement, with hundreds of contractors and sub-contractors involved, there must necessarily be some whose work, compared with others, is inconspicuous.

Every dollar's worth of material, however, had to pass the rigid test of the Pennsylvania Railroad's Board of Engineers, and houses, although relatively small, are entitled to the standing which recognition by such a board automatically grants.

On the Newark Extension and on the Meadows Division, from the Harrison Yards to Bergen Hill Tunnels, the Wayne Iron Works furnished all of the pipe railing.

In the terminal proper it furnished much of the pipe railing and approximately 1,000 steel lockers for the P.R.R.'s employees and the members of the Y.M.C.A., whose rooms are in the building.

They also furnished all the pipe railing on the retaining walls of the "inverts" in the Sunnyside Yards; approximately 15,000 feet of seven feet high iron fence around the Sunnyside Yard boundaries; much of the ornamental railing on the highway bridges crossing the yards, and 500 lockers for the various service buildings.

The Wayne Iron Works has been identified with much of the elevation and bridge work of the Pennsylvania Railroad Company during recent years and has installed above one hundred miles of pipe railings, bridge railings and other forms of iron fencing during that time.

The company was incorporated in 1893.

Its works are located at Wayne, Pa., and the officers of the company are George W. Powell, president, and C. M. Wetzel, treasurer.

As is obvious, railroad contracts are a specialty of the company, and their large and rapidly increasing business may be ascribed to quality of product, reasonable prices, and facilities for handling contracts of the largest size.

HARDWARE

THE hardware for the Pennsylvania Terminal Building was chosen as carefully and with as rigid an adherence to standards of quality as the other material used. The knowledge and experience of the architects was joined to the analytical reasoning of the engineers and the articles submitted were given the approval of both architects and engineers before adoption. The functions and the designs satisfy the architects and the reliability, the suitability and the operations meet the requirements of the engineers.

In a building such as this, grandly monumental in effect, the use of small ornamental details would be manifestly inappropriate. Therefore no ornament is employed in the hardware, but each piece is designed to carry the impression of strength and mass, and perfectly proportioned for the place in which it is to be used. Every outline and detail bears the stamp of the highest type of artistic effect for the place—a rich simplicity, suitability and appropriateness—unobtrusive, but with an appearance of strength and solidity. The long escutcheons in ordinary use were abandoned and plain knobs set in round roses substituted, with a simple ring or collar encircling the locking cylinder. On doors where pulls were required a handle set in rosettes was adopted, and the other side of the door was equipped with push bars which served an additional function of protecting the glass set in the door. The butts were extra heavy, with ball bearings which serve both to reduce the effort required to move the doors, and to ensure the minimum of friction and a length of service equal to the life of the building itself. Overhead stops were provided to all the traffic doors, made strong and substantial and firmly attached, heavy expansion bolts being employed when necessary to anchor them to the granite. Corbin door checks, which have proven their value for heavy service by long use upon the doors of many of the large railway stations of the country, were used throughout this building, after being subjected to severe tests.

All of the hardware is of bronze metal. A dull finish was adopted, in general, which the action of the salty air of New York will gradually deepen into those rich tints of antique bronze which cannot be successfully produced by artificial means. In the toilet rooms, however, the hardware was heavily nickel plated, facilitating cleansing and a sanitary condition.

The best types of Corbin cylinder locks were adopted, the Corbin system of master and grand master keys being employed. By this system, two absolutely independent series of key changes are provided in a single cylinder, using the same key way, and the security, inviolability and possibility of expansion to meet any required number of sets of locks or combination of changes so favorably impressed the engineering department as to secure its adoption not only for this building but for practically all others east of Philadelphia, a uniform system of master keying being perfected for this use.

In every respect, the hardware is giving satisfactory service and pleasing the maintenance department in a manner which has justified the selections made.

CONDUITS

JUST as the vital organisms of the human body are concealed from view and are rarely thought of, just so it is in the case of tunnels, either subaqueous or those under the land. Little do we realize while speeding along in comfort that concealed in the concrete benches on either side of us there are conduits carrying the power, telephone and telegraph cables—just as the veins and nerves perform the functions of the human body. There are approximately four hundred duct miles of power tile conduits and in addition six hundred duct miles of telegraph and telephone conduits required for the operation of the New York Tunnel Extension of the Pennsylvania Railroad. A part of this installation was effected by the Great Eastern Clay Products Company of 39 and 41 Cortlandt Street, New York City, they having furnished conduit to the contractors for the tunnels under Bergen Hill, N.J.; the cross-town tunnels under Thirty-second and Thirty-third Streets, New York, and the contractors having charge of the excavation of the station site. This company, of which R. W. Lyle is president and general manager and W. C. Kimball is secretary and treasurer, operates an extensive plant turning out fireproofing, wall coping, flue linings, vitrified electrical conduits and special clay products.

Lewis L. Clarke   Henry Japp   Lord Cowdray   Ernest W. Moir   H. D. Forbes

S. PEARSON & SON, Inc.

Contractors for the East River Tunnels

THE four East River Tunnels of the Pennsylvania Railroad, on account of their large diameter and the difficult strata they pierce, are generally considered the most difficult subaqueous tunnel construction ever attempted. The construction of this work of nearly five miles of twenty-three foot tubes required 100,-000 tons of cast iron lining, reinforced by two feet of concrete, to hold out the quicksands and the river above, and involved the largest subaqueous tunnel contract ever placed.

The construction required about five years and was accomplished by using compressed air to hold back the river. The air pressure required depends on the depth of water above the point considered, every 2 feet of water above the tunnel represents about one pound of air pressure in the tunnel. As the tunnels are 23 feet diameter, the pressure necessary at the bottom of the tunnel was 10 lbs. greater than that required at the top.

If the air pressure was kept low enough to prevent the river bed from being blown off, then the quicksand and water flowed in at the bottom causing the tunnel to settle, while if the pressure was kept high enough to prevent settlement in the quicksand, then the roof blew off. It was only by dumping 500,000 cubic yards of stiff clay from scows to reinforce the river bed that a pressure was maintained which kept the bottom dry enough to prevent the tunnel sinking below grade.

The workmen, or sand-hogs, worked in pressures up to 40 lbs. to the square inch above atmosphere, and 42,000,000,000 cubic feet of air were compressed and forced into the tunnels. At times, as much as 20,000 cubic feet of air per minute escaped from one tunnel alone, causing a sufficient disturbance in the river above to deflect a ferry-boat from its course.

Forty-two nationalities were represented in the 2,500 men required to carry out the work which was prosecuted day and night continuously in 3-hour shifts for the highest pressures.

Mr. Alfred Noble was the Engineer in charge for the Railroad Company; he is considered to be the greatest living American engineer. His judgment is appealed to in important undertakings, as, for instance, the Panama Canal, the greatest construction work in the world, owes in no small measure its present design to him.

He is loved and respected by all who know him and takes all responsibility when things go wrong while giving credit to his subordinates when good work is done.

The contractors who staked their capital on the correctness of their bid and carried out the work successfully, are the well-known American firm of contractors, S. Pearson & Son, Inc., which is incorporated in the State of New York and is at present engaged on the construction of 10½ miles of the New York State Barge Canal. The firm of S. Pearson & Son is well-known all over the world. The latest of the great works they have undertaken include the National Harbor at Dover, England, and the Tehuantepec Railroad, in Mexico, with the harbors on the Atlantic and Pacific sides of the Isthmus. They operate this railroad for the Mexican Government and it is carrying a large traffic, 1,000,000 tons of freight being trans-shipped across the Isthmus last year.

The President of the Company, Lord Cowdray, (better known as Sir Weetman Pearson) is a great organizer and financier. His boldness in great things as well as his mastery of details puts him easily first amongst the builders of great works in all parts of the world.

The Vice-President of the Company, Mr. E. W. Moir, is a distinguished engineer whose experience and knowledge of subaqueous tunnel work is looked up to by the profession. In 1890 he acted as engineer for S. Pearson & Son on the old Hudson tunnel, building 2,000 feet of this tube with cast iron lining and the present day shield method attaining a speed of 10 feet per day when the Baring Bank crash suspended further operations. The shield which he used and left in position ready for going ahead was opened up by Mr. Jacobs, under Mr. McAdoo, and completed the first Hudson tunnel in 1904.

Mr. Lewis L. Clarke, Director of the Company, takes great interest in the construction work. As President of the American Exchange National Bank he wins the admiration of all for the judgment and energy with which he manages this well-known institution.

Mr. Henry Japp, Director and Managing Engineer, was in charge of the construction work, and Mr. Henry D. Forbes, Director and Secretary and Treasurer, handled the financial and clerical part of the work.

CHARLES E. FRASER   JAMES H. BRACE   GEORGE C. CLARKE

FRASER, BRACE & COMPANY
Engineering Contractors

AS a result of association during the construction of the Pennsylvania Terminal, the corporation known as Fraser, Brace & Co. was formed toward the completion of that work. The president, Charles E. Fraser, was superintendent for S. Pearson & Son, Inc., at the Manhattan end throughout the period of driving the East River Tunnels. James H. Brace, secretary and treasurer, was first engineer of alignment of the East River Division and afterward resident engineer on construction of the Thirty-third Street tunnel from Seventh Avenue to the middle of the East River.

When the tunnels were designed and the contracts let for their construction, it was believed that the piston action of the trains would furnish all the ventilation necessary for the tubes. This, however, could only positively be determined under actual working conditions and to make provisions for forced ventilation the construction shafts on each side of the East River were designed to be permanent structures. The original contracts, however, only provided for the outer lining of these shafts, leaving the details of the inner lining with its complicated system of air ducts to be worked out later.

The poor ventilation of the subways which were put into operation between the time the contracts were let and the completion of the tubes decided the management of the Pennsylvania Terminals to take no risks of a similar result.

The permanent lining of the shafts was planned with a system of ducts through part of which fresh air could be forced into the tunnels in the direction of the moving trains by fans in the head houses, at the top of the shafts, and through other the bad air could be forced out by the action of the trains. Provision was also made in separate conduits for power telegraph and telephone cables and for access to the tunnels by stairways. The work involved, among other things, the placing of 13,300 cubic yards of concrete.

The lower portion of the shafts at Manhattan had been lined at the time they were sunk with a temporary timber lining. It was necessary to replace this timber by permanent waterproof walls. Aside from removing and replacing the timber lining the chief difficulty of the work consisted in the construction of the concrete forms, which were extremely complicated. It was found advisable to build them complete at the surface, then take them apart in sections and rebuild them at the foot of the shaft. The contract was made for this work early in October, 1909, and by the middle of January it was so nearly completed as to offer no further obstruction to train movements.

Besides the shaft lining, Fraser, Brace & Co. also placed the reinforced concrete floors on the Bridge Approach and Honeywell Street Viaducts across the Sunnyside Yard.

The corporation has also constructed for the State of New York, the elevator shaft and tunnel at the Niagara Reservation and is just completing a contract for the intake section of the power development of the Canadian Light and Power Company of Montreal at Valleyfield, Quebec, Canada. Under this contract a coffer dam was built and about 185,000 cubic yards of earth and 95,000 cubic yards of rock excavated from the bed of the Beauharnais Canal and intake gates constructed containing 7,500 cubic yards of concrete and 200 tons of structural steel. The Canal is parallel to the St. Lawrence River and there was a continual leakage of water into the canal requiring at times twelve ten and twelve inch centrifugal pumps for its removal. Despite this, the work was completed in a little over a year.

The Company is now beginning the construction of some piers for a bridge replacing the present structure of the Central Railroad of New Jersey over the Elizabeth River.

Messrs. Fraser and Brace are both members of the American Society of Civil Engineers. The former is a member of the Canadian Society of Civil Engineers and the latter of the Western Society of Engineers of Chicago.

The officers of Fraser, Brace & Company believe that despite the apparent tendency toward the formation of large corporations to do engineering contracting, there is room on difficult construction for a concern with a moderate capital that will only undertake such work as its responsible officers can personally supervise in the field.

Since this article was written, Mr. Geo. C. Clarke, formerly Resident Engineer at the Penn. Terminal and the Tunnel Approaches in Long Island, has joined this Company as Director and Chief Engineer. Mr. Clarke is also a member of the American Society of Civil Engineers.

The Company has been successful in securing two large contracts for hydro-electric developments near Shelburne Falls, Mass.

POWER GENERATING EQUIPMENT FOR RAILROAD TERMINAL ELECTRIFICATION

Westinghouse Machine Company

THE reliability of the source of power supply is so plainly one of the most important factors in electrically operated terminal systems, that the proposition need not be argued. Without continuity of service, the running of trains would be interrupted, schedules sacrificed and the patronage of the road imperiled. Therefore, the choice of the primary motive power must be founded upon the most improved and rational lines to the end of securing this indispensable security of operativeness. Accompanying the rigid demand for permanency of the power source, comes the requirement of larger capacities, which, owing to their magnitude, call for the highest attainment and skill in the production of electric generating equipment. With such forethought, central supply stations have been constructed which exhibit noteworthy engineering development in each and every department. The modern steam turbine forms the center of this progressive movement, and has made practicable the present-day high-powered unit.

The power equipment of the Pennsylvania tunnel and terminal system represents very important innovations in generating machinery. All new units added to the Long Island station to care for the load produced by the electric locomotives and shuttle trains are of the highly developed type of double-flow turbines, comprising two low-pressure reaction elements placed end to end with a high-pressure impulse wheel between them. These machines constitute the highest development in turbines, which, though originated in America, have also gained popularity in England and on the Continent, owing to their great mechanical and economical advantages. The exterior construction is shown in cut; a general view of the engineroom of the Long Island City power station.

Another element of the station equipment worthy of note is the new type of condenser employing the Leblanc air pump and turbine drive, the signal advantage of which is that the

TURBINE ROOM, LONG ISLAND CITY POWER PLANT

Turbine types of engines involve no large wearing surfaces and no reciprocating parts subject to jar, vibration and maladjustment. Consequently, the advantages of low friction loss, comparatively negligible oil consumption and small maintenance expense are very marked. Great flexibility and low cost of attendance in the steam turbine are also very significant. Considering these advantages in connection with its most moderate first cost and small expense of installing, the steam turbine must necessarily be regarded as one of the most prominent causes contributing to the success of existing electrified systems.

ideal vacuum may be regularly obtained, with maximum simplicity of operation and virtual freedom from interruption of service.

The plant at the terminal station proper is equipped with two large non-condensing turbines which generate current for lighting and auxiliary power purposes, and also furnish a large proportion of the exhaust for station heating in cold weather, thus constituting an essential factor in the various operating economies which typify the entire terminal equipment.

COAL HANDLING MACHINERY AT LONG ISLAND CITY POWER HOUSE

THE Hoisting Tower and Cable-Car System in connection with the Long Island City Terminal of the Pennsylvania Railroad was designed, furnished and installed by the Robins Conveying Belt Co. of New York.

The hoisting tower, which has a capacity of ninety tons of coal per hour, is notable because of its high lift, the problems introduced thereby, and its novel controlling system. It is operated by steam engines and requires but one man to control the motions of the coal-digging bucket, which has a capacity of one and three-fourths tons.

The lift of the bucket is about 170 feet, varying with the tide and the amount of coal in the barge. A maximum hoisting speed of 1,500 feet per minute is used, overspeeding being prevented by throttling the steam pressure.

LONG ISLAND CITY POWER HOUSE—GENERAL VIEW

There are three independent engines, each having a keyed drum and a post brake. No friction clutches are used. One engine closes and opens the bucket and is equipped with a device for stopping it automatically. Another engine moves the trolley in and out between limits automatically governed. The ropes are reeved in such a manner that the rope stresses in the trolley are balanced to prevent a runaway. The trolley will remain in any position without being locked. The main engine, which is direct connected, hoists and lowers the bucket independently of the other engines, and has an automatic stop at the upper limit of travel.

On account of special rope-reeving, the horizontal travel of the trolley has no effect on the lift of the bucket. The latter, which weighs about 6,000 pounds, raises in its descent a counterweight of such a mass that the bucket speed is readily controlled without using the post-brake to prevent overspeed. Without this balance control, the powerful post-brake, which is sixty inches in diameter, would be set afire after a few operations.

All of the links and brakes are thrown by small steam engines, the operator merely throwing the valves of these engines. This avoids all laborious effort on his part, which would tend to reduce his efficiency and lower the capacity of the tower.

The operator's platform is located about thirty feet above the barge. As his view is entirely unobstructed he is able to land the bucket in the barge to the best advantage. After the loaded bucket passes his level, it remains out of his sight during the time it ascends to the boom level, while being trolleyed in and dumping into the hopper, and until it again passes before him on its downward trip. After the filled bucket is started upward all subsequent motors are controlled automatically, including the starting of the trolley inward, the stopping of the bucket in its ascent, the dumping and the reversal of the operation. The operator cannot change these functions, but he can stop everything at once by throwing a steam lever.

The small lever-handling engines which throw the brakes and reverse links are geared and interlocked to give the control described. Each engine operates a train of gearing from a drag link attached to one crank-pin of each of the three engines.

In the engine-room are three large dials which indicate the positions of the bucket and of the trolley, and show whether the bucket is open or closed.

This fully automatic control was furnished because a machine was desired which could be operated by any boiler-room hand of good intelligence and without the possibility of accidents, and which would handle coal at a uniform rate and at conservative speeds.

The coal after being dropped from the grab-bucket falls into a receiving hopper which feeds it to a crusher driven by a steam engine. The crushed coal, stoker-sized, is fed alternately to two weighing hoppers equipped with beam scales. Each hopper has a capacity of 3,000 pounds, equal to the charge of one of the cable cars.

These cars pass around a loop of the track encircling the tower, and are disengaged from the cable for a few moments as they pass under the weighing hoppers to be charged.

This cable railway which is about 1,700 feet long is installed on a level trestle 101 feet above the wharf, up to the point where the cars enter the monitor of the boiler-house. Here they pass around the loop over the concrete coal bunker into which they discharge their loads automatically.

The curves around which the cable passes are of special design. All curve idlers run on hollow cold-drawn shafting supported at top and bottom, and have central grease lubrication.

The drive has two grooved drums only one of which is driven, the tail drum being tilted, an arrangement commonly used in traction elevators. At the point where the cars are disconnected to be loaded, the space or gap between the ingoing and outgoing cables leading to and from the drives, is only two feet. Here the cable is deflected by a pair of forty-eight inch sheaves which turn on a common shaft. This gap is bridged by the impetus of the incoming car, after the grip has been released to stop and load. The cable railway system easily takes care of the normal capacity of the hoisting tower.

LONG ISLAND CITY POWER HOUSE—COAL HANDLING TRESTLE
FROM TOWER

THE UNITED ENGINEERING AND CONTRACTING COMPANY

Builders of the Manhattan Crosstown Tunnels

WM. H. SCHMIDT
V. President and Treasurer

INCORPORATED under the Laws of the State of New York in March, 1899, by men who had managed other companies, who desired to go into business for themselves.

D. L. Hough, President, after graduating from the Engineering Department at Yale, learned the trade of machinist and boiler-maker, and has been successively Managing Engineer for the Camden Iron Works; Chief Engineer and General Manager of the East River Gas Company; Manager of the General Contract Work of the Barber Asphalt Paving interests; an Engineer Officer in actual service during the Spanish-American War; and was appointed Consulting Engineer to the Receiver who completed the Battery to Brooklyn Tunnel for the Rapid Transit Commission.

Wm. H. Schmidt, Vice-President and Treasurer, is a graduate in engineering of Cornell University; is a Director of the Germania Bank; a Director of the Sicilian Asphalt Paving Company; and has had considerable experience in mining operations in the West.

Paul G. Brown, Vice-President and Managing Engineer, studied engineering at Cornell University, and has been successively Assistant City Engineer of Chicago where he took charge of the construction of two of the water works intake cribs and the connecting tunnels under Lake Michigan, done days' work by the City; and was for five years in charge of the maintenance of the water supply system of that City; Managing Engineer for the construction of a five mile water works tunnel in Cincinnati; Consulting Engineer to the contractor who built two cribs and two intake tunnels for the City of Cleveland; Superintendent for a Pittsburgh contracting concern in charge of deep foundation work for bridges; General Superintendent for the contractor excavating the New York Central Terminal; and for the Long Island end of the Belmont Tunnel at Forty-second Street.

W. C. LANCASTER
Elec. and Mech. Eng.

W. C. Lancaster, Electrical and Mechanical Engineer, is a graduate of the University of Virginia; served his apprenticeship in the Schenectady Works of the General Electric Company. It is he who has successfully worked out the electrical operation of contractors' plants in the City of New York, which has now been adopted by practically all the local contractors.

S. P. Brown, Assistant Managing Engineer in charge of Concrete Work, is a graduate of the Massachusetts Institute of Technology; has had wide experience in reinforced concrete work, and is now Chief Engineer for MacKenzie, Mann & Company, Ltd., building a railway tunnel under Mt. Royal, Montreal.

PAUL G. BROWN
V. President and Man. Eng.

The special "battleship" bucket, around which the plant for the Crosstown Tunnels was designed, was so successful in the reduction of costs of excavation and the annoyance to the public in the handling of excavated material that it has been adopted by practically all the contractors to whom sections of the new subway have been awarded.

Other contracts executed by The United Engineering and Contracting Company are—

An electric drive pumping plant for clearing Dry Docks No. 2 and No. 3 in the New York Navy Yard.

The foundations on both sides of the East River for the approaches for the Williamsburg Bridge.

D. L. HOUGH
President

The whole of the Scherzer Rolling Lift Bridge over Newton Creek, joining the Borough of Brooklyn with the Borough of Queens.

A tunnel through Watchung Mountain, forming a part of the Newark Water Works Aqueduct.

A tunnel, Thirty-ninth Street, South Brooklyn, for the Brooklyn Heights Railway Company.

The water supply for the Long Beach Improvement.

The excavation in rock for the Vanderbilt Hotel.

The road bed equipment for seven miles of electrified elevated structure in the Borough of Brooklyn, City of New York, for the Long Island Railroad Company.

The rectification, depression and double-tracking of the Port Morris Branch of the New York Central Railroad in the Borough of Bronx, including a tunnel through St. Mary's Park.

A complete water power development, including dam and power house, for the Lehigh Power Company, Pennsylvania.

Now at work on five miles of the Erie Barge Canal at Lockport, N.Y., and the water supply system at Glendale for the Long Island Railroad Company.

Its officers are managing the Cuban Engineering and Contracting Company, now building the $7,000,000.00 sewage system in Havana, consisting of sewers of every size from six inches up to eighty-four inches in diameter, with out-falls for the surface water into the Harbor, a pneumatic shield driven tunnel under the Harbor for the house drainage, complete electric drive pumping plant for the main pumping station and the sublifts, a tunnel in rock under Cabana Fortress, and an out-fall into the Gulf Stream.

S. P. BROWN
Asst. Man. Eng.

REFRIGERATION
The Brunswick Refrigerating Company of New Brunswick, N. J.

TWO ELECTRICALLY DRIVEN AMMONIA COMPRESSORS, COMMISSARY
DEPARTMENT, SUNNYSIDE YARD

ONE-HALF TON REFRIGERATION PLANT, PULL-
MAN CAR SERVICE, SUNNYSIDE YARD

THE refrigerating plant at Sunnyside Yards, Commissary Department, is a duplicate unit consisting of two electrically driven ammonia compressors.

The plant is used for cooling the various refrigerators of the Commissary Department in connection with the Pennsylvania Railroad's dining car and restaurant service. These refrigerators are divided into a number of individual units or compartments for the storage of fresh and salt meats, poultry, fish, fruit, dairy supplies, ice cream, and an infinite variety of foodstuffs characteristic of the Railroad's service, and they are cooled by means of direct expansion of the ammonia through coils located in the various compartments—in some cases in overhead chambers; in others, on the walls.

Each compartment is fitted with control valves for the regulation of the temperature best suited to the goods stored. The plan proper consists of two 4 ton, single acting, single cylinder, Brunswick ammonia compressors of the eccentric driven inclosed type, cross connected and driven by belt from 10 horse-power direct current motors, the necessary electric current being supplied from the company's power plant.

The great advantage and economy of mechanical refrigeration is well demonstrated by this simple installation. The condition in which stores are kept, the elimination of trouble consequent upon icing the refrigerators, and the promotion of sanitation as well; the general convenience of the whole installation, together with low cost of operation as compared with the antiquated refrigerating system employing melting ice, has demonstrated the superiority of the mechanical system beyond question.

It may be safely said that the same result could not be obtained in an ice-cooled refrigerator at any cost, since the perfect regulation, evenness of temperature, dryness and sanitation so easily obtainable with mechanically cooled refrigerators are beyond the range of possibility with a melting ice system.

The advantages of the Brunswick system are numerous: High efficiency, durability of construction, simplicity in every detail from the design of the compressor to the operation of the system, all demonstrate that the reputation of the Brunswick machine for this class of work is well deserved.

A point which illustrates the simplicity of the apparatus is the fact that the plant is operated under the supervision of the engineers at the company's power plant, which is located a considerable distance from the building containing the refrigerating plant, the machine being started and the valves adjusted by the engineer on duty at the power plant; it is then left to operate without any attention save an occasional visit from one of the engineers, which is more in the way of a general inspection than any necessary attendance. Under these conditions uniform temperatures are maintained throughout the various refrigerators.

The little half-ton Brunswick plant shown in the accompanying illustration is installed immediately alongside the refrigerator, and well illustrates the compactness and flexibility of the Brunswick system. The entire plant, including refrigerator and machinery, is located on the first floor and operated by the steward's attendant. Here, also, the direct expansion type of installation is employed, the refrigerator being fitted with an overhead cooling compartment in which are coils and brine storage tanks for the producing and maintaining of the temperature when the machine is shut down.

MODERN BUILDING CONSTRUCTION

George A. Fuller Construction Company

ONE of the wonders of the Western world is the sky line of New York City—a never-ending wonder even to the metropolitan himself as he approaches his home city by water from any point of the compass; a marvel to him who enters the country at the New York City gateway.

Truly it is marvelous; and equally truly, it is, to a remarkable degree, a monument to the genius of the late George A. Fuller—a pathfinder in his life work—and to the building corporation he created, the George A. Fuller Company.

Logical it is that to the Fuller Company was entrusted the work of building the greatest structure the Western Hemisphere has ever seen—the New York City terminal of the Pennsylvania Railroad Company. A genius for figures discovered that the old City Hall of America's metropolis could be set down, flagpole and all, under the great vaulted waiting-room, that in contour is so reminiscent of the ancient Baths of Caracalla, yet overtops in size and in dignity any other structure the world has seen.

More granite was used in its erection than was ever before utilized in a single piece of building construction.

The building, land it occupies, the river tunnels that made it possible, the immense problems that were overcome in its completion, represent an investment of $100,000,000.

And this building was reared, from foundations up, by the George A. Fuller Company.

It is a significant fact that the first skyscraper the visitor to this country sees, as his ship comes up the "Narrows" of New York Harbor, is a Fuller building. It is the majestic Whitehall Building, rising to a height of thirty-two stories from the grass-plots of Battery Park.

A glance at the buildings erected by the Fuller Company would indicate that the construction problems of a nation had been laid upon the doorstep of this house for solution.

When far-off Ottawa, Canada, desired an edifice that would be an honor to the fine old tradition of the city, the building of the Château Laurier was entrusted to the Fuller Company.

When the National City Bank of New York took over the old Custom House and decided to turn it into a banking house, it was the Fuller Company that removed every vestige of brick and plaster from the interior of the building, and, with the four bare walls as a shell, completed what is generally conceded to be the most practical and one of the most beautiful banking buildings in the world.

In the Downtown Building, in New York, the Fuller Company completed a construction record that will stand against time. Eight stories were standing; the specifications called for an addition of fourteen stories in the shortest possible time. The contract was signed October 17, 1910. Six months later, almost to the day, the completed twenty-two stories were turned over to the owners, with floors polished and windows cleaned, ready for tenants.

It is about twenty-five years since Mr. George A. Fuller, originally a young architect from New England, began to erect in Chicago the Tacoma Building, which was the first American skyscraper. This building marked the introduction of a new type of architecture. It also marked the beginning of the assumption by one company of the responsibility for the complete erection and equipment of large buildings. Both ideas originated with Mr. Fuller. The skyscraper was destined to solve a perplexing commercial problem affecting the property interests of great municipalities. It was also destined to inaugurate in all American cities great vertical expansion. Cities grew *upward,* instead of *outward.* Business was concentrated.

By one of those tricks of Fate, the company responsible for the first skyscraper was called upon to destroy the first concrete building consigned by ever-pressing Progress to the wrecker's pick and sledge.

The Baltimore *News* wanted an eighteen-story home; but before a foundation-stone could be laid, the paper's old home—a six-year-old, reinforced concrete building—must come down.

"Can't be done," said experts. "That's just what reinforced concrete is for—to stay, and not to be torn down."

Then a Fuller engineer looked over the job. He squinted up and down the old *News* building, pictured the fun of ripping off floor after floor, and then served notice on the paper to get out without delay.

"It's a tough bit of wrecking," he said, "but down she comes!"

And down she came! Hydraulic-drills bit into the concrete until the steel reinforcing-rods were laid bare. A white-hot glow, a few swift strokes from air-driven chisels, and the rods designed to bind the building together against all time gave way like threads.

The George A. Fuller Company needed no introduction to Baltimore—nor to any other city, for that matter—for it was in this city that the building world had one of its most emphatic demonstrations of the marvelous efficiency in the term "Fuller-Built."

After the great fire had swept Baltimore there were mighty few structures still standing in the path of the flames. In the midst of the ruins, block after block leveled around them, stood four "Fuller-Built" office buildings, stone-facing and frame work intact, and ready for occupancy the instant their interiors could be restored. The salvage on these buildings ran as high as eighty-five per cent.

Since George A. Fuller built his first skyscraper, the company that bears his name has superintended the erection of about 250 imposing structures, representing a total cost in excess of $300,000,000.

Representatives of the company point with pride to two full blocks on the Lake Front of Chicago in which every building—and there are seven large ones, including the University Club, the Athletic Club, and Montgomery, Ward & Co.—is the product of the Fuller organization. This is doubtless the most unique evidence of one builder's predominance in building history.

Of the many thousand who visit the New York Hippodrome every year, few realize the problems that faced the builders of it.

When the plans were submitted, few contractors would have cared to undertake a work so unprecedented. They called for a theater to cost $1,750,000, and to be larger than any other playhouse in the world. The dome was to cover nearly an acre in area, exceeded only by the Pantheon at Rome, and the stage was to be thirty-eight feet larger than that of La Scala, the famous opera house of Milan, which, until now, has had no rival in size.

The Fuller Company took the contract. Ground was broken July first, and on the twelfth of April, the following year, amid exclamations of wonder and delight from six thousand people, the first performance was given. New York —no, America—possessed the largest theater in the world!

The Fuller Company has reduced the art of building to an exact science. Serious mistakes and delays are practically eliminated. It operates a great manufacturing plant, whose products are million-dollar office buildings, great hotels, and beautiful theaters, all made to order and turned out complete "while you wait."

The president, Mr. Paul Starrett, and the vice-presidents, Mr. Walter H. Clough and Mr. W. A. Merriman, who are attached to the New York office, Mr. Leslie Witherspoon, who is in charge of the Western business, located at Chicago, Mr. James Baird, in Washington, and Mr. J. Edward Fuller, in Boston, are all young, aggressive men of great executive capacity, promoted from the ranks.

Institutions planning the erection of new homes, architects who have a problem before them that demands quick action with absolute certainty of result, are invited to correspond with the offices of the company, The George A. Fuller Company, 111 Broadway, New York City. Branch Offices: Chicago, Marquette Building; Boston, Board of Trade Building; Philadelphia, Morris Building; Washington, Munsey Building.

SERVICE BUILDINGS IN SUNNYSIDE YARD, LONG ISLAND CITY, N.Y.

JOHN W. FERGUSON CO., BUILDERS

NOT the least important feature of the great terminal of the Pennsylvania Railroad system entering New York are the buildings for motive power and other facilities at Sunnyside Yard, Long Island City, which were built by the John W. Ferguson Co. of Paterson, N.J.

If one stands on the Honeywell Street Viaduct which crosses the extensive Sunnyside Yard and looks west towards the East River, the first building in view is the massive Boiler House and Sub-station, 253 ft. long x 50 ft. wide, in which are located the boilers, engines, transformers and generators furnishing power, light and steam for the various buildings and yard purposes.

Beyond the Boiler House is the Battery Repair Building, 102 ft. x 67 ft.—and looking towards the river is to be seen the Stores and Lavatory Building, 162 ft. x 67 ft., and the Stores and Commissary Building, 258 ft. x 67 ft., where all the supplies are carried for the Pullman and dining car service for the trains leaving the New York Station.

In the distance may be seen smaller buildings used for the storage of supplies and cleaning of the Pullman cars.

From the same viewpoint, looking in the opposite direction down the yard or to the east, may be seen the Inspection Building and Machine Shop, 160 ft. x 71 ft., and the Oil and Lamp House, 67 ft. x 51 ft., which buildings are essential to the inspection and upkeep of the electric locomotives and cars which pass in and out of the main station.

In addition to the above buildings in the Sunnyside Yard, the Ferguson Company erected the various Signal Towers in Long Island City and at the Manhattan Transfer Yard near Newark, as well as two Blower Houses over the main tunnels on the Long Island side, and two on the Manhattan side of the East River, in which is installed elaborate machinery for ventilating the various tubes under the river.

In all, this company has erected some twenty buildings for the Pennsylvania Tunnel & Terminal Railroad Co. in connection with the general improvement of the New York Station.

Some idea of the magnitude of the construction work embodied in these buildings can be obtained from the following figures covering the principal items of material used:

Structural steel	1,890,550 lbs.
Brick	2,194,500
Portland cement	18,630 bbls.
Broken stone for concrete work	6,900 cu. yds.

If the stone alone were loaded on ordinary freight cars, it would require 345 cars to transport it, making about ten average train loads.

The buildings were designed by the Pennsylvania Tunnel & Terminal Railroad Co.'s Engineering Staff and the work was done under the supervision of the following officials:

ALFRED NOBLE, Chief Engineer, East River Division.

GEORGE GIBBS, Chief Engineer, Electric Traction and Station Construction.

LOUIS H. BARKER, Resident Engineer.

E. R. HILL, Asst. to Chief Engineer, E. T. & S. C.

JOHN W. FERGUSON

JOHN FRANCIS O'ROURKE

President of the O'Rourke Engineering Construction Co., Contractors for the North River Tunnels

JOHN F. O'ROURKE was born in Ireland about fifty years ago and was brought to America by his parents when he was still an infant. He was educated in the public schools and after graduating from them he entered Cooper Union, taking the five-year engineering course and graduating with the degree of Bachelor of Science, to which was subsequently added those of Civil Engineer and Mechanical Engineer. About twenty years ago he was married to Katharine B. Innis, of Poughkeepsie, a member of the well-known family of pioneers in the chemical and dyewood industries of the country.

His engineering career started in the office of Charles Guidet, a well-known contractor. While with Mr. Guidet he served, when only seventeen years of age, as superintendent on the construction of the first elevated railways. Mr. O'Rourke next entered the office of Edward Boyle, then the most prominent civil engineer in New York, as a student. Since that time he has been connected with engineering work, either as engineer or contractor.

Among the larger enterprises with which he has been connected are the Elevated Railway, the West Shore Railway, the St. Croix River bridge of the Wisconsin Central Railroad, the Chignecto Ship Railway between the Bay of Fundy and the Gulf of St. Lawrence, various Harlem River bridges and the Poughkeepsie bridge. The last-named structure has, with one exception, the deepest subaqueous foundations in the world and the project was prose-

JOHN FRANCIS O'ROURKE

cuted by Mr. O'Rourke, who was the chief engineer, in such a vigorous manner that the last pin was driven in the river trusses on the second anniversary of the signing of the contract. The construction of tall buildings opened up another field for Mr. O'Rourke's ingenuity and he has provided the foundations of many of the noted skyscrapers. The pneumatic caisson was first used for foundation work by Mr. O'Rourke, when he installed the foundations of the Commercial Cable Building. The same kind of foundation was provided by him for the New York Stock Exchange, where the caissons were formed into a continuous dam, the masonry being connected from caisson to caisson. This was a new departure and a successful one for although forty feet of water surrounds the deep cellar of this building it is absolutely dry. He also laid the foundations of the Hanover Bank Building, the Atlantic Mutual Building, the Blair Building, the City Investing Building, the New Whitehall Building and a number of others.

Probably his best-known works are the construction of the tunnels of the New York Central & Hudson River Railroad north of Forty-second Street, New York City, and that of the Pennsylvania Railroad tunnels under the North River to the station in New York City. Both of these projects were carried out with great skill and the speed with which the latter was accomplished, as well as the character of the work itself, has placed Mr. O'Rourke and his company in the front rank of large engineering constructors.

Gamewell Emergency Alarm System

THE Emergency Alarm System furnished by the Gamewell Fire Alarm Telegraph Company, and installed throughout all of the Pennsylvania Tunnels, is one of the important and interesting services maintained for the protection of the public.

Signal boxes are located at frequent and regular intervals throughout the tunnels, and are connected by special circuits with special devices controlling the power circuit breakers in the several power stations. Each of these emergency boxes is capable of transmitting two different signals, one indicating "Fire" and the other "Emergency."

In the event of fire or accident, the operation of an emergency box will instantly cause the circuit-breakers controlling the third rail in the particular section where such box is located, to be thrown and the power thus cut off from the rail. This operation is immediately and automatically followed by the transmission of a location signal over the entire system, thus notifying responsible officials of the exact location where such emergency has occurred.

This system, therefore, makes directly for the safety of life and property, by immediately removing the dangers of a "live" rail in the vicinity of an accident, and by enabling the officials of the road to quickly and intelligently place other protective measures in operation.

CHAPTER 1
PENNSY'S ELECTRIC
TRACTION BACKGROUND

Without a doubt the Pennsylvania Railroad Company's entrance into New York City's Manhattan Island, represented one of the most courageous and complex engineering feats of the twentieth century.

Underwater tunnels ruled out operation of steam powered trains. Electric motive power was essential, for upon it the success of the project depended. And both gearless, initially, and later geared side-rod drive electric locomotives were, until the coming of alternating current locomotives, an inseparable part of Penn Station.

As for the electric locomotives of class DD1, that played so vital a part, they proved an unqualified success with their gearless jack-shaft side-rod drive. In carrying millions of passengers to and from Penn Station, they once and for all removed the Hudson River barrier that had so long tied Pennsy trains to the New Jersey shore.

All this was made possible by the new concept of a high-powered electric locomotive, novel in the United States, the famed DD1's. Later came the L5 group and their sub-classes with their geared jack-shaft, side-rod drive, but they were not primarily meant to replace class DD1, for nothing at the time as far as the Pennsy was concerned could have done that. When we see what these DD1's could do in regard to operating performance as recorded in Chapter 6, this viewpoint becomes readily understandable.

Electrification of the Pennsylvania Tunnel and Terminal Railroad, between Sunnyside Yard, Long Island City, N.Y., and Manhattan Transfer, N.J., 13.66 miles in length, was not, however, the Pennsy's first use of electric powered passenger trains. It is, therefore, appropriate at this point to review this railroad's earlier ventures in electric traction.

As far back as 1895, the Pennsylvania Railroad had inaugurated electric traction for passenger service on their Burlington and Mount Holly Branch. It is interesting to note that this application was just slightly pre-dated by the Baltimore & Ohio Railroad's electrification in Baltimore, Md., that same year. The Pennsy electrification was purely a local transit system, and electric locomotives were not used. Multiple-unit (MU) cars similar to those used on interurban lines provided the service.

One of my Baldwin colleagues, Edward O. Elliott, former Chief Draftsman of the Philadelphia & Reading Railway, at Reading, Pa., designed some of the finest steam locomotives on this road to ever grace American rails, was the engineer of this Pennsy project. He designed the steam power plant, supervised the installation of its equipment, together with the trolley system, and design of the cars.

Although a comparatively small electrified operation, to Elliott goes the distinction of being the first to electrify Pennsy trackage for passenger service. It is this writer's view that Mr. Elliott receive recognition for this initial application of Pennsy electrification, hence this reference regarding his association with it. Eddie Elliott, like my friend Paul T. Warner, was a fountain of knowledge concerning locomotives, and to hear either of them discourse on this subject was a treat.

A larger and more significant electrification project was completed on the Long Island Railroad in 1905. In 1900 this road had become a part of the Pennsy, and electrified passenger train operation began on some of its western lines in 1905. Trains of multiple-unit equipment using direct current at 650 volts, fed this power to the cars

Notice to public indicating commencement of service between Hudson Terminal, New York, to PRR train shed in Jersey City, on July 19, 1909.

from an over-running type third-rail. At that time these trains terminated their runs at Flatbush and Atlantic Avenues, in Brooklyn, N.Y. Power was supplied by a large power plant to serve the Pennsylvania Railroad and the Long Island Railroad. It was adjacent to the East River, just a bit north of the Long Island Railroad station, in Long Island City, that still operated trains from, and to, that point with steam power. From there ferryboats made connection with Manhattan at east 34th Street, and James Slip. Later, due to the construction of Penn Station, most Long Island Railroad passenger trains ran directly from and to that point as well as the Brooklyn terminal. The Penn Station service began on Thursday, September 8th, 1910, with a LIRR, MU train, thereby, preceding Pennsy electric locomotive train operation from the huge station which commenced at 12:01 a.m., on Sunday, November 27, 1910.

Another large electric traction project for passenger service was put into operation in 1906 on another Pennsy subsidiary line, the West Jersey and Seashore Railroad. This was a double-tracked, and, at some places a triple-tracked railroad between Camden and Atlantic City, N.J., for a distance of 64.4 miles. At Newfield Junction, a single track branch diverged to the Cape May Division, where electric powered trains ran for 10 miles to Millville, N.J., where steam locomotives took over for points south. Service on the electrified line was provided by MU car trains operated at 650 volts DC, from an over-running third-rail, and from an overhead trolley wire at certain loca-

tions. Cars were originally of wooden construction, but later, steel cars with clerestory roofs similar to those first used on the Long Island Railroad, went into service. Later, this same WJ&SS RR., was instrumental in developing the final electric locomotive design that inaugurated train operation in Penn Station; but more of this anon.

In 1906 still more electrified passenger train operation took place on a portion of the Cumberland Valley Railroad, another Pennsy line. This was in its operating features much like the Burlington & Mt. Holly Branch, and regarded mainly as an interurban road. Like the WJ&SS RR., the Cumberland Valley line has long since ceased straight-electric operation.

Another electrified section of the Pennsylvania Railroad appeared when part of the New York Division went into operation on October 1, 1911. Hudson & Manhattan rapid transit MU trains then ran between downtown New York's Hudson Terminal buildings at 30 and 50 Church Street and Manhattan Transfer, N.J. In this way H&M received trackage rights on the Pennsy, which later in turn obtained a station in downtown New York for their inbound and outbound trains. Later in 1911, the H&M was extended west of Manhattan Transfer, on their own elevated structure operating trains to Fourth Street, Harrison, and a terminal at Park Place, Newark, N.J.

For this longer run between Hudson Terminal and Newark, different and more powerful MU cars were used than the original Stillwell car.

Pennsy's first application of electric traction was also believed to be the first use of electrified train operation for high-speed passenger service on a steam railroad. Motor car No. 1, at extreme left of picture was built by Brill, in Philadelphia, Pa. Motor car No. 1, was hauling a standard PRR open platform wooden coach for an experimental run on June 3, 1895. Regular service began on July 22, 1895, between Burlington, and Mount Holly, New Jersey. I believe a fire ultimately destroyed the power plant completely, whereupon, the Pennsy discontinued electrified operation and went back to steam power.

These new cars had a class M-38 designation with some furnished by the H&M, and were so lettered in gold leaf on their Pennsy tuscan red sides. Others were supplied by the Pennsylvania Railroad and were so indicated in similar painted coloring.

Prior to this long range electrified train service, a steam powered shuttle service operated between Manhattan Transfer and Jersey City. This was not wholly satisfactory as passengers still had to make another change to H&M trains at Exchange Place station, many feet below the old Jersey City Terminal, and its huge imposing train shed of beloved memory. Nevertheless, since July 19, 1909, this mode of transportation provided all rail pas-

senger service between stations on the Pennsylvania Railroad and downtown New York. Some passengers, however, still took the splendid Pennsy tuscan red ferryboats that sported double decks and several had double stacks. But after the opening of Penn Station on November 27, 1910, the 23rd Street ferry, and that which sailed to the Brooklyn Annex, were discontinued. But Pennsy patrons could still avail themselves of the two remaining ferries to Cortlandt or Desbrosses Streets, New York, which continued to operate for some years after 1910.

It might be pertinent here to point out that the H&M was the first railroad company to operate standard gauge electrically propelled trains

under the Hudson River. This brought to reality a nebulous dream that had long been suggested and actually attempted at times, once with disastrous and fatal results. William Gibbs McAdoo, was the dynamic force behind the H&M success, and it was due to him and the far-sighted cooperation of Pennsy President Alexander Johnston Cassatt, that it all came to pass.

The Hudson & Manhattan Railroad Company is now know as PATH (Port Authority Trans-Hudson Corporation) since September 1, 1962. Now PATH trains run directly to Pennsy's station in Newark, though, after electrification of the Pennsy's main line, H&M trains still using the old

M-38 class cars did likewise. Use of the old elevated structure was discontinued and Fourth Street, Harrison station was moved to the main line. Today, however, newer and speedier MU car trains take passengers from the towering Trade Center buildings in New York to Newark.

For a detailed description of H&M, from its inception to PATH, this author heartily recommends an excellent book titled, RAILS UNDER THE MIGHTY HUDSON, by Brian J. Cudahy. Included is a graphic description of Manhattan Transfer, that endows this locale with a mystique rarely met with in the field of railroad operation.

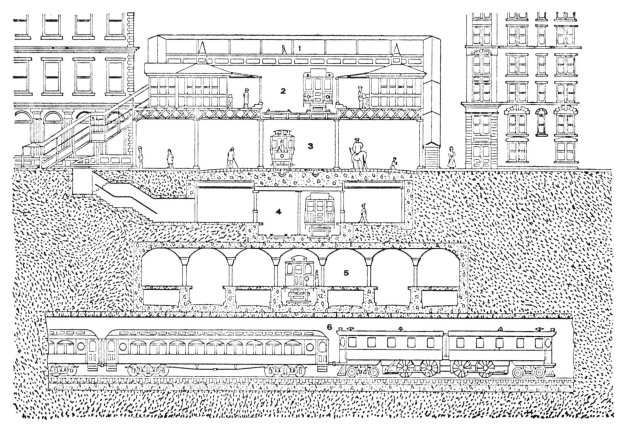

CROSS-SECTION ON SIXTH AVENUE AT 33d STREET.

1	Foot Passage	4	Proposed Rapid Transit Subway
2	Manhattan Elevated R.R.	5	Hudson and Manhattan R.R. Station
3	Street Surface and Metropolitan St. Ry.	6	Pennsylvania R.R. Tunnel

Fig. 33.

A ten-car train bound for New York, passing Marion, in west Jersey City. Train was made up of tuscan red cars of class M-38.

Many years later we see a stoker-fired K4s class engine No. 5367, bound for Point Pleasant, N.J., with an express train. Eastbound an H&M train still using M-38 class cars operating on DC from the third-rail is approaching Journal Square Station, originally known as Summit Avenue Station, in Jersey City. Photo also taken at Marion.

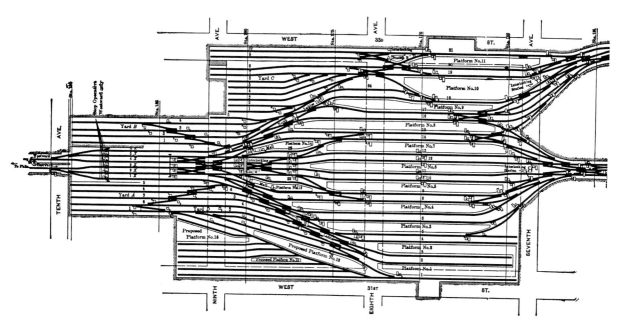

GENERAL TRACK PLAN PENN STATION, NEW YORK

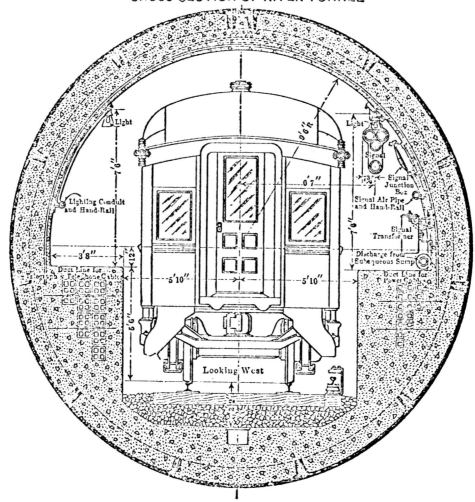

Cross section of PRR tunnel under Hudson River.

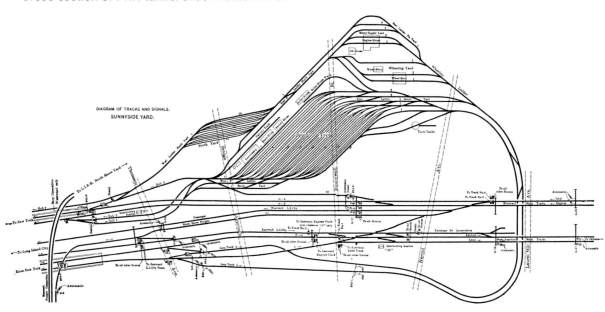

Diagram of Tracks and Signals at Sunnyside Yard.

CHAPTER 2
PROBLEMS FOR A COMMITTEE

A brief description of Penn Station's electric locomotives has been given in the first part of this book. But a more detailed account of events leading to the final choice of these locomotives is covered in this second part.

Engineers of the highest competency could make certain the success of the underwater tunnels, and other engineering difficulties. Architects would, and did, provide a beautiful station building fully expressive in presenting the proper image of the great railroad for which it was built, while its constructional durability could guarantee a life span of centuries to come. But to insure successful finality of this momentous project, electrification, and electric locomotives, were a vital ingredient; and there came the big problem.

With quick characteristic decisiveness, President Cassatt, appreciating the urgency of this situation appointed a special four man Committee to investigate existing designs, and develop by experiment or otherwise, a suitable electric locomotive for the exacting conditions of the proposed service. The Committee consisted of George Gibbs, Chief Engineer Electric Traction, and Station Construction, who acted as Chairman, Alfred W. Gibbs, General Superintendent of Motive Power, Pennsylvania Lines East, David F. Crawford, General Superintendent of Motive Power, Pennsylvania Lines West, and Axel S. Vogt, Mechanical Engineer, Pennsylvania Railroad, Altoona, Pa.

The Committee was well chosen. These four gentlemen, with George Gibbs, as Chairman, were authorities on the subject of locomotive design. They concentrated mainly on mechanical details and set specifications regarding train hauling demands. Westinghouse Electric &

Manufacturing Company (now Westinghouse Electric, or plain Westinghouse, as I shall refer to it) was commissioned to work out the details of the electrical equipment to meet the service requirements.

An important question to settle at the start was which electrical current to use for train propulsion. In view of the predominance of direct-current (DC) at the time, and which was known to be reliable as proved by its extensive use in the United States on rapid transit lines, and lengthy suburban electrified railroads, its use was deemed advisable. Furthermore, the Locomotive Committee preferred to conform to the DC system already installed on the Long Island Railroad, and proposed for the Hudson & Manhattan Railroad. They, therefore, decided against alternating current (AC), making it plain, however, that the decision to use DC for locomotive and multiple-unit car operation was not a blanket endorsement for this form of power for possible extensions of future Pennsylvania Railroad electrified trackage. Only the particular circumstances at the time dictated its use.

By 1905, the Committee had produced two electric locomotives originally numbered 10001, and 10002, to possibly operate in the New York Terminal and Tunnel area of the Pennsylvania Railroad. Both units consisted of two four-wheel trucks with motors for each axle. In each case the trucks were articulated at the center, and carried the necessary draft gear at their ends, thereby, having the drawbar pull transmitted through the truck frames, and not through the cab superstructure.

The distribution system which fed power to cars and locomotives, was by the over-running type of third-rail, at 650 volts, DC. This, as has been noted, matched that on the Long Island and future Hudson & Manhattan Railroads.

These two experimental locomotives had their mechanical parts built at the Juniata Shops of the Pennsy at Altoona, Pa., but were equipped with electrical equipment at the East Pittsburgh Works, of Westinghouse, where they were completely assembled for road service. Motor No. 10001 was built in August 1905, and No. 10002, in September 1905. Both featured box-cab, superstructures, and were dismally plain in appearance with long overhanging roofs at each end.

The motor drive for No. 10001, was the old nose-suspended, or "wheelbarrow" direct-geared arrangement. This drive had a pinion on the motor shaft directly driving a gear on the axle. One end of the motor frame was carried in bearings on the axle; the other end by proper nose suspension on the truck frame. Disadvantages of this arrangement were the low center of gravity of the motor's considerable unsprung weight, and gear wear, particularly that of the pinions. Nevertheless, this form of drive, quite common on comparatively small-wheeled rapid transit MU cars as well as present day diesel-electric locomotives has wide application. This is due to the necessity for much required headroom above the trucks. In one instance that needed by passengers in MU car trains, and room for the "high-boy" diesel engine on diesel locomotives.

The motors of No. 10001, were in pairs between pairs of axles, and in consequence the gyratory, or revolving disturbance was less than where the motor center coincided with that of the axle. On the other locomotive, No. 10002, the gearless quill drive was used. With this arrangement the armature of the motor was not mounted on the axle directly, but on a quill, or hollow tubular shaft through which the axle passed without touching it. Inside the quill was a radial clearance separating the outside diameter of the axle from the inner diameter of the quill. This distance was enough to allow vertical movement of the axle while permitting the motor to be rigidly fastened and spring supported on the truck frame. At each end of the quill was a plate, from which projected several round pins. These pins fitted into corresponding sockets on the inside of each wheel hub, which was made specially large for the purpose.

Springs of special design were placed between the pins and the sides of the sockets, and when the quill revolved the wheels propelled the locomotive.

Locomotives Nos. 10001, and 10002, were designed for a maximum speed of 45 mph., on level track. They could develop 1,350 horsepower with a normal train, for at the time it was intended to limit terminal electric operation to the haul through the tunnels from the west portal at Bergen Hill, N.J., to Penn Station, and Sunnyside Yard, in Long Island City, N.Y. Practically all this portion of the line is on heavy grades for a short distance only, and a slow speed would make for economy while not prohibitive as to time consumed. Later, it was planned to extend the terminal run to Harrison, N.J., on the west, and possibly to Jamaica on the east, involving level stretches of about ten miles from either end of Penn Station. Thus it became necessary to adapt the locomotives to the higher speed conditions normally made in main-line operations, and the two locomotives were modified electrically to provide a maximum speed of 65 mph.

Tests with these locomotives on the Long Island Railroad had shown their hauling power and successful operation at the slow speed for which they were originally designed, but when speeded up it was found that they became quite destructive to track. At speeds greater than 45 mph., they developed a tendency to rhythmic side swaying, or "nosing," and produced excessive lateral, or heavy side pressures at the rail heads.

It was, therefore, decided by the Committee to arrange a series of road tests to bring out more fully the details of electric lomomotive design affecting tracking operation at high speed. These tests were to record as far as practicable the comparative lateral rail pressures at various speeds with several types of steam and electric locomotives. A special recording device for the purpose was devised and placed on a stretch of tangent and curved track near Franklinville, N.J., on the newly electrified West Jersey & Seashore Railroad, to which reference has been made in Chapter 1.

The next Chapter has outline diagram drawings of Nos. 10001, and 10002, and other locomotives that provided much informative data relating to the track tests are also illustrated.

The electric locomotive second from the right, adjacent to the DD-1, is allegedly No. 10001. After the West Jersey track tests it went to the Penn Station area where it operated as No. 8, in switching service in December, 1910. At that time the Pennsy used a four digit group of 3900 series numbers to designate electric locomotives. Motor No. 8, was listed on their records as No. 3950. These 3900 numbers were also later used on the DD1's with each semi-unit carrying a different cab number. This enabled enginemen to identify defects in the cab or cabs involved with precision, and shopmen to quickly duplicate equipment, such as compressors, and electrical control details. In May, 1916, No. 8, went to the Long Island Railroad, where it became No. 323, and remained there until scrapped in August 1937. Building in background was the Sunnyside engine house where electric locomotives were maintained. Heaviest repairs, however, were made at the Meadows Shops, in New Jersey. On the Long Island Railroad No. 323 was known as "Phoebe."

What appears to be the same picture and location taken from the other side of the track, is supposedly No. 10002, Pennsy's second main line electric locomotive, and was so listed on the photograph. It was assigned No. 9, in December, 1910, but on Pennsy records was listed as "Odd 3951." Motor No. 9, operated in switching service at Penn Station, and Sunnyside, until scrapped July, 1, 1937. Both locomotives had similar cab superstructures. Pennsy men used to call No. 9, "The covered wagon."

CHAPTER 3
ROAD TESTS AND ANSWERS

As the West Jersey & Seashore Railroad was available regarding current and voltage, an experimental track with special ties which would make a permanent record of the lateral or side impacts of the locomotives was prepared in 1907 near Franklinville, N.J. It was expected that the bad oscillations would occur on curves, if anywhere, therefore, only one end of each tie was arranged to register the impacts.

The line drawings show one of the recording ties; the other rail being so constructed that the rail was free laterally resting on rollers, resisted against outward movement by a bracket carrying a strip of boiler plate, movable longitudinally at will. Against this strip rested a one-inch steel ball which in turn bedded in a plunger bearing against the outside face of the rails which were of Pennsy standard weighing 100 pounds per yard.

Records obtained in this manner simulated a series of glorified Brinnell tests with the depth of the one-inch ball in the boiler plate being taken as a measure of the impact. After each run the plates were slipped longitudinally and adjusted to touch the ball, each single plate taking the record of 30 or more runs.

The recording ties, 80 in number, extending over five rail lengths or a total distance of 165 feet, were laid on a one-degree curve in the south-bound track near Franklinville. It was here that the first tests were made. At the completion of the runs on the curved track, the recording ties were removed to the tangent track north of the Franklinville station where the trials were completed. Four trips were used for the tests on the curves, and seven for those on the tangent.

Other apparatus used in the tests consisted of speed recorders on the locomotives, and in some runs a seismograph was placed on the locomotives having three pendulums, giving vibrations in vertical, transverse and longitudinal direction.

Two West Jersey & Seashore Railroad steam locomotives were included in the tests, one, No. 6034, class D16b, of the American (4-4-0) type, built in 1904, and the other, No. 6020, class E2, of the Atlantic (4-4-2) type, built in 1902. Driving

wheels were 68 and 80 inches respectively, and both engines were built at the Pennsy's Juniata Shops, Altoona, Pa.

We have seen how the Locomotive Committee came up with two electric locomotives, namely, Nos. 10001 and 10002, which were used previously on the Long Island Railroad then sent to the West Jersey. To further delve into the subject of locomotive stability at speed, a brand-new 1,000 hp. passenger electric locomotive No. 028, built in January 1907 by Baldwin-Westinghouse for the New York, New Haven & Hartford Railroad, of the 0-4-4-0 type, was also tested. This locomotive like No. 10002, had a motor for each axle using a gearless quill drive. Its traction motors, however, differed from the other electric locomotives in their being arranged for DC, and/or AC. Mechanical parts were built by Baldwin using Westinghouse electrical equipment.

New Haven locomotives of this type ran into Grand Central Terminal where third-rail DC operation prevailed. At Woodlawn Junction, the New Haven locomotives switched from the New York Central's Harlem Division, to the New Haven, and a changeover to AC operation was made. There the pantographs collected single-phase current at 11,000 volts, with a frequency of 25 cycles, from an overhead catenary system. Control equipment suitable for running on DC or AC, was contained within the cab, giving this locomotive, No. 028, and others like it built in 1907, for the New Haven, decided flexibility.

Unlike Nos. 10001 and 10002, the New Haven locomotive No. 028, did not have its trucks linked together. Instead, their two four-wheel powered trucks were pivotally connected to the cab underframe which carried the draft gear details. This may have accounted somewhat for their superior tracking when compared with the pioneer Pennsy electric locomotives. Nonetheless, it was deemed advisable after the locomotives had operated on the New Haven some time, to add a two-wheel pony truck at each front end of the four wheel driving trucks. This truck was designed by

This locomotive was not included in the track tests but illustrates a symmetrical wheelbase. It was of the 2-4-2 Columbia type, built by Baldwin in 1893. On the road this engine and others like it showed a marked tendency for much side swaying against the rails at high speed. The objectionable actions of such wheel arrangements in general were confirmed by electric locomotives with symmetrical wheel arrangements on the West Jersey track tests.

Baldwin, and materially improved the stability of these New Haven locomotives. These locomotives usually operated in multiple, two units for a train, and they achieved outstanding performance records.

Another electric locomotive that proved to set the final base design, was furnished gratuitously by Westinghouse, was tested and numbered 10003. It had an eight-wheel American type wheel arrangement and was built in 1907. The performance of this particular locomotive on both curved and tangent tracks put it in the class of the best records made by the two steam locomotives.

Locomotive No. 10003, was so superior in lessened nosing, or lateral side swaying against the rails under all conditions, and speeds, that it became the basis for the standard DD1 class design built for the tunnel and terminal service. This locomotive was, however, equipped for AC operation which necessitated provision for DC operation. Electrical equipment to permit this was placed in a separate car that always accompanied the locomotive on DC trackage.

Through the courtesy of the Franklin Institute in Philadelphia, I am enabled to present the following summation from an engineer prominently associated with the track tests. This was an engineer of high repute, Alfred W. Gibbs, and in his talk at the Franklin Institute, on November 19, 1921, who as a former member of the Locomotive Committee, spoke as follows.

"The outstanding fact seemed to be the superior performance of the locomotive with the non-symmetrical wheel arrangement over that with

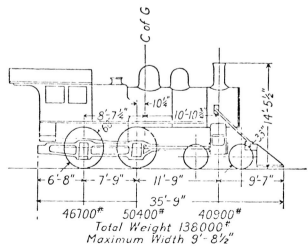

American Type (4-4-0) Locomotive.

129

the double four-wheel motor-driven trucks. The articulated truck arrangement was undoubtedly the worst of the combinations, but how much of this was due to the low center of gravity and how much to the articulation setting up a snaking motion was not definitely established.

"It is to be noted that one of the double-truck motor-driven locomotives (No. 10002) and one with two driving axles and leading truck (No. 10003) had the same height of center of gravity, and the latter was decidedly the better. The comparison is the more interesting because in both of these locomotives the same quill-drive type is used.

"The action as the result of the tests was the condemnation of both types of articulated electric locomotives and the preparation of an entirely new design.

"The new design consisted of two eight-wheel American type locomotives coupled back to back, each driven by one motor in the cab and coupled by cranks and rods to a jack-shaft placed in the horizontal axis of the driving wheels, and coupled to them by rods, as in the case of steam locomotives. In this design were embodied not only the non-symmetrical wheel spacing of each semi-unit, but also the elevation of the center of gravity of the spring-borne portion. This design was completed and locomotives built and tested in time to start the operation of the New York Terminal in 1910, and the locomotives have satisfactorily performed that service ever since.

"It is not claimed that the question of stability is fully understood. The selection of available wheel arrangements was very limited, but prompt decision was imperative. It is felt that this investigation should be considered as only a starting point for a much more extensive one, which should determine the most desirable arrangement of wheels, of height of center of gravity, and method of motor drive.

"So far as this particular investigation was concerned, the question of electric system was not involved, but, of course, a full discussion of the characteristics of steam and electric locomotives cannot ignore such questions.

"Since this set of tests with single-ended ties, other series have been made in which ties were arranged to record at each end. More ties were used so as to lengthen the test track. As for the equipment, the test included different methods of coupling the semi-units of electric locomotives; also studying the effect of depressions purposely placed in the approach track, the effect of different amounts of end clearance in the axle boxes, variation in the amount of counterbalancing in steam locomotives, etc. The whole accumulation of data is too voluminous to be included in one paper. Although considerable practical information of value has resulted from various trials,

The non-symmetrical steam locomotive of the American 4-4-0 type of the Penna. RR., class D16b, turned in a fine performance. This type was noted for its smooth running. Photo shown, however, is of a class D16a engine which had 80-inch drivers while the D16b had 68-inch drivers.

130

An engine of class E2 similar to the one used in the West Jersey track tests. Note that it was of the non-symmetrical 4-4-2 Atlantic type. This locomotive turned in a fine performance as did the American type, and apparently bore out the possibility that non-symmetrical wheel arrangements combined with a high center of gravity reduced lateral thrust impacts against the rails.

there is much work yet to be done before the questions of stability are really understood. It is to be regretted that the selection of electric locomotives did not include greater variations in the wheel base, the method of articulation and height of center of gravity, but it is believed that the work already done is a very good starting point for future investigations."

The final conclusions of Mr. Gibbs, could well be pertinent today in view of difficulties encountered on trucks for high-speed operation on some diesel and electric locomotives. Further in-depth track test studies may well cast light on the cause of these troublesome actions.

In connection with the track tests the Locomotive Committee expressed their appreciation to Westinghouse for their wholehearted cooperation in every instance concerning the tests and search for the most efficient locomotive. Many helpful suggestions were made by them and successfully acted upon. Electrical equipment for the first two locomotives, Nos. 10001 and 10002, was also furnished at Westinghouse's own expense, while No. 10003, with mechanical parts by Baldwin was wholly paid for by Westinghouse.

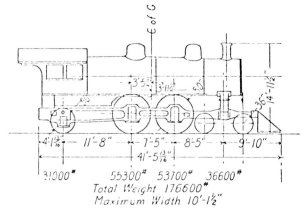

Atlantic Type (4-4-2) Locomotive.

FIG. 12.

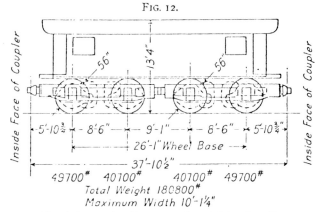

Electric Locomotive, No. 10,001, Geared Drive Type B.

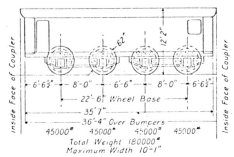

Electric Locomotive, No. 028, Quill Drive, Type C. Pivotted Truck.

FIG. 16.

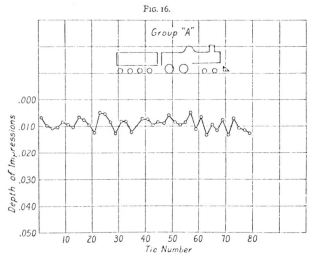

Steam Locomotive, American Type (4-4-0), Speed 83.5 M.P.H. on Curve.

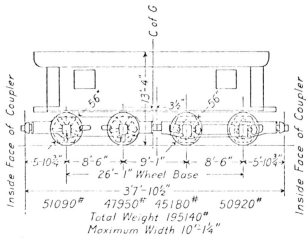

Electric Locomotive, No. 10,002, Quill Drive Type C.

FIG. 14.

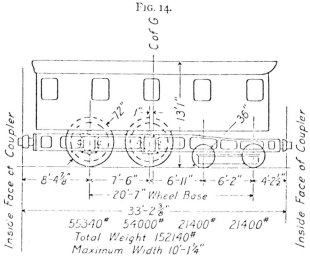

Electric Locomotive, No. 10,003, Quill Drive Type C.

Considered from various standpoints these locomotives ranked as follows:

As regards wheel-base:

	Total Wheel-base	Distance center to center of trucks.
Electric Loco. No. 10,003	20' 7"	17' 6"
Electric Loco. No. 028	22' 6"	14' 6"
Steam, American Type (4-4-0)	22' 9½"	19' 6"
Electric, No. 10,001 and No. 10,002	26' 1"	17' 7"
Steam, Atlantic Type (4-4-2)	30' 9½"	

As regards center of gravity:

	Vertically	Longitudinally
Electric Loco. No. 10,002	42½" above rail	3½" from center
Electric Loco. No. 10,001	45¼"	Centrally
Electric Loco. No. 028	55"	Centrally
Electric Loco. No. 10,003	55"	1" ahead of front drivers
Steam, American Type, (4-4-0)	63"	10¼" ahead of front drivers
Steam, Atlantic Type, (4-4-2)	73"	41¼" ahead of rear drivers

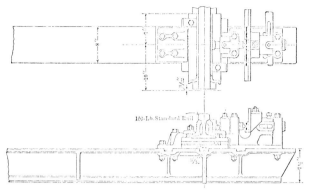

SPECIAL TRACK TIE AND REGISTERING DEVICE
FOR LOCOMOTIVE TESTS.

A rare picture of an electric locomotive similar to No. 028, of the New York, New Haven & Hartford Railroad.

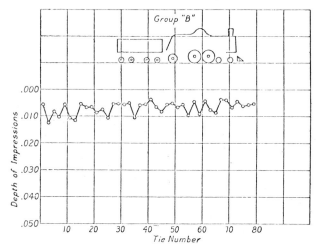

Steam Locomotive, Atlantic Type (4-4-2), Speed 95.7 M.P.H., on Curve.

FIG. 18.

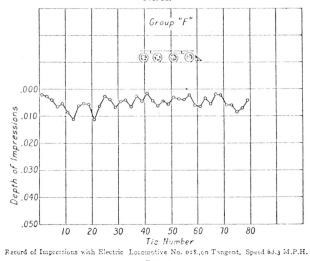

Record of Impressions with Electric Locomotive No. 10,008, on Tangent, Speed 83.3 M.P.H.

FIG. 23.

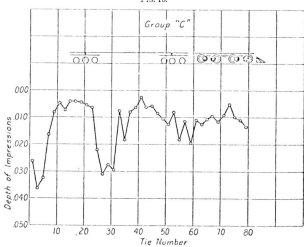

Electric Geared Locomotive, No. 10,001, Speed 71.5 M.P.H., on Curve.

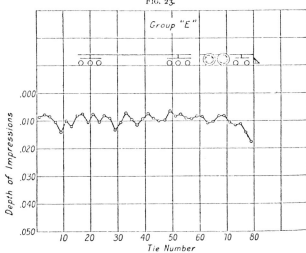

Record of Impressions with Electric Locomotive No. 10,003, (4-4-0), Speed 82.6 M.P.H. on Curve.

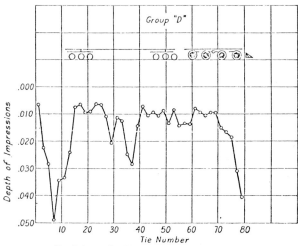

Electric Locomotive, No. 10,002, Speed 68.3 M.P.H., on Curve.

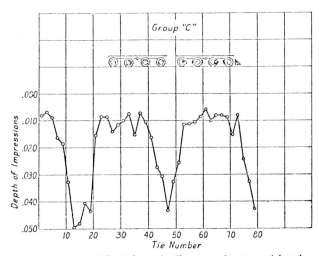

Record of Impressions with Electric Locomotives Nos. 10,001 and 10,002., coupled speed 71.6 M.P.H., on curve.

The severity of the impacts from the impressions measured statically is indicated by the following notes on rail pressures at speeds above 60 miles per hour:

Group A—Steam Locomotive.

No. 6034, Type D-16b (4-4-0).

Maximum readings of 6 runs, speeds between 60.07 and 83.2 M.P.H.

At 60.07 M.P.H.—Impression .0135"—Pressure 7250 lbs.

At 80.0 M.P.H.—Impression .0141"—Pressure 7580 lbs.

Average—74.3 M.P.H.—Impression .0123"—Pressure 6610 lbs.

Group B—Steam Locomotive.

No. 6020, Type E-2, (4-4-2).

Maximum readings of 7 runs, speeds between 59.6 and 95.7 M.P.H.

At 71.2 M.P.H.—Impression .0129"—Pressure 6930 lbs.

At 80.8 M.P.H.—Impression .0159"—Pressure 6550 lbs.

Average—74.4 M.P.H.—Impression .0123"—Pressure 6500 lbs.

Group C—Electric Locomotive No. 10,001.

Forward, No. 2 end ahead.

Maximum readings of 6 runs, speeds between 61.1 and 71.3 M.P.H.

At 71.3 M.P.H.—Impression .0272"—Pressure 14620 lbs.

At 67.9 M.P.H.—Impression .0193"—Pressure 10370 lbs.

Average—64.5 M.P.H.—Impression .0165"—Pressure 8870 lbs.

Reversed, No. 1 end ahead.

Maximum readings of 4 runs, speeds between 60.9 and 70.1 M.P.H.

At 62 and 70.1 M.P.H.—Impression .0289"—Pressure 15530 lbs.

At 69.7 M.P.H.—Impression .0298"—Pressure 16000 lbs.

Average—65.7 M.P.H.—Impression .0267"—Pressure 14350 lbs.

Group D—Electric Locomotive No. 10,002.

Maximum readings of 4 runs, speeds between 60.8 and 60.8 and 68.1 M.P.H.

At 62.8 M.P.H.—Impression .039"—Pressure 20960 lbs.

At 66.0 M.P.H.—Impression .0311"—Pressure 16720 lbs.

Average—64.4 M.P.H.—Impression .0291"—Pressure 15640 lbs.

Group E—Electric Locomotive No. 10,003 (4-4-0).

Forward, bolster free.

Maximum readings of 8 runs, speeds between 60.8 and 88.3 M.P.H.

At 63.3 M.P.H.—Impression .0123"—Pressure 6610 lbs.

At 72.38 M.P.H.—Impression .0125"—Pressure 6720 lbs.

Average—74.1 M.P.H.—Impression .0113"—Pressure 6070 lbs.

Forward, bolster blocked.

Maximum readings of 6 runs, speeds between 60.0 and 83.9 M.P.H.

At 75.1 M.P.H.—Impression .0179"—Pressure 9620 lbs.

At 83.9 M.P.H.—Impression .0193"—Pressure 10370 lbs.

Average—73.5 M.P.H.—Impression .0149"—Pressure 8010 lbs.

Reversed, bolster blocked.

Maximum readings of 5 runs, speeds between 65.5 and 84.0 M.P.H.

At 65.5 and 70 M.P.H.—Impression .0115"—Pressure 6180 lbs.

At 68.2 M.P.H.—Impression .0117"—Pressure 6290 lbs.

Average—74.04 M.P.H.—Impression .0106"—Pressure 5700 lbs.

Reversed, bolster free.

Maximum readings of 5 runs, speeds between 60.4 and 77.5 M.P.H.

At 68.9 M.P.H.—Impression .0289"—Pressure 15530 lbs.

At 70.2 M.P.H.—Impression .0281"—Pressure 15100 lbs.

Average—68.9 M.P.H.—Impression .0236"—Pressure 12700 lbs.

Group F—New Haven Electric Locomotive No. 028.

Maximum readings of 9 runs, speeds between 60 and 88.3 M.P.H.

At 70.7 and 72.6 M.P.H.—Impression .0197"—Pressure 10370 lbs.

At 70.8 M.P.H.—Impression .0186"—Pressure 10000 lbs.

Average—71.7 M.P.H.—Impression .0149"—Pressure 9000 lbs.

CHAPTER 4
TWO PILOT MODELS

From the foregoing experience gained in the service tests of the four different types of electric locomotives, and two steam engines, it was decided to make a radical departure from general practice in the final design of the high-speed locomotives for the tunnel and terminal equipment. Acting in conformity with the favorable impression made by the American type steam locomotive, an attempt was made to pattern the locomotive mechanically on the fundamental characteristics of modern steam locomotive design in the following manner:

1. High center of gravity of the machine as a whole, and especially of the heavy electric motor portion;
2. The large proportion of the total weight spring-borne, and equalized by a system having considerable amplitude of motion;
3. An unsymmetrical distribution of wheel base of the locomotive;
4. A combination of driving and carrying wheels.

All the above features, it was thought, would produce ease of riding flexibility in tracking, and the reduction of destructive action to the roadbed by heavy masses moving at high speeds.

In accordance with this viewpoint it was decided to build two high-powered pilot models which would encompass the above four salient points.

In 1909 the Pennsy ordered 24 electric locomotives of class DD1, and two pilot models were built. The first was numbered 3998, built October 1909, and this number appeared in large numerals on the sides of each cab or semi-unit. In April 1910, another DD1 was built and numbered 3999. Later renumbering of these two locomotives has puzzled certain folks. I am, therefore, including the official renumbering plus a notation from the Pennsylvania Railroad Day Book, kept by the Company's secretary

No. 32 3996 Odd DD1 unit Juniata 2048-2
        10/09 Westinghouse Eqt. cut up 9/47
        3997 Odd DD1 unit Juniata 2048-1
        10/09 Westinghouse Eqt. cut up 9/47

No. 33 3998 Odd DD1 unit Juniata 2049-2
        4/10 Westinghouse Eqt. cut up 9/47
        3999 Odd DD1 unit Juniata 2049-1
        4/10 Westinghouse Eqt. cut up 9/47

Day Book notation for August 1909 recorded as follows. "No. 3998, construction number 2048, and No. 3999, construction number 2049, sent to Westinghouse from Juniata Shops, August 1909." Thus No. 32, Odd DD1, as shown by the construction number was the locomotive originally numbered 3998, and the first motor of class DD1. Later all DD1's received two digit road numbers carried in the headlights and cab sides, but they also retained the four digit numbers in small lettering on each semi-unit.

These two locomotives 3998 and 3999 deserve a Chapter of their own, for with the exception of some changes and small additions they pioneered the design for the whole subsequent fleet of 33 DD1 class locomotives.

We have seen previously the four main characteristics which were desired for the proposed electric locomotives. In describing their

The first DD1 (later classified Odd DD) on the Westinghouse Interworks Railway in 1909. I am quite sure I can name three of the gentlemen on the extreme right of the picture. Reading from right to left, namely: David F. Crawford, George Gibbs, (I am not certain of the third member of the group, could be Alfred W. Gibbs, or E. Rowland Hill) next is Axel S. Vogt, Pennsy's outstanding Mechanical Engineer, and the highest paid in the United States. We can be pretty sure then, that at least three members-possibly four- of President Cassatt's select Locomotive Committee were there.

general details we can do no better than to quote the Locomotive Committee Chairman, George Gibbs, who stated as follows: "To accomplish these results, required an important modification in the customary method of mounting and connecting the electric motors; instead of being placed concentric with or in the plane of the axles, and direct-mounted or geared to them, they are placed on the main frames above the wheels, and driving connections are made with rods. The locomotive is double, or articulated, each half being similar to an "American" type, or eight-wheeled steam locomotive, in the wheel arrangement, frames, and running gear. These halves are

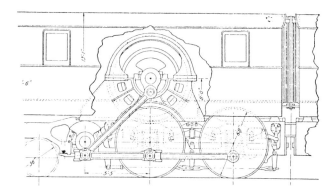

Original design of traction motor in each Odd DD semi-unit Nos. 3998 and 3999. This motor like a later design rested on the main frame rails, but the lower half of the motor casting was not diagonally fastened to the jack-shaft casting as on other DD1's that followed and featured 72-inch driving wheels. Unlike the later DD1 traction motors, the vertical center line of the armature shaft coincided with that of the forward pairs of drivers in each unit.

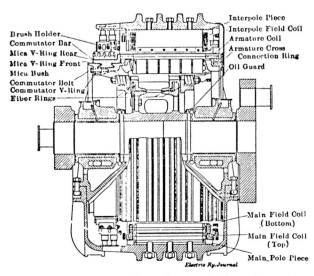

Pennsylvania Locomotives—Sectional View of 2000-hp Motor

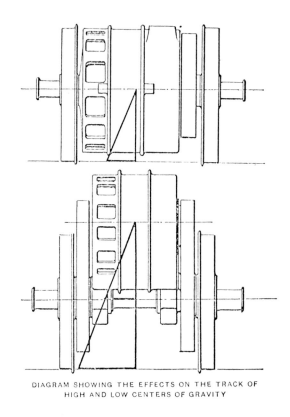

DIAGRAM SHOWING THE EFFECTS ON THE TRACK OF HIGH AND LOW CENTERS OF GRAVITY

While a locomotive with a high center of gravity is more liable to overturn at excessive rates of speed, there is no question that the low center of gravity puts more stress upon the outer rail of the curve and its tie connections. This may be illustrated by the accompanying diagram, in which it will be seen that while the centrifugal force is the same for locomotives either with high or low center of gravity with the weight, speed, and radius of curvature, yet the high center of gravity throws an increased weight upon the outer rail, thus forcing it more tightly to the ties and reducing the shearing of the horizontal centrifugal force.

permanently coupled back-to-back by a drawbar and equalizing buffer connection. Each half has its own cab, and carries above the frame one series-wound electric motor, having interpoles and a divided main-field winding. The large space available for the motor enabled its design to be liberal in all parts, and its location makes the entire motor accessible for inspection. The motor shaft, or axle, carries quartered cranks which are connected by rods to a cranked jack-shaft set between the frames and having its center in the plane of the driving axle center. From this shaft, rod connections are made to the wheels, as in steam locomotives. All moving masses of the rods and cranks are revolving, and are susceptible of accurate counterbalancing. The system adopted for motor control enables one motor to be out of service and the locomotive to be operated in emergency by the remaining motor; also, two or more locomotives may be coupled together and operated as a single unit. The division of the fields into sections for manipulating the field strength, gives four, instead of the usual two, running positions of the speed controller, and thus also, economizes current during acceleration.

"Special attention has been given to the arrangement of control and other apparatus in the locomotive cabs, to enable all parts to be readily

Motor No. 3999, in Penn Station yard, west of Eighth Avenue, New York. Date was August 20, 1909, before station was opened for revenue train operation. This locomotive duplicated No. 3998 and was also listed later as an Odd DD. (See text in this Chapter 4)

accessible for inspection and adjustment, such as electrically-driven air pumps for brakes and control, pneumatic sanding devices, contact shoes for the third-rail, overhead pantagraph shoes, sleet scraping devices for removing ice and snow from the third-rail, automatic train stops for applying the brakes and shutting off power in case of over-running signals in the tunnel, etc.

"In fixing the capacity of the locomotive, the probable maximum and average train weight was established, and the unit was designed for the most economical distribution of equipment for the Terminal service. It is obvious that on a short run the condition of starting a train from rest and accelerating on the tunnel grades fixes the maximum train which can be hauled rather than the limitation of motor capacity due to the heating. The maximum weight of train to be hauled by one locomotive under the given conditions was specified as 550 tons trailing load; the actual capacity, however, in intermittent service has approximated 700 tons trailing.

"Each DD1 locomotive had two direct-current, field-controlled, series motors, with cast-steel frames.

Weight of each motor complete with cranks	43,000 lb.
Height of center of gravity from track	8 ft. 2¹³⁄₁₆ in.
Top of motor frame above cab floor	5 ft. 6½ in.

"A sample locomotive of this design (No. 3998, F.W.) was built, placed under road test in October 1909, and run 15,000 miles on a continuous test, with a train of 400 tons trailing; also, complete dynamometer car tests were made of the hauling capacity, speed, and other characteristics."

Locomotive No. 3998 in February 1910, was test running between Dunton and Rockaway Park, Long Island, with a 450-ton train as a test for the tunnel work between Harrison, N.J., and Long Island City, Long Island. It operated at speeds of 50 to 60 mph., and occasionally exceeded 70 mph.

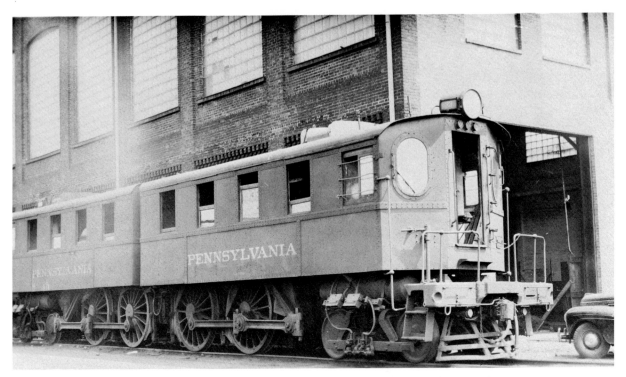

In 1947 locomotive No. 33 (originally No. 3999) stood outside the Meadows Shops, waiting to be scrapped. Both Nos. 32 and 33 retained their 68-inch drivers, solid disc truck wheels, and steam locomotive "big ends" that simulated those used on class E3 Atlantic type engines. As unfortunately happened later with many Pennsy steam and electric locomotives, it had been "uglified" with cab roof ends cut away and a sort of home-made ventilator replacing the Globe ventilators that had dissipated heat from the grid resistors most satisfactorily for many years.

The runs averaged 170 miles per day, without any delays due to failures. All these tests took place on the Long Island Railroad, which had been electrified in this area since 1905. Power was supplied from the large Pennsy owned power plant in Long Island City, on the East River. Up to the coming of AC electrification on the Pennsy, this plant powered all Pennsy electrically hauled trains using DC. In the later 1920's Public Service Electric Company of New Jersey, also began to supply power for DC operation. Pennsy's power plant furnished power to the DC operated Long Island Railroad, which since 1905, had greatly extended their electrified trackage.

A small pantograph on each cab roof collected current at certain switches, and "ladder tracks" where the continuity of the third-rail had to be broken. Overhead third-rails were employed at these points and quite an elaborate and graceful steel catenary shaped structural system supported them in the open area of the New York Terminal. Provision was also made for automatically stopping a train if the locomotive passed a stop signal in the tunnels. When the signal indicated stop, a trip-stop device went into operation. If the locomotive then attempted to pass the signal, it made contact with the trip-stop, which resulted in an automatic brake application and train stoppage.

It was first planned to equip the DD1 locomotives with train heating boilers. Later, this idea was discarded in favor of heating the cars from service plants at Penn Station, New York, and the huge Sunnyside passenger car storage yard in Long Island City, reputed to be the largest in the world. Heat was sufficiently maintained in this manner for the average run of 14 minutes from Penn Station to Manhattan Transfer.

Further information regarding a vital element in the design of the DD1, follows next in more detail than previously referred to in this Chapter.

The question of transmission of electrical energy into mechanical power for propulsion of the locomotive is of great importance in the design of an electric locomotive. This concerns the "traction motor drive" and accordingly was the cause for much study. Norman W. Storer, an engineer connected with the Railway Department of Westinghouse, who was directly involved with this detail had this to say: "The question of transmission between the motors and the driving wheels was considered by the Committee with the greatest care, and it was only after a very exhaustive study that the side-rods were adopted; and, while the Committee fully recognized the difficulty in the design and the disadvantages of the side-rods, it was felt that, on the whole, they were more reliable and safer than any other form. I believe that the test has shown the wisdom of the choice of side-rods, though I do not like their use on electric locomotives. The problem is very different from that of steam locomotives, because in the latter the power of only one cylinder is transmitted through any driving pin, and the two sets of rods are independent of each other, except as connected through the wheels. On the electric locomotive, however, the two sides are connected rigidly through the motor shaft, and at certain points in the revolution, the entire power developed by the motor must be transmitted through a single pin. This makes it necessary to have all pins and rods heavier than those in a corresponding steam locomotive. The motor and jack-shaft bearings must also be designed to carry enormous reciprocating pressures. This will be better understood when it is shown that the registered maximum dynamometer pull of 79,200 lb. corresponds to a pressure of 120,000 lb. on the crank pin. I have stated my dislike of side-rods on electric locomotives, but lest I be misunderstood, wish to say that if the same problem were presented to me at the present time (Year 1910, F.W.) I would vote for side-rods, just as before. No other transmission system could handle the service as well without a very radical change in all the plans. If the weight is to be confined to four pairs of drivers, if a single unit is desired, as at the present time, side-rods are practically the only form of transmission between motors and wheels which would give the satisfactory operation secured on this locomotive."

At one time on a dynamometer test run with No. 3998, a maximum drawbar pull of 79,200 lb. was registered. This corresponded to a coefficient of adhesion of about 38 per cent, which was very high and creditable. At that time (Year 1910, F.W.) some of the largest Mallet steam locomotives did not develop higher drawbar pull, and on a level track could not travel at the speed of a DD1.

These two pilot models in their day were probably the most powerful locomotives in horsepower rating ever built. No. 3398 and 3399, later Nos. 32 and 33, respectively, were part of the order for 24 DD1's ordered in 1909 and built in 1910. In the next Chapter we shall see how the following 22 DD1's of 1910 were somewhat modified.

CHAPTER 5
DD1's ON THE HIGH LINE —
1910 to 1924

In this Chapter we shall see how close the newer and more numerous DD1 class locomotives adhered to the pilot models.

Nevertheless, some changes were deemed advisable in the light of operating experience with Nos. 3998 and 3999. This new group was numbered from No. 10 to 33, or the total number of DD1's ordered in 1909. Included were the two "Odd DD1's" Nos. 32 and 33. These two locomotives operated mostly in switching service in Sunnyside Yard. I do not recall ever seeing either one hauling a train over the "High Line" as the Pennsy embankment on the Jersey meadows and long eleven span viaduct over the huge Erie Railroad, Croxton Yards was called.

The changes that were made on Nos. 10 to 31, and the nine additional DD1's built in 1911 numbered 34 to 42, were as follows:

1. Jack-shaft housing was diagonally bolted direct to lower half of traction motor casting.
2. Two more pairs of Globe ventilators were added making a total of six.
3. Driving wheel diameter increased to 72 inches from original 68 inches.
4. Change in big ends of main rods on first pairs of drivers and jack-shafts.
5. Circular windows in end doors of some locomotives.
6. Spoked truck wheels instead of solid disk type.
7. Revised location for main air reservoirs.
8. Overhang of cab roofs was cut away more at sides.
9. Some locomotives had curved hand railings, or grab irons at ends of pilot beams.
10. A cover about manhole size on the roof at the rear left-hand side of each semi-unit of the complete locomotive covered an opening to permit application of an electric flash train heating boiler. It never

seems to have been used and, as noted in the previous Chapter the plan was abandoned.

Another feature of the DD1's was a fiber friction clutch, so that in case a short circuit developed while the locomotive was running at high speed the tendency of the armature to come to a sudden stop would not be disastrous to the side rods.

The circuit breaker in the control circuit was set for a specific amperage overload, and the enginemen were instructed to operate with great care when the current reached a figure of 2700 amperes. A heavy red mark on the cab ammeter indicated when this point was reached.

The cab of each unit could be completely removed apart from the running gear and this included electrical control equipment, air compressor, and all cab fittings.

A great advantage that the DD1's possessed was the comparative dryness of the tunnels where the most critical sections of their operation occurred.

In a talk given before members of the Franklin Institute, in Philadelphia, Pa., Mr. Alfred Noble, considered to be the top American Civil Engineer of his day, was in charge of the four tunnels constructed under the East River regarding their engineering details. In that connection he had this to say concerning leakage in the river tunnels of the Pennsylvania Railroad. "The cast iron lining is an effective water proofing, and, while not absolutely water-tight, the leakage is insignificant. A sump of some form is provided at the lowest point of each tunnel or pair of tunnels and pumped out when necessary by pumps regularly installed. The daily leakage in the 5½ miles of river tunnels of the Pennsylvania Railroad is 2300 gallons. The magnitude of this may be better appreciated by stating that it amounts to one drop per lineal foot of tunnel every 17 seconds, or by stating that the entire amount of leakage for one day would be

This a posed publicity shot probably takes on the non-electrified Pittsburgh Division. Note absence of third-rail. Motor No. 3977, was built in July 1910, (see Roster, Chapter 9) and later ran on the High Line as No. 22.

removed in one or two minutes by a pump of the capacity ordinarly used by contractors for foundations. The pumps provided at the new dry docks of the Brooklyn Navy Yard would remove the leakage in about two minutes."

The following lists the weights of the four components making up a semi-unit, or one-half of a complete DD1.

Cab complete	22 tons
Motor, less motor cranks	21 tons
(43,000 lb. with motor cranks)	
Running gear	18 tons
Chassis	17 tons
	78 tons

or 156 tons for total locomotive.

Natural ventilation sufficed for the DD1's, but if they would have been used on longer runs than originally intended, air blast cooling would have been used, thereby, greatly increasing their power output. The high-up location of the traction motors, one in each cab, did much to keep them free from dust, dirt and water, which militated against motors closer to the track which at times caused troublesome situations causing delays to trains. This was another plus for the DD1's.

Concentrating all power in one traction motor per cab, or a total of two motors, meant a lower first cost, and decreased subsequent maintenance costs for developing the same power.

A change was also made in the location of the traction motors in each semi-unit cab. In the first two pilot models Nos. 3998 and 3999, later Nos. 32

and 33, the vertical center line of the motors both coincided with that of the vertical center line of the forward drivers on each unit. On the final design of the 31 additional locomotives the vertical center line of the motors was five inches in back of the forward drivers vertical center line in each cab. These were the motors that were fastened diagonally at one end of the jack-shaft housing, unlike Nos. 32 and 33.

Those traction motors measured 5 feet, 6½ inches from the cab floor to the top of the motor casting. Height from the rail top to the center of gravity of the complete locomotive was 63.75 inches. This figure almost duplicated that of the smooth running D16b class American type engine in West Jersey, which measured 68 inches.

The mechanical design of class DD1, was done in the Mechanical Engineer's drawing room of the General Superintendent of Motive Power at Altoona, Pa. Electrical equipment was designed and furnished by Westinghouse, and all 33 DD1 class locomotives were assembled ready for road service at Westinghouse in East Pittsburgh, Pa.

All in all the design proved fundamentally sound and showed that the Locomotive Committee, Altoona and Westinghouse, had despite the apprehension of some critics, and their doleful prognostications, produced a highly efficient, economical, and noteworthy electric locomotive. One still exists at the Pennsylvania State Railroad Museum, at Strasburg, Pa. It was originally old No. 36, built in 1911. If ever refurbished into her pristine glory, it will be well worth a visit.

1   *Overhead Contact Shoe*
2   *Contact Shoe Pantagraph Base*
3   *Headlight Lens*
4   *Grid Resistance Ventilator*
5   *Bell Rope Stand*
6   *Bell*
7   *Sand Box Opening Cover*
8   *Sand Box Body*
9   *Combined Inter-cooler Pipes and Sand Box Support*
10 *Air Compressor Gear Case*
11 *Air Compressor Motor Case*
12 *Upper Half of Motor Field Frame*
13 *Lower Half of Motor Field Frame*
14 *Jack Shaft Counter-weight*
15 *Motor Rod*
16 *Jack Shaft Cross Tie*
17 *Main Rod*
18 *Side Rod*
19 *Semi-Elliptical Driving Spring Fulcrum and Brake Hanger Support*
20 *Brake Lever*
21 *Brake Clog*
22 *Semi-Elliptical Driving Spring*
23 *Spring Rigging Equalizer Beam*
24 *Driver Brake Rod*
25 *Delivery End of Sand Pipe*
26 *Safety Bar between Semi-Units*

27 *Draft Gear Casting between Semi-Units*
28 *Draft Gear Chafing Block*
29 *Pedestal Jaw Cap or Binder*
30 *Driving Wheel Tire*
31 *Jack Shaft Pedestal Cap*
32 *Main Frame of Engine*
33 *Main Air Reservoir*
34 *Cable*
35 *Bus Line Fuse Box*
36 *Third Rail Shoe Beam Bracket*
37 *Third Rail Shoe Beam*
38 *Third Rail Shoe*
39 *Third Rail Shoe Adjusting Bracket*
40 *Control Reservoir*
41 *Bus Line Cable between Semi-Units*
42 *Bus Line Cable between Locomotives*
43 *Pilot*
44 *Engine Step*
45 *Bumper Beam*
46 *Coupler Head*
47 *Main Circuit Breaker*
48 *Control Groups*
49 *Grid Resistance Frame*
50 *Auxiliary Circuit Breaker*
51 *Motor Crank*
52 *Combined Fuse Box Support and Main Air Reservoir Bracket*

53 *Bolster Bracket*
54 *Engine Truck Wheel*
55 *Diaphragm between Semi-Units*
56 *Truck Brake Cylinder*
57 *Main Switch*
58 *Junction Box*
59 *Grounding Switch*
60 *Distributing Valve and Double Chamber Reservoir*
61 *Equalizing Reservoir*
62 *Brake Valve*
63 *Reducing Valve*
64 *Feed Valve*
65 *Bus Line Socket*
66 *Train Cable*
67 *Train Cable Jumper*
68 *Diaphragm Spring*
69 *Helical Driving Spring*
70 *Draw Bar between Semi-Units*
71 *Master Controller*
72 *Motorman's Seat*
73 *Cab Lifting Rod*
74 *Bulkhead*
75 *Bulkhead Door*
76 *Driver Brake Cylinder*
77 *Steam Heat Pipe*
78 *Reservoir Pipe*
79 *Brake Pipe*
80 *Signal Pipe*

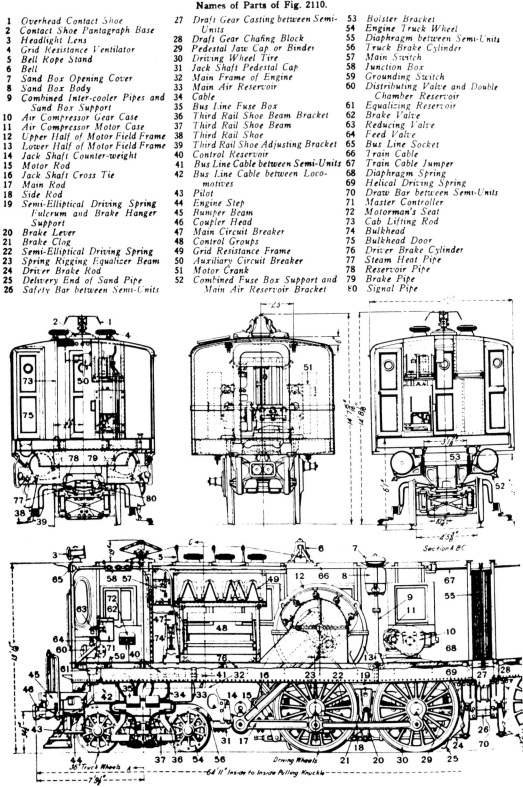

General arrangement of Control Apparatus in the Cab of Electric Locomotive Class DD1. It should be pointed out that the left-side motor crank is incorrectly "quartered." With the jack-shaft and driving wheel crank pins in the position shown, the motor or armature crank should be quartered likewise (see next illustration.)

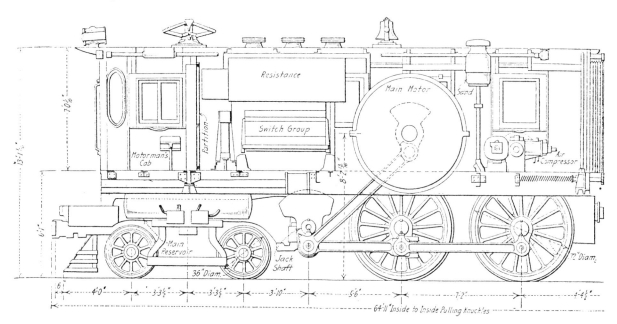

In this picture the left-side motor cranks are quartered correctly. Motor shaft, jack-shaft, and driving wheel crank pins are quartered in unison as they should be.

Courtesy of the Westinghouse Electrical & Manufacturing Company

THE RIVAL OF THE "TEA-KETTLE ON WHEELS"

The working parts of an electric locomotive of the type that is superseding steam locomotives for suburban traffic and for the hauling of freight trains over heavy mountain grades and through long tunnels

The exceptional simplicity of the driving gear of the final DD1 design. Note new casting of lower half of traction motors as compared with two pilot models. It is diagonally and directly connected to the jack-shaft crosstie casting. Main air reservoirs and brake cylinders are visible. Electrical control equipment, compressors for air brake, and third-rail shoes are yet to be applied. Photo was taken at Westinghouse East Pittsburgh Works, where all the DD1's were completely assembled and made ready for immediate road service.

For some time before Penn Station was operating revenue trains a regular dress rehearsal went into operation. Such a huge project calling for numerous power changes at Manhattan Transfer, on east and westbound trains could not depend on last minute improvisation. Here is a westbound tryout non-revenue run in late 1910, with typical all-steel cars with motor No. 14, in charge.

Motor No. 22, with another non-revenue train in tow, speedily approaches Manhattan Transfer.

Train emerging from the Bergen Hill, or Hackensack Portal, headed by motor No. 39, in 1914. This train and all others that follow in this Chapter are revenue passenger trains.

A panoramic view as a DD1 heads a train around the long curve that led in and out of the tunnels, and starts its trek over the Jersey meadows, in 1914. Sub-Station No. 3, on the left is where rotary converters turned AC into DC after transformers first stepped down the high-tension line current. From the converters it was then distributed to the third-rails.

Motor No. 21, at speed passing over the Belleville Road. Hackensack River swing drawbridge can be seen in back of train. On this bridge speed was restricted to 50-mph. Two tall steel towers, 181 ft.-4 in. in height above high water spanned the river by order of the then called War Department. These tall towers as well as smaller ones carried the high-tension transmission lines between Sub-Stations Nos. 3 and 4. Photo taken March 15, 1912.

At high speed the DD1 hauled train is nearing Manhattan Transfer.

Train is in sight of Manhattan Transfer and passing "S" tower (now "Hudson") opposite motor storage track at east end of the Transfer.

Arriving at the Transfer, motor No. 24, made a brief stop as car inspectors went to work. The DD1 was quickly uncoupled and given the "highball" to move away. The waiting steam locomotive then backed to the train and was speedily coupled to it. All this was done in the alotted time of four minutes though it has been done in two minutes. Trains at this point took on passengers from downtown New York and Jersey City, who arrived there on H&M trains on gauntlet track No. 7. Note that the original small 50 candle power headlamp has been replaced by the type used with Pennsy steam power, and window wipers have been added to the front windows. This would put the date up in the late 1920's after the L5PD sub-classes had come into service on these runs. After the steam locomotive was coupled, brakes were tested and a car inspector at the train's rear made sure they applied. One of the front-end car inspectors is walking toward couplers between locomotive and first car which happens to be a scenery car with two large doors at one end and the large door hinges are clearly visible.

For speediest operation to provide rapid track clearance engineer would stay put at the DD1's master controller after uncoupling and proceed west to a point just past first semaphore signal bridge. Helper had meanwhile moved to other end of motor, and gave hand signals to the engineer who then reversed the locomotive, and by signal indications moved to the motor storage track. In some cases, however, it was indicated that the motor was to return "light" to Penn Station. This occasionally happened when ample motor power was available at the Transfer for incoming trains and a power imbalance existed at Penn Station or Sunnyside. Here we see that motor No. 26 has stopped and is ready to move east.

Engine No. 2437 built at Juniata in 1910, pulls away from Manhattan Transfer, after taking over from the DD1. With saturated steam spurting from open cylinder cocks, train No. 5, the Pennsylvania Limited, was hauled by the big K2 Pacific in reverse consist order over the New York Division, with the open platform end of the observation car coupled to the tender. This was due to the Limited running via Broad Street Station, Philadephia, which was a stub, or dead-end terminal. West from Broad Street, the train ran with the observation car at rear of train and parlor-baggage, or club car at the head end coupled to a Philadelphia Division engine. No. 2437 was a New York Division engine, with engineman Jim Maloney at the throttle that Sunday on June 25, 1911, when Charley Chaney's post-card size Graflex camera caught this gem of a bygone yesterday.

An exceptionally rare view of "N" tower at the west end of Manhattan Transfer. This tower handled the outgoing steam locomotives on the outbound storage track, and in the distance a K2 class Pacific waits for its DD1 hauled train from New York. Courtesy of James J. Lynch, Jr.

An inbound train for Penn Station arriving at Manhattan Transfer. The locomotive, No. 1737, is of special interest as it was built in May 1914, and was the original K4s class locomotive of a world famous fleet of Pacifics.

A class DD1 on the motor storage track at the east end of the Transfer. The locomotive in this picture hauled a two-car train carrying the pictures of President Calvin Coolidge's inauguration. But without the sign it could have been any DD1 waiting for an inbound train.

Motor No. 11, hauling the eastbound Broadway Limited. Semaphore signals were arranged for reverse operation if desired. High tension latticed steel transmission line poles can be seen at left. All pictures that follow show typical eastbound runs of DD1's in action.

Train No. 20, the Keystone Express, heeling to the curve as it nears the Bergen Portal of the south tunnel. Motor No. 26, in charge.

Closer to the tunnel's mouth DD1 No. 12, is ready to pass under the last signal bridge before entering the Bergen Hill Portal. Motor No. 12 is hauling a Philadelphia-New York, "Clocker" and observation car of the westbound Broadway Limited is passing under the signal bridge.

Train No. 56, the combined New York-New Orleans Limited and the "FFV" of the Southern and Chesapeake & Ohio Railroads respectively, plunges down into the tunnel past the concrete retaining walls. At this point speed was reduced to about 30 mph., per the rules, and the "two longs and two shorts" of the compressed air whistle were given. Year was 1914.

After Train 56 had stopped at Penn Station, and unloaded passengers and baggage, it usually had a sizeable wait, and then proceeded under Manhattan Island and the East River tunnel until it came out into the open in Long Island City. Here we see it approaching the loop tracks that led into what the Pennsy called the "world's largest passenger car yard." I never heard anyone successfully challenge that statement.

Approaches to Sunnyside Yard in Long Island City, N.Y. Courtesy James J. Lynch, Jr.

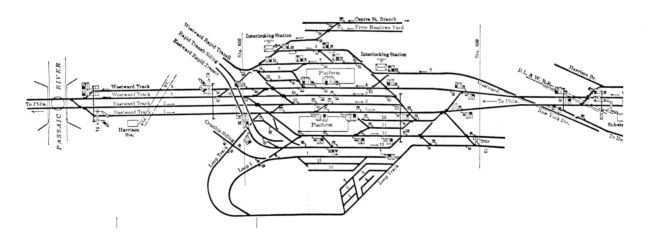

Track layout at Manhattan Transfer in the early years of its operation. Despite some minor changes this general plan was retained until its abandonment in 1937.

	CLASSIFICATION		Odd 3951	Odd DD 3996 to 3999 Incl.	DD 1	FF 1
1	Wheel Arrangement		0-4-4-0	4-4-4-4	4-4-4-4	2-6-6-2
2	Wheel Diameters	In.	56	36-68-36	36-72-36	36-72-36
3	Journal, End Trucks	In.	-----	5½ x 10	6½ x 12	6½ x 12
4	" Drivers	In.	6 x 11	10 x 13½	10 x 13½	11 x 15
5	" Inside Trucks	In.	-----			
6	Wheel Base, Driver	Ft. In.	26-1	24-1	24-1	38-8
7	" Base, Total	Ft. In.	26-1	55-11	55-11	63-11
8	Length Coupled	Ft. In.	38-9	64-11	64-11	76-6½
9	Width, Maximum	Ft. In.	10-1½	10-7	11-2½	10-1½
10	Height Over Cab Roof	Ft. In.	13-4	13-1	13-1⅛	14-8
11	" Maximum, Trolley Down	Ft. In.	14-6⅞	14-8¾	14-8¾	15-6
12	Drive, Type of		Gearless	Jack Shaft	Jack Shaft	Gears and Jack Shaft
13	Current Collectors		3rd Shoes and Collector	3rd Shoes and Collector	3rd Shoes and Collector	Pantograph
14	Line Voltage		650 D. C.	650 D. C.	650 D. C.	11000 A. C.
15	Main Motors, Class and Voltage		D. C. 300	D. C. 650	D. C. 650	3 Phase 850
16	" " Make and Type		Westinghouse 2-103, 2-129	Westinghouse 315	Westinghouse 315-A	Westinghouse 451
17	" " Number of		4	2	2	4
18	" " Ventilation		Forced	Natural	Natural	Forced
19	" " Gear Ratio		-----	-----	-----	21 to 106
20	" " Gear Type of		-----	-----	-----	Double Helical
21	" " Rotor, Diameter	In.		56	56	41¾
22	" " Rotor, Weight,	Lb.				
23	" " Weight	Lb.				
24	Control, Master Type		Electro Pneumatic	Electro Pneumatic	Electro Pneumatic	Electro Pneumatic
25	" Master Oper't'g Current		20 V	20 V	20 V	30 V
26	" Main Type		Grids	Grids	Grids	Transformer
27	Compressors, Number and Type		1 C 60 2-Stg.	2-C-60 2-Stage	2-C-60 2-Stage	2-Vertical 2-Stage
28	" Capacity	Cu. Ft.	60	60	60	150
29	Blowers, Number and H. P.		-----	-----		2-50
30	" Capacity	Cu. Ft.	-----			
31	Wt. on Rail, End Truck	Lb.	-----	62000	57000	38000
32	" " 1st Drivers	Lb.	51090	52000	49750	73000
33	" " 2nd Drivers	Lb.	47950	52000	49750	72000
34	" " 3rd Drivers	Lb.	45180	52000	49750	70500
35	" " 4th Drivers	Lb.	50920	52000	49750	73000
36	" " 5th Drivers	Lb.				74500
37	" " 6th Drivers	Lb.				76500
38	" " 7th Drivers	Lb.				-----
39	" " 8th Drivers	Lb.				-----
40	" " All Drivers	Lb.	195140	208000	199000	439500
41	" " Inside Truck	Lb.	-----		-----	
42	Wt. of Engine, Total	Lb.	195140	332000	313000	516000
43	" " Mechanical Parts	Lb.	100000	205000	194000	258400
44	" " Equipment Parts*	Lb.	95140	127000	119000	257600
45	Rating Continuous	H. P.	423	1580	1580	4000
46	" Tractive Power	Lb.	10940	10800	10200	73000
47	" Speed	M. P. H.	14.5	54.8	58	20.5
48	Ratio: Wt. on Drivers to Continuous T. P.		17.8	19.2	19.5	6.02
49	Maximum Tractive Power	Lb.	38400	66000	50000	140000
50	Ratio: Wt. on Drivers to Max. Trac. Power		5.08	3.15	3.98	3.14
51	Compressor H. P. Rating					
52	Maximum Speed mph.				80	

*)Includes All Electrical Equipment, and Air Brake Parts Except Foundation Brake and Air Brake Cylinder.

Specifications for No. 3951, (originally No. 10002) Odd DD (nos. 32 and 33) originally Nos. 3998 and 3999 respectively. Also included are "specs" of "Big Liz" the giant FF-1 class locomotive, and final DD1 design.

Engine No.	Train No.	Engineman	Train Name
12	213	Scanlon	NY.-Phila. Exp.
42	211	O'Neal	NY/-Phila. Exp.
14	180	Jordan	---------- Phila.-New York-New Haven Exp.
11	209	Haddon	NY.-Phila. Accom.
14	25	Jordan	Metropolitan Express
20	109	Lee	NY-Washington Exp.
26	505	Stern	B&O (The Capitol Limited)
35	215	Tabor	NY-Phila. Exp.
38	205	Stern	NY-Phila. Accom.
13	27	Stern	Commercial Express (all DD-1 Class)
41	609	Dillman	Lehigh Valley RR (The Black Diamond)
25	185	Hoffman	ACL, Sou. Ry. Exp.
28	217	Vandervoor	NY-Phila. Exp.
35	709	Tettman	NY-Long Branch Exp.
22	219	Costello	NY-Phila. Accom.
29	117	Chevalier	NY-Wash. Exp.
30	501	Talle	B&O RR (The National Limited)
12	179	Scanlon	Boston-Philadelphia Exp.
34	1073-1st.	Hogan	NY-Atlantic City Exp. (The Nellis Bly)
42	1073-2nd.	Matthews	NY-Atlantic City Exp. (The Nellie Bly)
36	221	Vanleharldorf?	NY-Phila. Exp.
37	711	Roberts	NY-Long Branch Exp.
41	5	Dillman	Pennsylvania Limited
26	119	Sterry	NY-Wash. Exp.
31	223	Wilkinson	NY-Phila. Exp.

An authentic record of trains leaving Penn Station on March 20, 1920 hauled by DD1 motors. This record only represents some of the numerous trains that left the Station. Only one train was eastbound, No. 180, all the rest were westbound. Conductors wrote down the train consists in longhand, and it was not easy to do at times, hence, it was difficult to decipher the names of the enginemen, as in the case of train No. 221, the 10:00 a.m. "Clocker" to Philadelphia. These were the CT-220 reports. Train No. 180, was made by a New Haven conductor, as this was a New Haven train that proceeded eastward over the Hell Gate Bridge route.

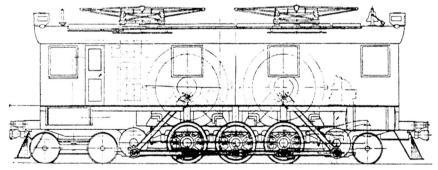

SKELETON DIAGRAM OF ELECTRIC LOCOMOTIVE.

It has been said that "Imitation is the sincerest form of flattery." Did the joint effort of Pennsy and Westinghouse, prompt the latter's arch rival, General Electric, to design the locomotive illustrated? Such a unit was partially built with a sort of make-shift shelter over the four wheel truck in 1909 and tested. One big departure from the DD1, was the fact that it was powered by AC, but the gearless jack-shaft, side-rod drives were in evidence. Perhaps they had the New Haven in mind as a possible customer.

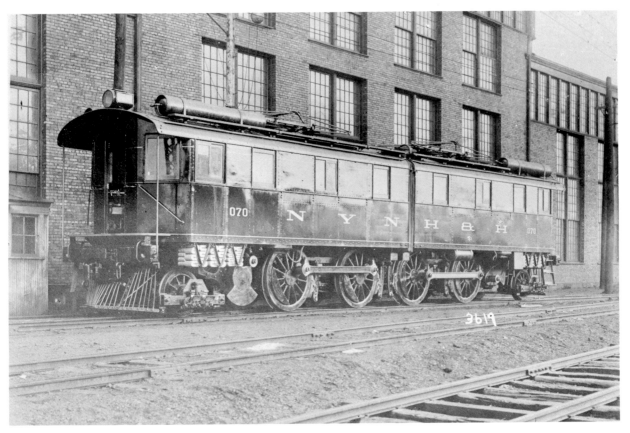

A locomotive, No. 070, was built for the New York, New Haven & Hartford, Railroad in 1909, which more closely simulated Pennsy's DD1. Photo was taken at the Westinghouse Works, East Pittsburgh, Pa., where the locomotive was completely assembled. Mechanical parts were built by Baldwin. This locomotive could operate on AC or DC, and was suitable for passenger or freight service. Unit No. 1, contained a train-heating boiler, and oil fuel tank; a water storage tank was contained in unit No. 2. Under-running third-rail shoes and overhead pantographs enabled the locomotive to operate into Grand Central Terminal, New York and the New Haven main line. It appears that neither the GE and New Haven locomotive were ever duplicated and may well be regarded as experimental units. The New Haven motor did, however, actually go into service.

CHAPTER 6
"LET'S LOOK AT THE RECORD"

A once well known politician when confronted with questions concerning political issues would reply, "Let's look at the record."

This same retort could be given to those who might question the design of class DD1. For the record, with crystal clear clarity, makes plain the fact that the Pennsy had a superb record breaker in their locomotive family.

These records point out the fine operating performance of class DD-1, also showing the minimal time out for repairs. These figures also indicate the locomotives low operating costs, plus ability to maintain schedules with a minimum of locomotive failures which reflect great credit on the design of the mechanical and electrical equipment.

Edward R. Hill, Partner of Gibbs & Hill, had this to say about the performance of class DD1, after the first ten months of operation following November 27, 1910, when the locomotives went into revenue service on the main line. It is herewith listed in the following table.

LOCOMOTIVE OPERATION

Locomotive mileage since November 27, 1910	759,940
Failures due to short circuits	2
Control failures	2
Total number of locomotive failures causing train detentions	4
Number of trains delayed by same	10
Number of miles per failure	189,985
Number of miles per train detention	75,994
Average time per train detention	min. 11.5
Average elapsed time between failures	days 77
Average elapsed time between detentions	days 30.8

Mr. Hill stated further, "In addition to the exceptionally reliable performance shown by the foregoing figures, the large margin in capacity of the locomotives has been of great value; each locomotive is guaranteed to handle a 550-ton train on the tunnel grades, while in actual daily service, single locomotives are used for handling 800-ton trains."

Mr. George Gibbs, the other Partner of Gibbs & Hill, prepared some authentic figures with information undoubtedly furnished by the Pennsylvania Railroad in some instances for the year 1911.

Mr. Gibbs' figured for the New York terminal service of the Pennsylvania Railroad, showed nine miles of main line, with about 6½ miles of level track and 2½ miles of heavy grade, in addition to an underground run of four miles from the station to the yards on Long Island. Practically all traffic was locomotive hauled, although there was a very small multiple-unit (MU) car service between Harrison, N.J. and New York; there was much switching and transfer.

The extra dry conditions of the tunnel permitted a higher coefficient of adhesion than designed, so that the locomotives were able to start a 650-ton train readily and occasionally an 800-ton train. Station service limitations kept the average locomotive performance to 26,000 miles per year (with a maximum of 56,000). Of a total 909,000 locomotive miles, 72 percent was in road service, and 28 percent in switching service.

Total operating costs per car mile of the Pennsylvania electric locomotives were compared with steam locomotives (1) on the New Jersey Division, and (2) on all Divisions as follows; electric 5.91 cents; New Jersey steam 8.83 cents; all steam 11.9 cents. The cost of lubrication was the same for all at 0.25 cents, while enginehouse expense was 0.58 cents for electrics, compared with 2.58 cents for both New Jersey and the all-Division steam (steam locomotive figures taken from pooled figures, as the Pennsylvania does not segregate locomotive figures according to class of service). The figures for repairs were probably higher than some expected, but were considered low on account of the exacting service, and the presence of expenses in the first year of operations which would not arise subsequently. Thus the heaviest items were for brake shoes, tire turning and structural changes; for instance, some of the

Steam locomotives were sent to Manhattan Transfer from the Meadows Enginehouse, and ready track for outgoing trains. Incoming engines after uncoupling from trains at the Transfer proceeded to the Meadows in reverse direction. Occasionally some came and went to Waldo Avenue Enginehouse, but this was not the usual procedure. Here we see engine No. 3150, class E2d, on June 18, 1911, slowly backing up to the steam locomotive storage track. Double-tracked jumpover bridge No. 79, is in the background. Track on the west side of the bridge was used for eastbound H&M trains, while the one next to it was a siding used to store H&M cars.

jack-shaft bearings had unsuitable babbitt, and many flat wheels were due to the inharmonious proportions of the original brake rigging. In the past year (1911) there have been only 16 locomotive failures, detaining 26 trains an average of 6.8 minutes. There were about 35,000 train miles per detention, and 56,000 train miles to each locomotive failure.

I had personally heard about "hot" jack-shaft bearings that the DD1's were first troubled with, but it was not long before they had that problem solved. Wait and see how this 1911 record improved through the years up to April 1916.

For the year 1912 we have several figures listed in tabular form which show some more interesting facts regarding these remarkably efficient locomotives. These are as follows:

The following data gives details regarding DD1 locomotive detentions and their causes.

My friend and associate, Paul T. Warner, at The Baldwin Locomotive Works, had this to say about these splendid DD1 class locomotives; During the first four years of service, these locomotives made the following record:

Miles run	3,974,746

Total engine failures	45
Total minutes detention	271
Miles per detention	88,328
Miles per minute detention	14,667

"The cost of maintenance, during this period, averaged 7.2 cents per locomotive mile; while during the year May 1, 1915 to April 30, 1916, the maintenance cost approximated only 3.5 cents per locomotive mile. It would be difficult indeed, to find any other locomotives that could show an equally creditable record."

Mr. Warner also stated that the service — prior to 1924 — was exclusively maintained by 33 DD1 locomotives. Trains of 14 cars weighing 1,000 tons were successfully handled, and 850-ton trains were frequently started on the 1.93 percent grades in the tunnels by one locomotive.

Ending this Chapter are three tables consecutively numbered that provide informative statistical data for year 1915, and up to April 1916.

These records prove the soundness of the DD1 design. It appears that no other electric locomotives in the United States — probably the world, could match the DD1's at the time period shown in the foregoing tables.

Light Atlantic No. 1044, class E3d, had coupled to its train at the Transfer, and was heeling to the curve that took the train in a south westerly direction. Note that the embankment adjacent to the jumpover bridge had not been completed. Date of this scene was June 18, 1911. Later that year the line was completed on the H&M RR., to Harrison, and Park Place, Newark, N.J.

PARTIAL LIST OF REPAIRS AND RENEWALS MADE AT SUNNYSIDE ENGINE
HOUSE DURING 1912

```
Arc chute sides replaced ........................................ 585
Arcing tips renewed ........................................... 168
Switch contacts renewed ........................................ 236
Main motor brushes replaced.....................................  67
Compressor brushes replaced .................................... 234
Contact shoes renewed........................................... 617
Main rod brasses reduced........................................  26
Jack-shaft brasses closed or reduced............................ 489
Jack-shaft brasses renewed .....................................  14
Motor bearings renewed .........................................   4
```

MAINTENANCE COSTS OF ELECTRIC LOCOMOTIVE UNITS
CENTS PER MILE

During 1912	Mechanical	Electrical	Total
June	1.51	1.01	2.52
July	2.18	0.85	3.03
August	2.86	0.66	3.52
September	2.46	0.97	3.43
October	2.84	0.79	3.63
November	2.84	0.90	3.74
Average	2.45	0.86	3.31

These costs include all operating overhead charges, such as the cost of general labor, supervision, heating and lighting of the shops and the like. They do not, however, include any charges for capital account nor charges due to repairs to buildings or machinery.

PENNSYLVANIA RAILROAD COMPANY, MANHATTAN DIVISION.
Electric Locomotive Detentions in Minutes During 1912.

| Month | ELECTRICAL | | | | MECHANICAL | | Total, All Causes | Mileage | Miles per Minute Detention |
	Fuses	Master Control	Motor Control	Misc. Electrical	Misc. Mechanical	Brakes			
January...	..	2	...	...	...	..	2	84,422	42,211
February..	..	5	6	5	...	..	16	78,100	4,881
March.....	..	3	...	...	...	..	3	82,573	27,524
April......	..	2	...	...	.:.	..	2	78,886	39,443
May.......	..	2	...	...	...	..	2	80,880	40,440
June......	..	5	...	...	...	2	7	80,013	11,430
July.......	...	...	...	...	...	..	.....	84,283	.....
August....	..	...	2	...	4	..	6	85,486	14,248
September.	..	...	5	...	4	2	11	83,950	7,632
October...	..	...	...	...	4	7	11	85,305	7,755
November.	..	...	6	...	...	..	6	84,473	14,079
December..	..	...	...	...	...	..	.....	86,221	.....
Total....	..	19	19	5	12	11	66	994,592	15,070

EXPLANATION OF DELAYS.

Master Control:
2 minutes. "J" switch not operating owing to oil on armature.
2 minutes. Grease on master controller drum.
2 minutes. Broken control battery plate.
3 minutes. Loose master controller finger.
2 minutes. "J" switch sticking; motors not operating in parallel.
1 minute. Bent finger on No. 2 controller plug.
4 minutes. Master controller finger loose.
3 minutes. Bridge relay finger not making contact; small piece of waste found under same.

Motor Control:
6 minutes. Circuit-breaker not resetting owing to glycerine in dash pot gumming, account cold weather.
6 minutes. Due to motorman not using power in proper manner and blowing breaker by notching up too rapidly.
2 minutes. Broken strap connection.
5 minutes. R-5 resistance strap breaking No. 2 motor.

Miscellaneous Electrical:
5 minutes. Shoe cable burning off.

Miscellaneous Mechanical:
8 minutes. Latch on engine coupler opening when starting.
4 minutes. Motor crank disk striking cover (stopped to examine same.).

Brakes:
2 minutes. Brakes failed to release promptly.
4 minutes. Defective air hose.
5 minutes. Loose finger on pilot governor of air compressor.

TABLE I—COST OF ELECTRIC LOCOMOTIVE MAINTENANCE, PENNSYLVANIA RAILROAD, 1915-1916

Month and Year	Mechanical	Electrical	Total	Total Locomotive Mileage	Cost per Locomotive Mile (Cents)
May, 1915......	$2,180.96	$995.12	$3,176.08	81,126	3.91
June, 1915.....	1,731.64	1,018.97	2,750.61	83,145	3.31
July, 1915......	2,499.72	1,439.21	3,938.93	88,792	4.44
August, 1915...	2,268.33	737.13	3,005.46	88,433	3.40
September, 1915	1,808.85	999.23	2,808.08	85,054	3.30
October, 1915...	2,118.38	847.78	2,966.16	83,121	3.57
November, 1915.	1,630.41	855.07	2,485.48	82,438	3.02
December, 1915.	2,105.56	927.29	3,032.85	84,677	3.58
January, 1916..	1,919.19	610.42	2,529.61	83,797	3.02
February, 1916.	2,342.45	859.26	3,201.71	80,819	3.96
March, 1916....	2,091.34	1,127.42	3,218.76	85,299	3.77
April, 1916.....	1,506.20	814.45	2,320.65	83,604	2.78
Totals	$24,203.03	$11,231.35	$35,434.38	1,010,305	3.51

Note: Mileage figures made up with two locomotive-units considered as one locomotive.

Costs include all charges for inspection, repairs and superintendence in electric zone; for work done on the electric equipment by steam locomotive shops; for material either purchased direct or through purchasing agent; and for freight except over Pennsylvania Railroad.

TABLE II—1915 RECORD OF VARIOUS OPERATIONS AT SUNNYSIDE
ENGINE HOUSE

Electric locomotives receiving classified repairs.............. 9
Electric locomotives receiving class 1 painting.............. 6
Electric locomotives receiving class 2 painting.............. 4
Electric locomotives receiving class 3 painting.............. 4
Locomotives held in shop for inspection and repairs.......... 465
Driving-wheel tires shimmed............................. 5
Engine truck-wheel tires shimmed........................ 3
Engine truck wheels applied............................. 64
Engine truck wheels removed for side play................ 3
Main motor armatures and fields painted.................. 2
Main motor bearings renewed............................ 18
Jackshaft bearings renewed............................. 24
Jackshaft bearings reduced............................. 631
Rod bushings renewed or reduced........................ 123
Rod brasses reduced................................... 143
Compressor armature commutators turned and slotted....... 16
Main motor resistances welded.......................... 53

TABLE III—NUMBER AND MINUTES DETENTION TO TRAINS DUE TO
ELECTRIC LOCOMOTIVES FROM 1911 TO 1915, INCLUDING TOTAL
MILEAGE AND MILEAGE PER DETENTION, PENN-
SYLVANIA RAILROAD

	1911		1912		1913		1914		1915	
Failures	No.	Min-utes	No.	Min-utes	No.	Min-utes	No.	Min-utes	No.	Min-utes
Mechanical	3	10	7	27	1	6	7	43	5	27
Electrical	11	71	10	31	4	35	8	48	5	16
Man	2	19	4	13	4	37	3	11	3	39
Total	16	100	21	71	9	78	18	102	13	82
Total mileage..	909,238		994,592		1,046,613		1,016,044		995,141	
Mileage per de-tention	56,827		47,362		116,290		56,447		76,550	

NOTE: Figures apply to trains on which trouble occurred and
do not include other trains delayed because of the failure.

TABLE IV—TRAIN DETENTIONS FOR CALENDAR YEAR 1915 DUE TO
ELECTRIC LOCOMOTIVES, PENNSYLVANIA RAILROAD

Cause of Detention	Minutes Delay to Train	Class of Failure
Main switch left open on one unit............	21	Man
Fuse blown in starting train.................	15	Man
Air hose	6	Mechanical
Air hose	7	Mechanical
Shunt-field resistance terminal broken........	5	Electrical
Control wire broken........................	1	Electrical
Circuit breaker opened and not reset.........	2	Man
Air hose	3	Mechanical
Contact shoe broken........................	6	Electrical
Spring hanger and sand pipe broken..........	6	Mechanical
Coupler knuckle opened.....................	6	Mechanical
Fuse failed	3	Electrical
Circuit breaker opened—overload...........	1	Man
Total	82	

Summary:
    Mechanical failures, 5.
    Electrical failures, 4.
    Total locomotive mileage. 995,141.
    Miles per locomotive failure, 110,570.

CHAPTER 7
THREE UNIVERSAL
SIDE-RODDERS

Long before the Pennsy actually began electrified train operation between New York, Philadelphia, Washington, D.C., and Harrisburg, Pa., they had contemplated such action. Even during development of class DD1, consideration had been given to electrifying the New York Division between New York, and Philadelphia.

But meanwhile conditions had changed and the Pennsy decided to abandon DC for long-range electrification. For future electrified trackage extensions alternating-current (AC) would be their standard.

Successful AC operation on the main line from Broad Street Station, Philadelphia, and Paoli, Pa., which went into operation September 12, 1915, and later when the Chestnut Hill Branch opened, March 30, 1918, over a period of years was greatly instrumental in making this decision.

In the early 1920's the idea of electrifying the Pennsylvania Railroad System (as it was then officially called) between New York and Washington, D.C., again surfaced. But at that time the situation regarding electric locomotive design was in a fluid state, and varied indeed were the designs then in use in the United States and Continental Europe. New progressive developments were on the way, but how soon they would appear no one could say with certainty. James T. Wallis, who had been made Chief of Motive Power of the entire System when the Pennsy went back to private ownership on March 1, 1920, wanted to get on with it.

Under his direct supervision, and working closely with Westinghouse, they combined forces to explore the possibilities of a powerful AC locomotive for long-distance main line operation. The result of this exploration was the construction of a unique electric locomotive in the field of railroad motive power.

In January 1924, an unusual looking Pennsylvania Railroad electric locomotive could be seen at the Juniata Shops. It was indeed an oddity; nothing like it among electric locomotives had ever been seen on the Pennsy, in fact, anywhere on the continents of North or South America.

Running gear and mechanical parts with its cab superstructure were built at the Juniata Shops in East Altoona, Pa., but electrical equipment was the product of Westinghouse at East Pittsburgh, Pa.

On its cab sides it bore road number 3930, and the railroad gave it a class L5 designation. It was of the 2-8-2 or 1-D-1 type, and its superstructure was of the steeple or center cab form with a hood at each end — the Pennsy's first steeple-cab locomotive. The letter "L" was appropriate for it stood for the Pennsy's 2-8-2 type Mikados, with a similar rigid wheelbase arrangement.

This cab measured 26 feet in length, with an overall width of 10 feet, 6 inches, while the hoods at each end were 16 feet, 9¼ inches in length. Each hood housed two Westinghouse type 418 single-phase commutator traction motors with a rating of 760 horsepower per motor. These motors were built to operate efficiently on either AC or DC, a fact which added materially to the locomotive's flexibility. Like class FF1, each pair of motors was geared to a jack-shaft, which by side-rods drove the adjacent pair of drivers. The driving wheels were arranged in two independent groups of two pairs each and were not connected by rods with each other. This caused some to refer to the type as a 2-4-4-2, or 1-B-B-1, but officially since there was no articulation between the two groups, the Pennsy considered them to be of the 2-8-2 type of wheel arrangement.

The four pairs of driving wheels were compactly grouped in a rigid wheel base of 22 feet, 3 inches. The center drivers were flangeless and 80 inches in diameter. Design of the end pony trucks with their 33 inch wheels was very carefully worked out. They were of the radial center-bearing type equalized with the main drivers through bell cranks by means of flat leaf springs placed trans-

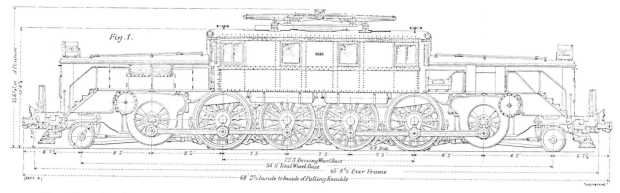

Elevation drawing of motor No. 3930 class L5, giving wheel base dimensions. These figures were duplicated on all L5 sub-classes as were the general mechanical features. Clasp brakes were used on all motors of the L5 group.

versely and resting on the swing links supporting the weight of the trucks. A side swing of ten inches each way was provided with a maximum resistance of one-fourth the weight on the trucks.

The main frame was composed of four main steel castings accurately machined and substantially bolted together to form a continuous framework extending the full length of the locomotive. Each end of the locomotive was formed into a separate cradle casting containing the jack-shaft and traction motors, with suitable bearing seats for both motors and jack-shaft. These two cradle castings were connected to each other by the two main side frames which were quite deep and located over the drivers.

An elaborate arrangement of motor and jack-shaft bearing lubrication was employed in an oil circulation system. Oil from a reservoir containing an adequate supply was automatically pumped when the locomotive was running, to a distributing manifold. From that point it flowed under low pressure to all the motor and jack-shaft bearings, thence returning to the reservoir. An indicator, which by means of small green lights showed whether all the bearings were being properly lubricated, was located in each operating cab.

Each jack-shaft was fitted with two flexible gears one on each end of the shaft. This gear (as on class FF1) was so arranged that through the action of flexible springs the motor torque (twisting and turning effort) was greatly cushioned, thereby, dampening out destructive effects of excessive vibrations.

Motor No. 3930 completely assembled and ready for the road in January, 1924. Tests were later taken on the Altoona test plant of this locomotive. Blower on right side of running board drew air in, rather than blowing it out for forced ventilation of traction motors. This air was drawn from a louver on the opposite side of the hood. To its left is a battery box for the control current used by the master controller at 32 volts DC. Hood to the left shows the louver which fed air to the blower on the opposite side. Supported on the cab roof is an AC pantograph centrally located. This is normally not the best place to put it if you have a choice.

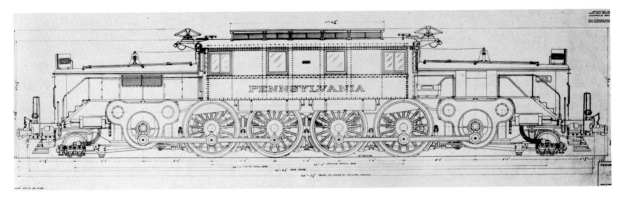

Like No. 3930, Nos. 3928 and 3929, originally had low hoods at each end, but small pantographs at each end of the cab roof collected DC from overhead third-rails in the open yard and under Penn Station. This occurred at tracks where the third-rail had to break its continuity, leaving too large a non-electrified gap. To enable the locomotive to receive a continuous supply of current at all times an overhead third-rail was installed. A steel cantilever form of construction of noticeable symmetry due to its curved top chords simulating a graceful catenary system, supported the overhead third-rails in the then open yard between the United States Post Office, on Eighth Avenue to a point somewhat west of Ninth Avenue. Unlike the L5, the L5A's had a louvered clerestory roof to allow free dissipation of heat from the resistance grids. A larger sized round-cased headlight similar to those used on Pennsy's newer steam locomotives replaced the small headlight first used on the DD1's and L5 locomotives.

These gears were driven by two pinions located on the armature shaft of each motor which meshed with the flexible gear on the jack-shaft. The pinions on the motors nearest to the adjacent driving wheels were made solid, while those on the outer motors were flexible. The reason for this was due to the fact that the space available was not sufficient to allow room for a flexible pinion. These flexible pinions were similar in construction to the gears and used duplicate flexible elements.

The part of the frame extending over the driving wheels was carried up to form a support for the equipment deck, the heavier pieces of equipment being bolted directly to the frame. This relieved the cab structure of equipment weight and permitted the cab to be made of light material and placed in position after the heavy equipment work was done.

This alternating current locomotive had traction motors of the interpole type which were force ventilated. In common with AC locomotives, a transformer was used to step down the trolley voltage and thus through the operation of transformer tap switches obtain smooth acceleration. The main transformer was oil insulated and cooled by circulating oil through a radiator arranged for forced ventilation.

Norman W. Storer of Westinghouse, an engineer with exceptional expertise in electric locomotive design, had this to say about the L5:

"This locomotive was designed for the maximum permissable axle load per driving axle, that is 75,000 pounds. There were good reasons for adopting gear and side-rod drive for class L5. In fact, a careful analysis showed that it was not only the best but the only type of drive possible for this locomotive after the general arrangement and type of motors and number of axles had been settled upon.

"With class L5 the power required per axle was entirely too great for any single-phase motor that could be geared to an axle. Each motor had a continuous rating of 760 horsepower at 23 mph. That was the amount of power needed for each driving axle. The motor was also too large and too heavy to have one side suspended on the axle and geared to it. The power output was too great for a twin motor geared to a quill to develop, as it would have required a pair of motors each having eight or ten poles, and a quill drive much heavier than any that had yet been attempted to develop the required power.

"Motors driving through side rods and jack-shaft only would have a prohibitive weight and dimensions so that there was no alternative to gears and side rods, even if this type had not been preferred. It was probably the largest of the type that could be built as an electric locomotive. The total weight on driving axles of 308,600 pounds is well proportioned to the tractive force, which was 50,000 pounds continuously and 100,000 pounds,

166

This locomotive exerted some influence on the three Universal electric locomotives. Its geared side-rod drive and some other details were used on class L5 and its sub-classes. It, therefore, deserves a place in this Chapter, although it never operated in the Penn Station area. In April 1917, the Pennsy and Westinghouse, produced a giant electric locomotive of the 2-6 + 6-2 articulated type, class FF1, numbered 3931. It could develop 7,640 maximum hp., and develop a continuous rating of 4,000 hp. This horsepower, and a starting tractive force of 140,000 lb. made it the most powerful electric locomotive ever built. No. 3931 featured regenerative braking, and was, I believe, the first and only Pennsy electric to use it. Modern Pennsy electrics use dynamic braking, and do not utilize the regenerated current for return to the trolley or sub-station. Designed primarily for the heavily graded Pittsburgh Division, west of Altoona, class FF1 never got to operate in that area. It did, however, work out its career in pusher service between Overbrook and Paoli, Pa. No. 3931 was scrapped in April 1940. There her huge size and power soon earned No. 3931 the sobriquet of "Big Liz."

maximum, as it called for 16⅔ percent adhesion at continuous rating and 33⅓ percent at maximum. As built No. 3930 stood as an example of symmetrical design, and a minimum number of parts for such a large output of power.

"The traction motors are the largest single-phase commutator interpole motors that have been built in this country. They have eighteen poles and are designed for a speed range from 23 to 35 mph.

"The weight efficiency of this locomotive is exceptionally high, the total is only about 200 tons which is about evenly distributed between the mechanical parts and the electrical equipment.

"Two of these locomotives are to be used with direct-current control equipment in the Pennsylvania Terminal in New York, where they will be operated in passenger service."

As the motors ran at approximately 580 rpm. for maximum locomotive speed, the result was 35 mph. geared for freight operation, and 70 mph. geared for passenger service."

Locomotive No. 3930, in February 1924, went into freight service on the 11,000 volt AC section between Overbrook, Pa., and Paoli, Pa. Here it cooperated with No. 3931, the huge box-cab locomotive "Big Liz," and the difference in size between them caused Pennsy men to refer to the

L5 as "Little Jenny." But with a starting tractive force of 100,000 pounds, and 50,000 pounds at 23 mph. "Little Jenny" was no puny specimen of a locomotive. Todays E44's don't rate that starting tractive force.

In February 1927 motor 3930, was given an L5PAW classification, and its external appearance showed some changes. The height of the hoods was raised and pantographs were located on each hood roof instead of on the cab roof. With the exception of their large sized pantographs and the omission of third-rail shoes, they conformed in external appearance to the L5PD class then operating in the Penn Station and tunnel area. The gear ratio was changed from 30:118 to 50:98 for higher speed. Ever the "rugged individualist" Pennsy, contrary to usual practice puts the pinion first and the gear second regarding gear ratios.

Later this original representative of class L5, again was re-classified and became class L5FAW presumably re-geared for freight service. The letters "P" and "F" in their classification indicating passenger and freight service respectively.

Finally in May 1944, No. 3930 was scrapped, outlasting all other locomotives of the L5 group which had all been scrapped before the end of 1942. "Little Jenny" had indeed proved herself a rugged performer, and probably ran up a higher

Specifications for classes L5 and L5a.

	CLASSIFICATION		L5	L5a	
1	Wheel Arrangement		2-8-2	2-8-2	1
2	Wheel Diameters	In.	33, 80, 33	33, 80, 33	2
3	Journal, End Trucks	In.	7 x 12	7 x 12	3
4	" Drivers	In.	11 x 15	11 x 15	4
5	" Inside Trucks	In.	—	—	5
6	Wheel Base, Driver	Ft. In.	22-3	22-3	6
7	" Base, Total	Ft. In.	54-11	54-11	7
8	Length Coupled	Ft. In.	68-2½	68-2½	8
9	Width, Maximum	Ft. In.	10-7	10-7	9
10	Height Over Cab Roof	Ft. In.	13-4⅞	13-4⅞	10
11	" Maximum, Trolley Down	Ft. In.	15-6	14-8½	11
12	Drive, Type of		Gears and Jack Shaft	Gears and Jack Shaft	12
13	Current Collectors		Pantograph	Pantograph and 3rd Rail Shoes	13
14	Line Voltage		11000 A. C.	650 D. C.	14
15	Main Motors, Class and Voltage		A. C. 350	D. C. 325	15
16	" Make and Type		Westinghouse 418	Westinghouse 418	16
17	" Number of		4	4	17
18	" Ventilation		Forced	Forced	18
19	" Gear Ratio		30 to 118	50 to 98	19
20	" Gear Type of		Spur	Spur	20
21	" Rotor, Diameter	In.	55	55	21
22	" Rotor, Weight,	Lb.	12000	12000	22
23	" Weight	Lb.	25000	25000	23
24	Control, Master Type		Electro Pneumatic	Electro Pneumatic	24
25	" Master Oper't'g Current		32V	32 V	25
26	" Main Type		Transformer Switches	Grids	26
27	Compressors, Number and Type		1-Vertical 2 Stage	1-Vertical 2 Stage	27
28	" Capacity	Cu. Ft.	150	150	28
29	Blowers, Number and H. P.		2-24	2-24	29
30	" Capacity	Cu. Ft.	8000	8000	30
31	Wt. on Rail, End Truck	Lb.	50000		31
32	" 1st Drivers	Lb.	79000		32
33	" 2nd Drivers	Lb.	76000		33
34	" 3rd Drivers	Lb.	75300		34
35	" 4th Drivers	Lb.	78300		35
36	" 5th Drivers	Lb.	—	—	36
37	" 6th Drivers	Lb.	—	—	37
38	" 7th Drivers	Lb.	—	—	38
39	" 8th Drivers	Lb.	—	—	39
40	" All Drivers	Lb.	308600		40
41	" Inside Truck	Lb.	—	—	41
42	Wt. of Engine, Total	Lb.	408600		42
43	" Mechanical Parts	Lb.	208600		43
44	" Equipment Parts*	Lb.	200000		44
45	Rating Continuous	H. P.	3070	3730	45
46	" " Tractive Power	Lb.	50000	37000	46
47	" " Speed	M. P. H.	23.0	37.8	47
48	Ratio: Wt. on Drivers to Continuous T.P.		6.18	8.34	48
49	Maximum Tractive Power	Lb.	100000	82500	49
50	Ratio: Wt. on Drivers to Max. Trac. Power		3.09	3.74	50
51	Compressor H. P. Rating		35	35	51
52					52

* Includes All Electrical Equipment, and Air Brake Parts Except Foundation Brake and Air Brake Cylinder.

mileage record than any other class L5 motor. Not only that but "Little Jenny" could also claim being the first and last of a bold and interesting design of an electric locomotive.

The foregoing covers class L5 only, but the Pennsy wanted to find out the capabilities of these locomotives (or motors as the railroaders called them) in heavy high-speed passenger service. And what better place to try this than in the New York tunnel and terminal area. Consequently two more locomotives similar to class L5 were built; No. 3928 in June 1924, and 3929 in January 1925. These two motors were first given a class L5a designation, and in January 1927, this was changed to class L5PDW.

But as we have noted previously, electrified trackage between Penn Station, Manhattan Transfer and Sunnyside used DC for train propulsion. To permit DC for high speed passenger service required DC control equipment for speed acceleration.

Operating on the principle of rheostatic speed control with 3,000 ampere, 650 volt electro-pneumatic unit switches, or contactors, that sent power through metal grid resistors, they cut out resistance until high speed was attained.

Over-running third-rail shoes, and master controllers duplicating those used on the DD1's in the New York Zone, as well as some other items were applied to those two L5a motors.

Another vital change was the gearing which used a 50:98 ratio for high-speed service. To change the gearing in the event of using the 30:118 for freight service, small hydraulic tools suitably designed were provided for either removing or pressing on both pinions and gears, so that this operation could be performed in any shop where facilities for handling these locomotives were available. One unique hand tool was a huge wrench about 500 pounds in weight which was used by the shop mechanics in removing or applying the large nut located on the outside end of the jack-shaft.

With this versatility, and for the power produced they were most certainly "Universal" locomotives.

CHAPTER 8
NEWCOMERS ON THE HIGH LINE

The two newcomers on the high-line, Nos. 3928 and 3929, were the first of their DC descendants. During the years from 1926 to 1928, 21 additional units were built. As these locomotives were arranged to operate in the New York Tunnel and Terminal Zone on DC, they were given an L5PD classification. This indicated that the locomotives were of the L5 class, geared for passenger (P) service, and operated on DC (D). A final letter denoted the name of the electrical equipment manufacturer. Thus the letter "B" stood for the American Brown Boveri Corporation, (later represented in the United States by (Allis-Chalmers). Letter "G" stood for General Electric, and "W" meant Westinghouse. Of the 21 L5PD's, there were seven L5PDB's, four L5PDG's, and ten L5PDW's, which including the three pioneer locomotives described in Chapter 7, gave a total of 24 locomotives of the L5 group. No others were ever built, and not one was spared for posterity.

A few departures from the original L5a class were made, and are obvious in the picture of No. 3929 when compared with the drawing of the L5a class. Blowers were omitted as forced ventilation was not used due partly to the characteristics of the traction motors when operating on DC. These motors were indeed large and heavy, for their 56-inch diameter rotors were just one-inch smaller than those on the huge DD1 traction motors.

The newcomers did fairly well, that is, they could handle heavy trains through the tunnels under both rivers with their severe mountain-like grades, and skim over the high-line at a right good pace, but if anyone expected them to displace the doughty DD1's, they failed to meet such anticipations. They proved to be more expensive to maintain by far than the DD1's. Traction motor brushes seemed to be continually wearing out on all of them regardless of the motor manufacturer, and they had more heavy and unwieldy parts to be moved during shop repairs. On the road they

pitched and rolled, it was said, like a rocking chair, besides being noisy inside the cab as well as outside. From my own experience this was quite the opposite compared with the DD1's which were noticeably quiet and smooth running. A shrewd English observer commented that this comparative roughness on the L5PD's was probably due to the "dumbell arrangement" which concentrated much weight at each end cradle supporting the two large traction motors, gears and pinions, and which was evidently not rectified by the spring equalization system. Then again, each manufacturer of electrical equipment differed from one another in many details. Brown Boveri, L5PDB's for example, used a reverser that the shop men called the "piano reverse" because it operated with mechanical fingers similar to those used on a player piano. Pennsy later realized the disadvantages of this procedure when the P5A's came along, and insisted on uniform electrical equipment from General Electric and Westinghouse.

There were also some complaints about excessive brake shoe wear. This however, was attributed possibly to the use of clasp brakes used on the L5PD's. With twice as many brake shoes applied to the drivers as on a DD1, such a condition was not unlikely. A report by a Special Duty Engineer, included in this Chapter touches on clasp brake action on the L5PD's, as well as their spring rigging that throws some light on this situation.

Another bad thing about the L5PD's, was the rigidity of their driving wheel base. Despite the flangeless center drivers they were prohibited from certain tracks in Sunnyside Yards, and Penn Station. They were not good on some sharp turn-outs either. This, as can be understood, gained them no popularity among the towermen. Compared with articulated tracking flexibility of the DD1's left much to be desired. It was also said that they were always having "grounds" in the automatic oil lubricator, resulting in "short circuits."

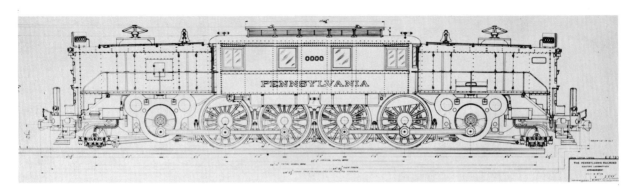

Elevation drawing of class L5PD. The clerestory roof dissipated heat from the resistance grids through side louvers which replaced the Globe type ventilators used on the DD1's for the same purpose.

In general, the L5PD's were considered an unsatisfactory locomotive. In fairness, however, one must recognize the fact that unlike the DD1 class, these L5PD's were not specifically designed for the New York Tunnel and Terminal service. Consequently, for such shuttle operations, they were out of their sphere of action for the work originally planned for them.

Coming events were also casting their shadows before, to paraphrase Thomas Campbell. In 1927 Westinghouse Electric produced a single-phase, series wound interpole traction motor of exceptional power. It could produce 500 horsepower, something unattainable until then, and soon upgraded to 625 horsepower. And yet it was small enough to fit within the main frames of an electric locomotive. This was a point of great moment, for it fitted in with the Pennsy's adherence to base their electric locomotive design on a steam locomotive concept. A review of their electric locomotives for main line operation clearly indicates this.

What they were aiming at with this new motor was to obtain more horsepower from independent driving axles without side rods. By arranging the traction motors in a twin, or tandem arrangement, pinions drove a gear fastened to a quill. Projections on one end of the quill fitted between spokes and by a spring-cup drive rotated the driving wheels. The object of the quill was to permit the motors to be rigidly fastened to the main frames, and yet, permit vertical play of the axles encased within the quill. This was done by providing sufficient radial clearance inside the quill. It was not a new idea; Westinghouse had used this twin motor drive years before on the New Haven and Milwaukee electrics. And in Europe this method of driving wheel propulsion was known as the Westinghouse drive.

Unquestionably this high powered traction motor was of much significance, for it was the catalyst that brought Pennsy's long-range, main line electrification plans together with practical reality. So much was this point recognized that Pennsy President, William Wallace Atterbury, and the Board of Directors, in 1928, authorized completion of the huge project that finally brought straight-electrified train operation between Penn Station, New York, and Washington, D.C., and as far south as Potomac Yards in Virginia. In 1938 electrification was extended from Paoli to Harrisburg, Pa., which resulted in the Pennsylvania Railroad operating more electrified track mileage than any other railroad in the United States.

With the appearance of this super-power traction motor, the side-rodders were doomed and their demise was imminent. The problem was what to do with the L5PD's. It did seem a shame to scrap fairly new locomotives that had cost a bit above $142,000.00 each. The L5, Little Jenny, had proved it could operate satisfactorily on AC from an overhead trolley wire. And, therefore, the point was raised, why not use these locomotives in AC territory, or give them to the Long Island Railroad? The Long Island, however, did not want them, but said they would gladly accept all the DD1's they could get! They knew the performance records of both classes and hence their attitude.

Later the Long Island Railroad received most of the DD1's, where, as expected, they continued to do fine work. To the surprise of some they performed splendidly not only in passenger service, but in freight where it was thought they would not do so well. It looked as though the DD1's could also claim to be "Universal" locomotives as well as class L5.

Meanwhile, what to do with the L5PD's? Mechanical parts were not new, being several years old, and DC electrical equipment would re-

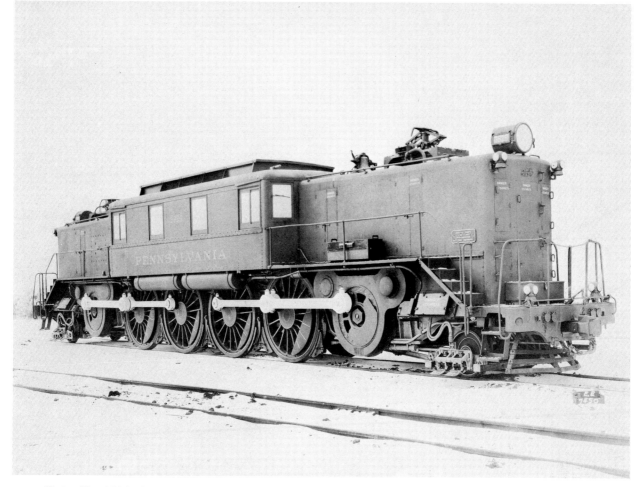

Motor No. 3929 after its conversion to class L5APDW. January, 1927, this motor and No. 3928, were later given a class L5PDW designation. This was done to coincide with the 21 class L5PD motors that were built between 1926 and 1928. Changes made in comparison with original motors 3928 and 3929 are self evident. Box-like receptacles on both bumper beams carried tools and spare air hoses. On this motor and on 3928 and 3930, protrusions covering flexible gears on the outer end were retained, but on the 21 other L5PD's they had the pinions covered as on the inner end of the gears; that is, flush with each other. Good close-up of over-running third-rail shoes, showing power cable leading to the fuse box and labeled "Danger 650 Volts." the two blowers, one on each side in front of the engineers windows had been removed as no forced ventilation was used when operating on DC in this specific service.

quire costly replacement to operate on AC. The Pennsy also felt that they would still have a good bit of a second-hand locomotive. They reasoned, therefore, why not pay more and get additional units of a new design of electric locomotive, embodying latest and better concepts of locomotive construction. And that is what they did. Subsequently all the L5PD's were scrapped in 1942.

Early in 1933, AC ended the DC monopoly in the Pennsy's tunnel and terminal area. Locomotives of other forms and types took over the roles performed by the side-rodders. Yes, Pennsy DC side-rodders had had their day, and are now but shadows of a nostalgic past, but oh, it was a great day while it lasted.

Westbound train for the south arriving on track No. 4, at Manhattan Transfer. Motor 7809, class L5PDG, is on head end, and will quickly uncouple for the K4s Pacific steam locomotive waiting on the steam storage track. Four minutes were allowed for this procedure.

An L5PD speeding a heavy westbound train over the high-line as it approached Belleville Road.

Picture taken by the author from the cab of a GG1, as it sped over the high-line shortly after leaving the Bergen Portal. Third rails are still in place, but upper quadrant semaphore signals used when the DC motors first and later ran here had given way to position light signals.

View taken from westbound H&M train on track No. 7, as it left Manhattan Transfer. Track No. 7, was on the northern side of the island platform.

If the L5PD's had been converted to AC operation provision for a train heating boiler, with oil fuel and water storage space would have had to been made for use with passenger trains. There would have been no room for a proper size boiler or sufficient room for a supply of oil and water on the L5 sub-classes. Chances are that a trailer unit for housing a train heating boiler with necessary fuel oil and water storage would have been used. This illustration shows such a "kitchenette" car used by the New Haven. In this way, when freight electric locomotives were called into passenger service during periods of heavy passenger traffic during the Yale-Harvard football games, freight motors could supplement the passenger motors quite satisfactorily.

A **"Clocker"** bound for Philadelphia pulls out of Manhattan Transfer on track No. 7. Engine was No. 5426, built in February 1927, by The Baldwin Locomotive Works, at Eddystone, Pa., construction number 59,807. This was one of the 75 K4s class locomotives built for the Pennsy by Baldwin.

An L5PD had uncoupled from its train and was moving east to the motor storage track, or perhaps the signals indicated that this motor move "light" to Penn Station, depending on the power situation or schedules of incoming trains. The helper on the running board is giving hand signals to the engineer at the far end of the center cab. This was routine procedure as it permitted rapid movement for track clearance for the outbound train, and quickly got the motor to the motor storage track. The engineer could not take time to change ends after the rapid uncoupling of the outbound train, and the DD1, or L5PD had to scoot away in a hurry. Then the engineman had to quickly reverse and keep moving for at times track occupancy was limited to seconds at the Transfer.

At Meadows Shops an L5PD rests alongside the old electric locomotive repair shop building. Note large size of door to permit entrance for the DD1's and L5PD's. Man in doorway affords interesting comparison regarding door and locomotive size with himself.

A class B1, 0-6-0 type switcher in Sunnyside Yard powered by AC. These non-side-rod drive locomotives used a pinion and gear drive. But from 1926, similar locomotives powered by DC collected from a third-rail and with a BB2 classification shifted or "drilled" cars in Sunnyside. They greatly relieved DD1's and L5PD's from switching duties, thereby, making more road engines available for main line service. In view of this assistance to the side-rodders they are worthy of notice in this book.

New York, Oct. 24, 1928

Mr. C.C. Hipkins
R.F. of E.

Sir:-

   I hereby submit the following report of my activities for
Wednesday October 24th.

Arrived at Mant'fr, 7.15 AM.
Rode engine #3922, hauling train #38 from Mant'fr, to N.Y.
Crew, Eng'r. W. Deakyne, Helper, H. Williams, Time 7.40 AM.
Arriving in New York, checked the night performance for
irregularities.
Observed the following engines and their movements in and
around Pa Sta, #23, 36, 39, 29, 7805.
Rode engine #39, hauling train #168 from N.Y. to SSide,
Crew, Eng'r. E.A. Titman, Helper J. Maupin, time 10.05 AM.
Checked the following engines, and their crews in SSide Yard,
Engine #6, #7812, #7808, #3929, and #39, also inspected
several L5 type engines, in order to determine if the Motors
were throwing oil from their bearings into the armatures.
Went to dinner 1.00 P.M. and returned at 1.35 P.M.
Inspected engine #7807 and found the brake cylinder piston
travel entirely too short, the late 99-B-1 air brake
instruction book authorizes 5 in. piston travel, and even this
is entirely too short on the L5 type engine, due to the fact
that the engine is equipped with a clasp brake, and whenever
one of the driving wheels is over a low spot in the tracks,
naturally it drops down and spreads the driving wheel rubbers,
which in turn takes up all the slack in the brake rigging,
resulting in all of the rubbers being drawn firmly against
the wheels.
Rode engine #7808, hauling train #29 from SSide to N.Y.
Crew, Eng'r. L. Cone, Helper, J. Pierciey, Time 2.10 P.M.
Rode engine #23 hauling train #29 N.Y. to Mant'fr, Time
2.55 P.M.
Crew, Eng'r. E. Jordan, Helper C. Carey.
Rode engine #7811, hauling train #228, time 3.45 P.M.
Crew, Eng'r. E. Flynn, Helper H.F. Mumm.
Rode engine #25 hauling train #735 N.Y. to Mant'fr, Time
5.10 P.M.
P.S. Engine #7807 cut off and sent to the engine house for brake
     adjustment.

                              Yours respectfully,

Authentic record made by   Special Duty Engineer
Special Duty Engineer, of
side-rodders operating in the
New York Terminal Zone, when
DD1's and L5PD's handled the
passenger traffic.

Specifications for all L5 sub-classes.

	CLASSIFICATION		L 5 P A W	L 5 P D B	L 5 P D G	L 5 P D W
1	Wheel Arrangement		2-8-2	2-8-2	2-8-2	2-8-2
2	" Diameters	In.	33-80-33	33-80-33	33-80-33	33-80-33
3	Journal, End Trucks	In.	7 x 12	7 x 12	7 x 12	7 x 12
4	" Drivers	In.	11 x 15	11 x 15	11 x 15	11 x 15
5	" Inside Trucks	In.	——	——	——	——
6	Wheel Base, Rigid	Ft. In.	22-3	22-3	22-3	22-3
7	" " Total	Ft. In.	54-11	54-11	54-11	54-11
8	Length Coupled	Ft. In.	68-2½	68-2½	68-2½	68-2½
9	Width, Maximum†	Ft. In.	10-7	10-7	10-7	10-7
10	Max. Ht. Over Cab	Ft. In.	13-8⅞	14-4⅞	14-4⅞	14-4⅞
11	Max. Ht. Trolley Down	Ft. In.	15-6⅝	14-8¹¹⁄₁₆	14-8¹¹⁄₁₆	14-8¹¹⁄₁₆
12	Drive, Type of		Gears and Jack Shaft	Gears and Jack Shaft	Gears and Jack Shaft	Gears and Jack Shaft
13	Current Collectors		Pantograph	Pantograph and 3rd Rail Shoe	Pantograph and 3rd Rail Shoe	Pantograph and 3rd Rail Shoe
14	Line Voltage		11000 A.C.	650 D.C.	650 D.C.	650 D.C.
15	Main Motors, Class & Voltage		A.C. 340	D.C. 325	D.C. 325	D.C. 325
16	" " Make & Type		Westinghouse 418	Brown Boveri Elm 1334-8-24	General Electric G E A 615-A	Westinghouse 418-A
17	" " Number of		4	4	4	4
18	" " Ventilation		Forced	Natural	Natural	Natural
19	" " Gear Ratio		50 to 98	53 to 95	53 to 95	50 to 98 / 53 to 95
20	" " Gear, Type of		Spur	Spur	Spur	Spur
21	" " Rotor, Diam.	In.	55	56¼	54.99	55
22	" " Rotor, Weight	Lb.	12000	10700	14500	12000
23	" " Weight	Lb.	21000	21500	25160	21000
24	Control, Master Type		Electro Pneumatic	Electro Pneumatic	Electro Pneumatic	Electro Pneumatic
25	" " Oper. Cur.		32V.	32V.	32V.	32V.
26	" " Main Type		Transformer Switches	Grids	Grids	Grids
27	Compressors, No. and Type		1-CA 150 2-Stage	1-Vertical 2-Stage	1-Vertical 2-Stage	1-CA 150 2-Stage
28	" Capacity	Cu. Ft.	150	150	150	150
29	Main Blowers, No. and H.P.		3-12	——	——	——
30	" " Capacity	Cu. Ft.	2-16000 1-8000	——	——	——
31	Wt. on Rail, End Truck No. 1	Lb.	50000	49000	No. 1-53600 No. 2-53600	48450
32	" " " 1st Drivers	Lb.	79000	74650	78500	74625
33	" " " 2nd Drivers	Lb.	76000	74650	76700	74625
34	" " " 3rd Drivers	Lb.	75300	74650	76600	74625
35	" " " 4th Drivers	Lb.	78300	74650	76600	74625
36	" " " 5th Drivers	Lb.	——	——	——	——
37	" " " 6th Drivers	Lb.	——	——	——	——
38	" " " 7th Drivers	Lb.	——	——	——	——
39	" " " 8th Drivers	Lb.	——	——	——	——
40	" " " All Drivers	Lb.	308600	298600	308400	298500
41	" " " End Truck No. 2	Lb.	——	——	——	——
42	Wt. of Engine, Total	Lb.	408600	396600	411000	395400
43	" " Mechanical Parts	Lb.				
44	" " Equipment Parts*	Lb.				
45	Rating Continuous, H.P. at Rail		3070	3120	1780	1560
46	" " Tractive Effort	Lb.	25000	19000	10000	9000 / 8800
47	" " Speed	M.P.H.	46	61.5	66.8	61 / 64.8
48	Ratio Wt. on Drivers to Cont. T.E.		12.34	15.7	30.8	31.1 / 34
49	Max. Tractive Effort	Lb.	54000	71800	80400	82500 / 75100
50	Ratio Wt. on Drivers to Max. T.E.		5.72	4.16	3.83	3.62 / 3.06
51	Compressor H.P. Rating		35	35	35	35
52	Maximum Speed	M.P.H.	70	78	80	70 / 76.5

177

A heavy train from Washington, D.C., passes the westbound Broadway Limited at the Belleville Road. I recall how the meshing pinions and gears gave out with a grinding sound as the big L5PDF worked the train up to speed.

This is how the double-tracked High-Line looked in the 1920's, before the AC catenary system replaced the third-rail method of current distribution. View was taken from Belleville Road looking east from the westbound track.

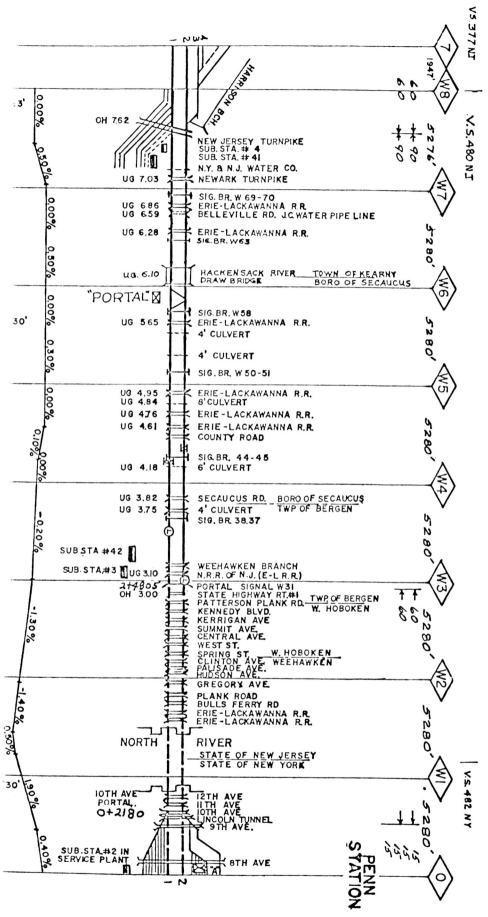

The High-Line in plan and profile as it appeared after AC operation of trains had taken over. Outside of Manhattan Transfer's disappearance, and apparently some slight tunnel grade reductions, it approximates the High-Line of the days when gearless and geared side-rodders ruled supreme.

CHAPTER 9
ROSTER OF ALL PENNA. RR.,
AND LONG ISLAND RR.,
CLASS DD1 SIDE-RODDERS

In this Chapter are listed all the DD1 and L5PD sub-class side-rod drive electric locomotives that operated on the Pennsylvania Tunnel & Terminal Railroad Company. Two other side-rodders are also recorded, No. 3931, the big FF1 class motor, and No. 3930, class L5, Pennsy's first steeple-cab locomotive. These two locomotives powered by AC operated only between Overbrook and Paoli, Pa., as freight service helpers.

Also recorded in a separate table are all Pennsy DD1's transferred to the Long Island Railroad. These locomotives were given three-digit numbers by the LIRR, and are listed in consecutive order.

Originally the DD1 class was assigned numbers in the 3900 series which were to be applied (and some were) to both cab sides in fairly large numerals under the operating compartment windows. Later two-digit numbers replaced the four-digit numbers on the cab windows and on the small original 50 candle-power headlight, as well as on

the doors at each coupler end of the locomotive. The illustration of motor No. 26, in Chapter 5, illustrates this quite clearly. Nevertheless, the four-digit numbers were retained and painted in small gold-leaf lettering over the rear cab openings adjacent to the Pullman vestibule diaphragms.

These different four-digit numbers on each cab unit enabled enginemen to identify a defect or failure with precision in making out a written report, which in turn aided the shopmen in quickly locating and correcting the condition. This together with other factors helped the DD1's in gaining their enviable record in producing high mileage per detention.

The tables tell the story, and it is significant that the rugged DD1's were still in service for a decade after the newer and more costly L5PD's had been obliterated.

Complete Roster of all DD1 electric locomotives

No.	Const. No.	P.T. & T.R.R. Road Nos.	Date Built	Disposal	LIRR Road Nos.
3952	2050-2	10	6-10	Scrapped 2-49	
3953	2050-1				
3954	2052-2	11	9-10	To LIRR on 1-28	348
3955	2052-1				
3956	2058-2	12	9-10	To LIRR on 1-23	347
3957	2058-1				
3958	2051-2	13	6-10	To LIRR on 6-27	339
3959	2051-1				
3960	2054-2	14	7-10	To LIRR on 12-44	358
3961	2054-1				
3962	2056-2	15	7-10	To LIRR on 4-28	351
3963	2056-1				
3964	2053-2	16	7-10	To LIRR on 12-44	359
3965	2053-1				
3966	2060-2	17	7-10	Scrapped No date recorded	
3967	2060-1				
3968	2055-2	18	7-10	To LIRR on 6-27	341
3969	2055-1				
3970	2057-2	19	7-10	To LIRR on 5-28	353
3971	2057-1				
3972	2061-2	20	7-10	To LIRR on 10-27	342
3973	2061-1				
3974	2059-2	21	7-10	To LIRR on 4-28	352
3975	2059-1				
3976	2062-2	22	7-10	To LIRR on 5-28	350
3977	2062-1				
3978	2064-2	23	7-10	Scrapped 9-47	
3979	2064-1				
3980	2063-2	24	7-10	To LIRR on 12-44	360
3981	2063-1				
3982	2065-2	25	7-10	To LIRR on 9-36	356
3983	2065-1				
3984	2066-2	26	7-10	To LIRR on 10-27	343
3985	2066-1				
3986	2069-2	27	7-10	To LIRR on 1-28	346
3987	2069-1				
3988	2067-2	28	7-10	Scrapped on 1-49	
3989	2067-1				
3990	2070-2	29	7-10	To LIRR on 8-33	354
3991	2070-1				
3992	2071-2	30	7-10	Scrapped on 8-47	
3993	2071-1				
3994	2068-2	31	7-10	To LIRR on 4-27	340
3995	2068-1				
3996	2048-2	32	10-9	Scrapped on 9-47	
3997	2048-1				
3998	2049-2	33	4-10	Scrapped on 9-47	
3999	2049-1				
3932	2236-2	34	5-11	To LIRR on 8-33	355
3933	2236-1				
3934	2240-2	35	6-11	To LIRR 6-27	338
3935	2240-1				
3936	2244-2	36	5-11	To Penna. St. Mus., Strasburg, Pa.	
3937	2244-1				
3938	2249-2	37	5-11	Scrapped on 2-49	
3939	2249-1				
3940	2253-2	38	6-11	To LIRR on 3-28	349
3941	2253-1				
3942	2254-2	39	6-11	To LIRR on 12-44	357
3943	2254-1				
3944	2255-2	40	6-11	Scrapped on 9-47	
3945	2255-1				
3946	2256-2	41	6-11	To LIRR on 1-49	345
3947	2256-1				
3948	2257-2	42	6-11	To LIRR on 10-27	344
3949	2257-1				

Roster of all Pennsy geared side-rod drive electric locomotives

Motor No.	Class	Shop	Const. No.	Date Built	Disposal
3922	L5pdw	Juniata	4082	10-26	Scrapped 9-42
3923	L5pdw	Juniata	4083	11-26	Scrapped 8-42
3924	L5pdw	Juniata	4084	11-26	Scrapped 6-42
3925	L5pdw	Juniata	4085	11-26	Scrapped 7-42
3926	L5pdw	Juniata	4098	12-26	Scrapped 5-42
3927	L5pdw	Juniata	4099	12-26	Scrapped 6-42
3928	L5pdw	Juniata	3904	6-24	Scrapped 8-42
3929	L5pdw	Juniata	3977	1-25	Scrapped 7-42
3930	L5faw*	Juniata	3852	1-24	Scrapped 3-44
3931	FF-1	Juniata	3232	4-17	Scrapped 4-40
7801	L5pdb	Juniata	4155	9-27	Scrapped 6-42
7802	L5pdb	Juniata	4164	10-27	Scrapped 7-42
7803	L5pdb	Juniata	4170	10-27	Scrapped 8-42
7804	L5pdb	Juniata	4171	10-27	Scrapped 2-42
7805	L5pdb	Juniata	4179	11-27	Scrapped 8-42
7806	L5pdb	Juniata	4180	12-27	Scrapped 7-42
7807	L5pdb	Altoona Works	4185	2-28	Scrapped 9-42
7808	L5pdg	Altoona Works	4189	3-28	Scrapped 4-42
7809	L5pdg	Altoona Works	4190	3-28	Scrapped 2-42
7810	L5pdg	Altoona Works	4191	4-28	Scrapped 7-42
7811	L5pdg	Altoona Works	4194	6-28	Scrapped 8-42
7812	L5pdw	Juniata	4149	4-27	Scrapped 7-42
7813	L5pdw	Juniata	4150	4-27	Scrapped 5-42
7814	L5pdw	Juniata	4156	5-27	Scrapped 5-42
7815	L5pdw	Juniata	4157	5-27	Scrapped 5-42

*Motor No. 3930 was class L5faw when scrapped. This motor had three classifications see Chapter 7.

Roster of Long Island Railroad DD1 locomotives in numerical order.

P.T. & T.RR. Co. or P.R.R. No.	LI.RR. Numbers	Date Transferred To LIRR	Final Disposal
35	338	6-27	Scrapped by 1952
13	339	6-27	Scrapped by 1952
31	340	4-27	Scrapped by 1952
18	341	6-27	Scrapped by 1952
20	342	10-27	Scrapped by 1952
26	343	10-27	Scrapped by 1952
42	344	10-27	Scrapped by 1952
41	345	12-27	Scrapped by 1-49
27	346	1-28	Scrapped by 1952
12	347	1-28	Scrapped by 1952
11	348	2-48	Scrapped by 1952
38	349	3-28	Scrapped by 1952
22	350	5-28	Scrapped by 1952
15	351	4-28	Scrapped by 1952
21	352	4-28	Scrapped 2-49
19	353	5-28	Scrapped by 1952
29	354	8-33	Scrapped by 1952
34	355	8-33	Scrapped by 1952
25	356	9-36	Scrapped by 1952
39	357	12-44	Scrapped by 1952
14	358	12-44	Scrapped by 1952
16	359	12-44	Scrapped by 1952
24	360	12-44	Scrapped by 1952
Total No.	23	of DD1's	

182

INDEX